JAPANESE
STEP BY STEP

SECOND EDITION

GENE NISHI

New York Chicago San Francisco Lisbon London Madrid Mexico City
Milan New Delhi San Juan Seoul Singapore Sydney Toronto

Library of Congress Cataloging-in-Publication Data

Nishi, Gene.
Japanese step by step : an innovative approach to speaking and reading Japanese / Gene Nishi. — 2nd ed.
p. cm.
Includes index.
ISBN 0-07-171362-X
1. Japanese language—Textbooks for foreign speakers—English. 2. Japanese language—Self-instruction. I. Title.

PL539.5.E5N56 2010
495.6′83421—dc22 2009051794

First published in Japan by Shufunotomo Co., Ltd.

3 4 5 6 7 8 9 10 11 12 13 14 15 16 QVS/QVS 1 9 8 7 6 5 4 3

ISBN 978-0-07-171362-7
MHID 0-07-171362-X

Interior illustrations by Toshiaki Suzuki

Bonus Audio Download

A bonus audio recording for this book can be obtained from mhprofessional.com. Simply follow these easy steps:

1. Go to mhprofessional.com.
2. Search for *Japanese Step by Step*.
3. Locate "Downloads" underneath the book's cover image.
4. Select story link to listen and/or download.

About the author

After graduating from the Engineering Department of Waseda University, the author worked as a technical advisor and as an instructor in Telecommunications Systems at the U.S. Military Headquarters in Zama, Japan, until he joined IBM. Starting as an instructor in the Education Department, he later became the manager of Computer-Communications, later working in IBM's Zurich Laboratory and at the Head Office in New York. He has also worked as a part-time lecturer in Communications Theory at Keiō University.

After retiring from IBM, the author established the Nishi Institute of Language Education for extensive research and practice in Japanese and English education.

Acknowledgements

I gratefully record my obligation to Mr. Shunichi Kamiya, Executive General Manager, International Department, Shufunotomo Co., Ltd. who has contributed to the publication of this book with suggestions, criticism, technical assistance and encouragement.

I am deeply indebted to Ms. Kimberly A. Scott, Ms. Kate Gorringe-Smith and Ms. Yumi Nakada, Editors, International Department, Shufunotomo Co., Ltd. for their capable editing, suggestions, guidance, and thoughtful cooperation.

I am grateful to Mr. Don Sayre, Mr. Jag Rao, Mrs. Peggy Rao and many other IBM colleagues who were enthusiastic students of the Japanese language and helped me establish the new study method.

I have found the following books to be particularly informative:

金田一春彦著（岩波新書）；日本語
寺村秀夫著（くろしお出版）；日本語のシンタクスと意味（I）、（II）
森田良行著（角川書店）；基礎日本語（1）、（2）、（3）

(I would recommend these books to the advanced learners who want to make a profound study of the language.)

Introduction

This book is designed to enable the reader to teach him or herself how to speak and read formal or refined Japanese, such as is used between adults and in business transactions, in the most effective way. First, let me explain how this book became a reality.

Requirements

When I was asked to teach the Japanese language to IBM employees who were stationed in Japan, I pondered over their requirements and conditions.

My students had been assigned to work in Japan for between three and five years. In preparation for their work, they all had to start learning Japanese from the absolute beginning, and yet they had to be able to speak the language as soon as possible. However, they were so busy in their work that they could spare only two to three hours a week for the study of Japanese. With so little time available, the study method had to be extremely effective.

Although their native language might be English, French, German, or Chinese, the "IBM language" is fundamentally English, so at work my students always spoke in English with their colleagues, including the Japanese employees. Then, when they went home in the evening, they spoke with their family members in their mother tongues. So they didn't have much chance to use colloquial Japanese. Instead, their immediate requirement was to learn formal Japanese, such as is spoken by educated adults both socially and in the business environment when talking with customers and traders.

Currently, the "direct method" of language teaching (using only Japanese to teach Japanese, not using the student's mother tongue) is in fashion. However, I thought this was rather ineffective when time was limited. Since all my students knew English, I decided to use English to explain the meaning and usage of Japanese, and to prompt understanding by comparing Japanese with English.

In order to meet these requirements and conditions, I embarked on the development of a new, logical, and systematic study method of the Japanese language, making the most of my computer engineer's mind.

Desu and masu

The first, and most important, step toward speaking refined Japanese is to master the formal sentence structure that ends with the polite word **desu** or **masu**. **Desu** is attached to nouns and adjectives, and **masu** is attached to verbs. I therefore discuss **desu** and **masu** in separate chapters.

Next, I express **desu**-ending sentences in two basic sentence patterns and **masu**-ending sentences in three basic sentence patterns. As these sentence patterns are merely skeletons, I then describe how you can modify and flesh out these skeletons to compose the most appropriate and sensible expressions as various needs arise.

Honorifics

Another important aspect of refined Japanese is understanding when and how to use respectful and humble words. Depending on who you are speaking to, you will need to know whether to make your speech respectful or humble before them (e.g. when speaking to an important client, or your superior at work), or whether to treat them as an equal (e.g. when speaking to a friend), or you may find yourself being rude quite unintentionally. I categorized these honorific words by nouns, adjectives, and verbs. In the case of verbs, I have given formulas for the honorific expressions, using symbols for simplicity and accuracy.

Accent symbols

In every English dictionary, pronunciation symbols are given with each entry. It is strange that although the accent in Japanese is just as important, most Japanese dictionaries do not provide such guidelines for pronunciation. In order to find out the correct accent, we have to consult a special dictionary such as the Pronunciation Accent Dictionary produced by NHK (the Japanese government broadcasting station). In this book I have designed and used accent symbols which should enable the reader to reproduce a satisfactory pronunciation without reference to a special dictionary.

In my childhood days, newspapers and books printed small **hiragana** characters (called "ruby") alongside difficult **kanji** characters, which greatly helped improve our ability to read **kanji**. In this book, **rōmaji** accent symbols (easier to read than **hiragana** ruby) are vertically aligned with kanji characters, showing not only the accent but also serving the purpose of "ruby."

にほんご
日本語
(**hiragana** ruby)

日 本 語
ni HON GO
(accent symbols)

Flow charts

I thought I could explain verb conjugations and derivations more concisely and intelligibly by using flow charts than by describing them in lengthy sentences. My students proved the effectiveness of this method. After they had gone through the charts several times, the charts remained in their memories, and eventually the conversion became spontaneous.

Counting units

The system of Japanese counting units is one of the hurdles that the learner has to jump over. By classifying these into several groups of common rules, I hope I have made them easier to master.

Hyphenating the words that constitute a phrase

As a phrase is a syntactic unit, the words that constitute a phrase should be uttered without a pause between them. To remind you of this rule, I have hyphenated such groups of words.

The building block approach

Since the building block approach is the main teaching method employed in this book, I strongly recommend that the learner starts to read from the beginning of the book and advances section by section, chapter by chapter as they are given, without skipping any.

Although "word for word" translations have not been given for each example, it is generally easy to make out which Japanese word corresponds to which English word by observing the sentence pattern. However, I still suggest that you keep a dictionary at your elbow for reference.

Unlike colloquial or slang Japanese, the more formal and refined Japanese that is spoken by educated adults is not so difficult to learn if you study logically and systematically. Victory is to you who study assiduously.

Gene Nishi
February, 2000

Table of Contents

Chapter 8 The Uses of "V_2'-Te" 160

Chapter 9 The Uses of "V_2'-Ta" 177

Chapter 10 The Uses of "V_1-Nai" 181

Chapter 11 Derivative Verbs 186

Chapter 12 Compound Sentences 196

Chapter 13 Complex Sentences 203

Appendices 229

Index 

English Syllables

A syllable is defined as a single uninterrupted sound forming part of a word or, in some cases, an entire word. For example:

el • e • phant	three-syllable word
bi • cy • cle	three-syllable word
u • ni • ver • si • ty	five-syllable word
con • scious	two-syllable word
peo • ple	two-syllable word
strength	one-syllable word

We know that there are only 26 letters in the English alphabet. But how many different syllabic combinations are there? According to the late Prof. **Minoru Umegaki** of **Tezukayama Gakuin** Junior College, as quoted by Prof. **Haruhiko Kindaichi** in his book ***Nihongo*** (**Iwanami Shinsho**, 1985) , there are more than 3,000 different syllables in English.

Japanese Syllables

What about Japanese? You will be surprised to know that there is no alphabet, and there are only 101 syllables in Japanese. It appears to be an easy language to learn, doesn't it? But wait. Only 101 syllables to compose hundreds of thousands of Japanese words! The consequence is as clear as day: there must be a huge number of homonyms and heteronyms in Japanese. A *homonym* is one of two or more words that sound the same but differ in meaning. A *heteronym* is one of two or more words that are spelled the same way but differ in meaning.

Homonyms and Heteronyms

Of course there are a few homonyms in English, like the words "pole" (telephone pole/the North Pole), meat/meet, and mail/male. Some examples of heteronyms are: "hour and minute"/"minute particles," and "to tear the letter to pieces in tears." As for the word "content," we place the accent on the first syllable when we say "the CONtent of the statement," and on the last syllable when we say "I am conTENT with it."

As I said before, we have an incomparably large number of homonyms and heteronyms in Japanese. Just to mention a few:

ame	rain, toffee
sake	salmon, rice wine
hashi	bridge, edge, chopsticks
hana	flower, nose, snivel, inception
seki	seat, cough, dam, the product of multiplication, family register
kaki	oyster, persimmon, summertime, the force of fire, fence
ishi	stone, volition, physician, posthumous child, dying wishes, death by hanging

Now do you think this is going to be a pretty kettle of fish?

Thanks to the Accent and to Kanji

Chaos is avoided by two means. In spoken Japanese, these words are usually pronounced with different accents, as with the English word "content." In written Japanese, different **kanji** characters are used to eradicate the ambiguity of these homonyms and heteronyms.

Now you can see that in the Japanese language, accent is particularly important when both listening and speaking, and knowledge of **kanji** is essential in reading and writing.

Accent is discussed in detail in CHAPTER 1 Section 2, and **kanji** in CHAPTER 2 Section 3.

CHAPTER 1 SECTION 1
Romanized Syllabary

Japanese syllables are arranged by sound groups to form what we call the "syllabary chart." (The basic chart is in **hiragana** shown in CHAPTER 2 Section 1.) There were attempts to romanize the syllables (that is to write their sounds using the English alphabet [**rōma-ji**]) to give foreign students easy access to the language. At present, there are two national standards on the romanized Japanese syllabary, namely:

1. The MOE style

(MOE = Ministry of Education)

2. The Hepburn style

The MOE style adopts a mechanical translation, that is more formulaic than an actual representation of the spoken sounds (e.g. **sa-si-su-se-so**, **ta-ti-tu-te-to**).

The Hepburn style was developed by Mr. James Curtis Hepburn, an American clergyman who lived in Japan during the latter half of the 19th century. His romanization reflects a more realistic sound of Japanese syllables (e.g. **sa-shi-su-se-so, ta-chi-tsu-te-to**), and is therefore more widely used. Although no statistics are available, I would say 99% of the romanized syllables that are currently in use are in the Hepburn style. So let's look at Mr. Hepburn's syllabary chart first. I want you to pay particular attention to the exceptions, which are marked with the grey background in the chart.

Romanized Syllabary, Hepburn Style

	a- column	ka- column	sa- column	ta- column	na- column	ha- column	ma- column	ya- column	ra- column	wa column
a-row	a	ka	sa	ta	na	ha	ma	ya	ra	wa
i-row	i	ki	shi	chi	ni	hi	mi	i	ri	i
u-row	u	ku	su	tsu	nu	fu	mu	yu	ru	u
e-row	e	ke	se	te	ne	he	me	e	re	e
o-row	o	ko	so	to	no	ho	mo	yo	ro	o

ga	za	da	ba	pa
gi	ji	ji	bi	pi
gu	zu	zu	bu	pu
ge	ze	de	be	pe
go	zo	do	bo	po

n

kya	sha	cha	nya	hya	mya	rya	gya	ja	bya	pya
kyu	shu	chu	nyu	hyu	myu	ryu	gyu	ju	byu	pyu
kyo	sho	cho	nyo	hyo	myo	ryo	gyo	jo	byo	pyo

Syllables

Each box of the syllabary chart represents a single sound or syllable. As you can see, a syllable is either a single vowel (**a**, **i**, **u**, **e**, **o**), or a combination of one or more consonants (**k**, **s**, **sh**, **g**, **ky** etc.) and a vowel. A single **n** is also a syllable.

The vowel **u** in the **u**-row of syllables is not always pronounced clearly. For example, **desu** may sound like **des**, **masu** may sound like **mas**, and so on.

Although the syllable located at the junction of the **ha**-column and the **u**-row is spelled **fu**, it should be pronounced like the English word "who" shortened.

The syllables in the first group are called the 50 voiceless sounds, because they are uttered without the vibration of vocal cords, while those in the second group are called the voiced sounds. (See CHAPTER 2 Section 1) The syllables in the third group are called the contracted sounds, because they are formed by joining two syllables and dropping the middle vowel, e.g. **kya** is formed by combining **ki** and **ya** and dropping the **i**.

Words

A *word* is a syllable or a combination of syllables that symbolizes and communicates a meaning. For example:

wa•ta•shi	*three-syllable word meaning* I
i•chi	*two-syllable word meaning* one
ku•ru•ma	*three-syllable word meaning* car

Phrases

A *phrase* is constituted by two or more words in sequence that form a syntactic unit. For example:

watashi-no	my
ichi-ji-ni	at one o'clock
kuruma-de	by car

Important

Syllables within a phrase are uttered without a pause between them. In this book, the words that constitute a single phrase are hyphenated, as shown above, to remind you not to pause between them. You may pause between phrases, depending on how rapidly you are speaking.

Also Important

In this book, when the English alphabet is used to express Japanese syllables and words, it is written in bold letters.

Spelling Rules

An apostrophe (') is used to separate the syllables when a single syllable **n** is followed by a single vowel syllable (**a**, **i**, **u**, **e**, **o**) or a **ya**-column syllable (**ya**, **yu**, **yo**).

kani	crab	*two-syllable word*
kan'i	simplicity	*three-syllable word*
shinai	within a city	*three-syllable word*
shin'ai	affection	*four-syllable word*
kinen	commemoration	*three-syllable word*
kin'en	no smoking	*four-syllable word*
konnyaku	root jelly	*four-syllable word*
kon'yaku	engagement	*four-syllable word*

A prolonged vowel, which is pronounced for the duration of two syllables, is written with a bar (macron) above the vowel like **ū**, **ō**, etc., except in the case of a prolonged **i** which is normally written as **ii**.

Tōkyō		*four-syllable word*
Kyōto		*three-syllable word*
ginkō	bank	*four-syllable word*
kūki	air	*three-syllable word*
byōin	hospital	*four-syllable word*
biyōin	beauty salon	*five-syllable word*

A silent syllable (choked break in your voice) is represented by the first of the two consonants in a double consonant, duplicating the consonant that follows.

hakken	discovery	*4-syllable word (2nd is silent)*
kesseki	absent	*4-syllable word (2nd is silent)*
shippai	failure	*4-syllable word (2nd is silent)*
okatte	kitchen	*4-syllable word (3rd is silent)*

Duplicating "**sh**" "**ch**" and "**ts**" is written as **ssh**, **tch** and **tts** respectively.

gasshō	chorus	*4-syllable word (2nd is silent)*
itchi	accord	*3-syllable word (2nd is silent)*
mittsu	three	*3-syllable word (2nd is silent)*

Practice

Count the number of syllables in the following words and pronounce them.

1. **Amerika**	America	19. **gen'in**	cause
2. **Igirisu**	U.K.	20. **kekka**	result
3. **Kanada**	Canada	21. **kitte**	postage stamp
4. **Ōsutoraria**	Australia	22. **hatten**	development
5. **Furansu**	France	23. **shinbun**	newspaper
6. **Doitsu**	Germany	24. **zasshi**	magazine
7. **Supein**	Spain	25. **shusseki**	present
8. **Chūgoku**	China	26. **kesshin**	determination
9. **Kankoku**	Korea	27. **muttsu**	six
10. **Nihon**	Japan	28. **shuppatsu**	departure
11. **ie**	house	29. **shutchō**	business trip
12. **iie**	no	30. **gyūnyū**	milk
13. **kuni**	country	31. **kōen**	park
14. **annai**	guide	32. **shin'yū**	close friend
15. **hana**	flower	33. **benkyō**	study
16. **han'i**	range	34. **yūbinkyoku**	post office
17. **kanai**	my wife	35. **gakkō**	school
18. **man'in**	fully packed	36. **sen'ō**	arbitrariness

Answers: Number of syllables

1. 4	7. 4	13. 2	19. 4	25. 4	31. 4
2. 4	8. 4	14. 4	20. 3	26. 4	32. 4
3. 3	9. 4	15. 2	21. 3	27. 3	33. 4
4. 7	10. 3	16. 3	22. 4	28. 4	34. 6
5. 4	11. 2	17. 3	23. 4	29. 4	35. 4
6. 3	12. 3	18. 4	24. 3	30. 4	36. 4

CHAPTER 1 SECTION 2

Accent and Intonation

This section will introduce you to the unique Japanese accent and intonation, and show you how to read the accent symbols I employ in this book. The accent adopted here is that of the standard Japanese language, as used by the media, and thus it is understood throughout the country.

English Accent

The Japanese and the English accent styles are completely different. Note the following example.

Let's say "good morning" in English.

Good **morn**ing!

The syllable "morn" is uttered louder. This is called stress accent or dynamic accent.

Japanese Accent

Let's say "good morning" in Japanese.

o	**ha**	**yō**		**go**	**za**	**i**	**ma**	**su**
	♪	♪—			♪	♪	♪	
♪				♪				♪
do	*re*	*re*	*re*	*do*	*re*	*re*	*re*	*do*

The preceding expression is pronounced as a two-level song using the *do* and *re* notes of the music scale. Unlike English, loudness does not change. This is called a pitch accent or musical accent. The intonation of two levels of pitch and constant loudness is normally maintained unless the utterance is fraught with emotions such as joy, anger, surprise, etc.

(The note *re* is 12% higher than the note *do* in pitch or tone frequency. In music, this is referred to as a "diatonic step.")

Accent Symbols

The following accent symbols are employed in this book:
Do level syllables are shown in small letters and *re* level syllables are shown in capital letters. Examples:

A•me	*re•do*	rain
a•ME	*do•re*	toffee / candy
HA•shi	*re•do*	chopsticks
ha•SHI	*do•re*	bridge
SA•ke	*re•do*	salmon
sa•KE	*do•re*	rice wine

A prolonged vowel is shown by double vowels, and the syllable is underlined in order to remind you that it is a prolonged vowel and there is no hiatus between the two vowels. Examples:

toOKYOO	*do•re•re•re*	**Tōkyō**
KYOoto	*re•do•do*	**Kyōto**
oBASAN	*do•re•re•re*	aunt
oBAasan	*do•re•do•do•do*	grandmother
byoOIN	*do•re•re•re*	hospital
biYOoin	*do•re•do•do•do*	beauty shop

Note

The double-vowel accent symbols which are not underlined are not prolonged vowels, and should therefore be pronounced with a hiatus between the vowels.
Examples:

oOKIi	big	toORI	street	koORI	ice	HOnoo	flame
toOI	far	TOo	ten	HOo	cheek	Ooi	many/much

So, written in accent symbols, "good morning" is:

oHAYOO goZAI-MAsu!

Important

In this book, when the English alphabet is used to express accent symbols, it is written in gothic (sans-serif) letters.

Intonation

As you may have noticed already, the accents on the first and second syllables of any Japanese word are of opposite levels (either *do•re* or *re•do*). However rapid speech may flatten out the sound levels, as discussed in the next paragraph.

Let us imagine a sentence consisting of two phrases.

	Phrase A	Phrase B
Sentence:	-------------------	-------------------

If the sentence is uttered rapidly, without a pause between the phrases, the accent of phrase B is affected by that of phrase A, as follows.

If the last syllable of phrase A is at *re* level and the first syllable of phrase B is at *do* level, this *do* changes to *re*. Example:

oHAYOO goZAI-MAsu (when uttered slowly)

oHAYOO GOZAI-MAsu (when uttered rapidly)

If the last syllable of phrase A is at *do* level, all syllables of phrase B change to *do* level. Example:

aRIgatoo goZAI-MAsu (when uttered slowly)

aRIgatoo gozai-masu (when uttered rapidly)

Practice the Japanese accent with the GREETINGS AND SIMPLE EXPRESSIONS in Appendix 1.

Chapter 2

KANA AND KANJI

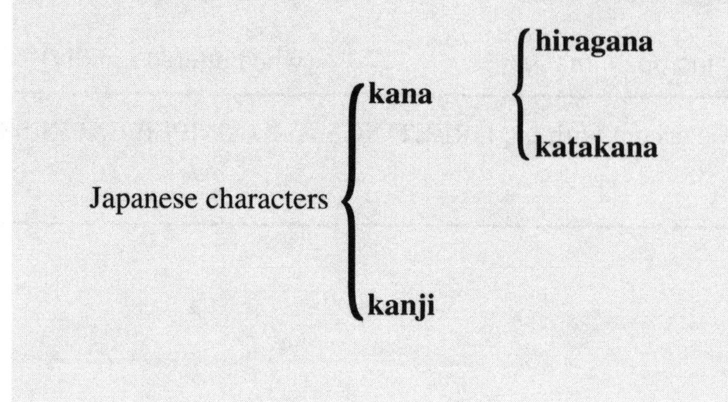

The Japanese language is normally written with **kana** and **kanji** characters (unless it is romanized) as we have seen in CHAPTER 1.

Kana

Kana characters, which were developed in Japan between 700 and 900 A.D., are phonetic characters, that is to say, one **kana** character represents a single sound and has no meaning in itself.

There are two styles of **kana** characters: **hiragana** and **katakana**. **Katakana** characters are used to imitate the sound of loanwords, that is, words borrowed from other languages, such as "coffee" and "butter." **Hiragana** characters are used to write any Japanese word except loanwords.

Kanji

Kanji characters started to develop in China over 3,000 years ago, and were introduced to Japan—where there was as yet no written language—between 400 and 700 A.D. **Kanji** characters are pictographs (characters that evolved from pictures) or ideograms (meaningful characters). For example, 山 means "mountain," and 川 means "river."

CHAPTER 2 SECTION 1

Hiragana

Hiragana is the basic characters set for the Japanese language. Each character represents one syllable. A contracted syllable, like **kya**, is written by combining a normal-sized character き (**ki**) with a second character, written at approximately a quarter of the size, ゃ (**ya**). This combination still depicts a single syllable.

Hiragana Syllabary

あ a	か ka	さ sa	た ta	な na	は ha	ま ma	や ya	ら ra	わ wa
い i	き ki	し shi	ち chi	に ni	ひ hi	み mi	い i	り ri	い i
う u	く ku	す su	つ tsu	ぬ nu	ふ fu	む mu	ゆ yu	る ru	う u
え e	け ke	せ se	て te	ね ne	へ he	め me	え e	れ re	え e
お o	こ ko	そ so	と to	の no	ほ ho	も mo	よ yo	ろ ro	を o

が ga	ざ za	だ da	ば ba	ぱ pa
ぎ gi	じ ji	ぢ ji	び bi	ぴ pi
ぐ gu	ず zu	づ zu	ぶ bu	ぷ pu
げ ge	ぜ ze	で de	べ be	ぺ pe
ご go	ぞ zo	ど do	ぼ bo	ぽ po

ん n

きゃ **kya**	しゃ **sha**	ちゃ **cha**	にゃ **nya**	ひゃ **hya**	みゃ **mya**	りゃ **rya**
きゅ **kyu**	しゅ **shu**	ちゅ **chu**	にゅ **nyu**	ひゅ **hyu**	みゅ **myu**	りゅ **ryu**
きょ **kyo**	しょ **sho**	ちょ **cho**	にょ **nyo**	ひょ **hyo**	みょ **myo**	りょ **ryo**

ぎゃ **gya**	じゃ **ja**	ぢゃ **ja**	びゃ **bya**	ぴゃ **pya**
ぎゅ **gyu**	じゅ **ju**	ぢゅ **ju**	びゅ **byu**	ぴゅ **pyu**
ぎょ **gyo**	じょ **jo**	ぢょ **jo**	びょ **byo**	ぴょ **pyo**

"Voiceless" to "Voiced" Sound Shift in English

There are a few cases of the voiceless (uttered without vibration of the vocal cords) to voiced (uttered with vibration of vocal cords) sound shift in English. Examples:

k-g distinction / distinguish
anxious / anxiety

s-z advice / advise
house / housing

t-d eat / edible

p-b purse / reimburse

f-v knife / knives
sift / sieve

"Voiceless" to "Voiced" Sound Shift in Japanese

The voiceless to voiced sound shift is extremely prevalent in Japanese. And, before I show you a few examples, we should note the very interesting way **hiragana** is constructed to cope with the shift. Observe the following:

k-g shift:

ka ki ku ke ko is written as かきくけこ
ga gi gu ge go is written as がぎぐげご

s-z shift:

sa shi su se so is written as さしすせそ
za ji zu ze zo is written as ざじずぜぞ

t-d shift:

ta chi tsu te to is written as たちつてと
da ji zu de do is written as だぢづでど

h-b-p shift:

ha hi fu he ho is written as はひふへほ
ba bi bu be bo is written as ばびぶべぼ
pa pi pu pe po is written as ぱぴぷぺぽ

Now you see that all you have to do to accomplish the shift in the Japanese **kana** writing is to add two dots (called **dakuten**) or a circle (called **han-dakuten**) to the upper right of the original voiceless characters. Clever, isn't it?

The voiceless to voiced sound shift in Japanese often occurs when two words are combined to make a *compound word*.

Examples:

k:	**kami**	paper	かみ
g:	**ori-gami**	fold + paper	おりがみ
s:	**sora**	sky	そら
z:	**ao-zora**	blue + sky	あおぞら
t:	**takara**	treasure	たから
d:	**ko-dakara**	child + treasure	こだから
h:	**hana**	flower	はな
b:	**ike-bana**	arrange + flower	いけばな

The word **hiragana** itself is the result of "k-g" shift from the original word of **kana**, and it means "plain **kana**."

Postpositions and Irregular Hiragana Usage

As the name implies, in English, *prepositions* (in, on, at, by, from, to, etc.) are always placed before a main word when used in assertive sentences (that is, in sentences that aren't questions).

The Japanese equivalent (**wa**, **ga**, **ni**, **o**, **e**, **de**, etc.), however, is always placed after a main word, and hence is called a *postposition*.

at 2 o'clock	**ni-ji-ni**	2 時に
in **Tōkyō**	**Tōkyō-de**	東京で
by train	**densha-de**	電車で

As shown in the preceding example, postpositions are always written in **hiragana**. Among many postpositions, however, the way of writing **wa**, **e**, and **o** in **hiragana** is irregular.

The postposition **wa** is written as は, which is otherwise pronounced **ha**, as in はな (flower), which is pronounced **hana**. (See CHAPTER 3 Section 4)

as for me	**watashi-wa**	私は

The postposition **e** is written as へ, which is otherwise pronounced **he**; for instance へや (room) is pronounced **heya**. (See CHAPTER 4 Section 8)

toward the station	**eki-e**	駅へ

The postposition **o** is written as を, which has no usage other than as a postposition. お (also **o**) is not used as a postposition. (See CHAPTER 4 Section 4 and 8)

through the park	**kōen-o**	公園を

Hiragana Spelling Rules

A silent syllable is represented by a small っ (**tsu**).

kekka	**kitte**	**kesseki**
けっか	きって	けっせき
result	postage stamp	absent

A syllable with a prolonged vowel (except **o**) is expressed by repeating the same vowel of that syllable.

For instance, the syllable ま (**ma**) includes the vowel sound **a** (あ). Therefore, a prolonged ま (**ma**) is written in hiragana as まあ.

o-kā-san	**o-nē-san**	**yakyū**
おかあさん	おねえさん	やきゅう
mother	elder sister	baseball

The second vowel after the prolonged **o** sound is expressed as う.

For instance, も (**mo**) includes the vowel sound **o** (お). However, a prolonged も (**mo**) is written in **hiragana** as もう, not もお.

o-tō-san	**ginkō**	**dōbutsu**
おとうさん	ぎんこう	どうぶつ
father	bank	animal
kōen	**hōritsu**	**rōjin**
こうえん	ほうりつ	ろうじん
park	law	old person

Note the difference between two consecutive vowels (**oo**) and a prolonged vowel (**ō**) in the following example. (See page 20)

(in **rōmaji**)	**Oosaka**	**Ōsaka***
(in **hiragana**)	おおさか	おうさか
(in **kanji**)	大阪	逢坂
(in accent symbols)	oOSAKA	oOSAKA

(* **Ōsaka** is the name of a hill in **Ootsu** city.)

Practice

あさひ	あめ	あす
Asahi	Ame	aSU
morning sun	rain	tomorrow

Practice (cont.)

いえ iE house	いぬ iNU dog	いす iSU chair
うま uMA horse	うし uSHI cow	うた uTA song
えいご eIGO English	えいが Eiga movie	えき Eki station
おとこ oTOKO man	おんな oNNA woman	おおどおり oODOori main street
かわ kaWA river	かぎ kaGI key	かさ KAsa umbrella
きもの kiMONO clothing	きつね kiTSUNE fox	きって kiTTE postage stamp
くつ kuTSU shoes	くし kuSHI comb	くも KUmo cloud/spider
けさ KEsa this morning	けむり keMURI smoke	けが keGA injury
こい KOi carp	こうえん koOEN park	こうじょう koOJOo factory
さる SAru monkey	さけ saKE rice wine	さかな saKANA fish

しろ	しま	しか
shiRO	shiMA	shiKA
castle	island	deer
すし	すずめ	すいどう
suSHI	suZUME	suIDOO
sushi	sparrow	tap water
せんせい	せいと	せっけん
seNSEi	SEito	seKKEN
teacher	student	soap
そら	そり	そろばん
SOra	SOri	soROBAN
sky	sleigh	abacus
たけ	たこ	たいこ
taKE	TAko	taIKO
bamboo	kite	drum
ちず	ちから	ちゅうしゃ
CHIzu	chiKARA	chuUSHA
map	power	injection
つき	つり	つくえ
tsuKI	tsuRI	tsuKUE
the moon	fishing	desk
てら	てがみ	てぶくろ
teRA	teGAMI	teBUkuro
temple	letter	gloves
とら	とけい	となり
toRA	toKEI	toNARI
tiger	clock	next door
なまえ	なし	なす
naMAE	naSHI	NAsu
name	pear	eggplant
にし	にわ	にんぎょう
niSHI	niWA	niNGYOO
west	garden	doll

ぬの nuNO cloth	ぬりもの nuRIMONO lacquerware	ぬかるみ nuKARUMI muddy road
ねこ NEko cat	ねずみ neZUMI mouse	ねぎ NEgi onion
のり noRI glue	のこぎり noKOGIri saw	のれん noREN shop curtain
はし haSHI bridge	はれ haRE clear weather	はがき haGAKI postcard
ひる hiRU noon	ひこうき hiKOoki airplane	ひつじ hiTSUJI sheep
ふね FUne ship	ふえ fuE flute	ふうせん fuUSEN balloon
へい heI fence	へや heYA room	へび HEbi snake
ほん HOn book	ほし hoSHI star	ほたる HOtaru firefly
まつ MAtsu pine tree	まち maCHI town	まど MAdo window
みみ miMI ear	みち miCHI street	みかん MIkan tangerine
むし muSHI insect	むね muNE breast	むぎ MUgi wheat

めいし
meISHI
business card

めがね
MEgane
glasses

めん
meN
face mask

もん
MOn
gate

もち
moCHI
rice cake

もくてき
moKUTEKI
purpose

やさい
yaSAI
vegetable

やね
YAne
roof

やかん
yaKAN
kettle

ゆき
yuKI
snow

ゆめ
yuME
dream

ゆうびんきょく
yuUBIn-kyoku
post office

よる
YOru
night

ようふく
yoOFUKU
Western clothes

よげん
yoGEN
prediction

らん
RAn
orchid

らせん
raSEN
spiral

らくだ
raKUDA
camel

りんご
riNGO
apple

りょかん
ryoKAN
inn

りょうり
RYOori
cooking

るす
RUsu
absence

るいじんえん
ruIJIn'en
ape

るつぼ
RUtsubo
melting pot

れんが
REnga
brick

れいぞうこ
reIZOoko
refrigerator

れっしゃ
reSSHA
train

ろうか
roOKA
corridor

ろんぶん
roNBUN
thesis

ろうそく
roOSOku
candle

わたし
waTASHI
I

わけ
WAke
reason

わに
WAni
alligator

CHAPTER 2 SECTION 2
Katakana

Katakana is another set of phonetic characters used to express the Japanese syllabary. **Katakana** characters are used to represent the sound of foreign names of persons, places and other loanwords.

Although it is difficult to simulate some foreign sounds with **katakana**, its representation is rather flexible, and the use of newly developed syllables (pictured with a grey background in the syllabary chart) is officially allowed in order to simulate foreign sounds as close to the original words as possible.

For example, both バイオリン (**baiorin**) and ヴァイオリン (**vaiorin**) can be used for "violin," both デザイン (**dezain**) and ディザイン (**dizain**) can be used for "design," and both ウイスキー (**uisukii**) and ウィスキー (**wisukii**) can be used for "whisky."

Katakana Syllabary

ア a	カ ka	サ sa		タ ta		ツァ tsa	ナ na	ハ ha	ファ fa	マ ma
イ i	キ ki	シ shi	スィ si	チ chi	ティ ti	ツィ tsi	ニ ni	ヒ hi	フィ fi	ミ mi
ウ u	ク ku	ス su		ツ tsu	トゥ tu		ヌ nu	フ fu		ム mu
エ e	ケ ke	セ se		テ te		ツェ tse	ネ ne	ヘ he	フェ fe	メ me
オ o	コ ko	ソ so		ト to		ツォ tso	ノ no	ホ ho	フォ fo	モ mo

ヤ ya	ラ ra	ワ wa		ガ ga	ザ za		ダ da	バ ba	ヴァ va	パ pa
イ i	リ ri	イ i	ウィ wi	ギ gi	ジ ji	ズィ zi	ディ di	ビ bi	ヴィ vi	ピ pi
ユ yu	ル ru	ウ u		グ gu	ズ zu		ドゥ du	ブ bu	ヴ vu	プ pu
イェ ye	レ re	エ e	ウェ we	ゲ ge	ゼ ze		デ de	ベ be	ヴェ ve	ペ pe
ヨ yo	ロ ro	ヲ o	ウォ wo	ゴ go	ゾ zo		ド do	ボ bo	ヴォ vo	ポ po

キャ kya	クァ kwa	シャ sha	チャ cha		ニャ nya	ヒャ hya		ミャ mya	リャ rya
	クィ kwi								
キュ kyu		シュ shu	チュ chu	テュ tyu	ニュ nyu	ヒュ hyu	フュ fyu	ミュ myu	リュ ryu
キェ kye	クェ kwe	シェ she	チェ che		ニェ nye	ヒェ hye			
キョ kyo	クォ kwo	ショ sho	チョ cho		ニョ nyo	ヒョ hyo	フョ fyo	ミョ myo	リョ ryo

ギャ gya	グァ gwa	ジャ ja		ビャ bya		ピャ pya
	グィ gwi					
ギュ gyu		ジュ ju	デュ dyu	ビュ byu	ヴュ vyu	ピュ pyu
	グェ gwe	ジェ je				
ギョ gyo	グォ gwo	ジョ jo		ビョ byo	ヴョ vyo	ピョ pyo

ン n

Katakana Spelling Rules

A silent syllable is represented by a small ッ. (This rule is the same as in **hiragana**.)

dokku	**koppu**	**poketto**
ドック	コップ	ポケット
dock	cup, glass	pocket

A prolonged vowel is represented by a bar "ー" (This rule is different from **hiragana**.)

kōhii	**chokorēto**	**chiizu**
コーヒー	チョコレート	チーズ
coffee	chocolate	cheese

Practice

Read the following words and see if you can identify the original words.

アメリカ aMERIKA America	カナダ KAnada Canada	イギリス iGIRISU U.K.
フランス fuRANSU France	オーストラリア oOSUTORAria Australia	ドイツ DOitsu Germany
スペイン suPEin Spain	ニューヨーク nyuUYOoku NewYork	ロンドン ROndon London
パリ PAri Paris	ベートーヴェン beETOoven Beethoven	バッハ BAhha Bach
ショパン SHOpan Chopin	アジア Ajia Asia	ヨーロッパ yoOROppa Europe
エンジェル Enjeru angel	クリーム kuRIimu cream	ケーキ KEeki cake

サラダ
SArada
salad

マカロニ
maKARONI
macaroni

ジュース
JUusu
juice

オフィス
Ofisu
office

スパゲッティ
suPAGEtti
spaghetti

ミュージック
MYUujikku
music

チェック
CHEkku
check

デュエット
DYUetto
duet

ヴィーナス
VIinasu
venus

アパート
aPAato
apartment

ボールペン
boORUPEN
ballpoint pen

ミシン
MIshin
machine

ヌード
NUudo
nude

アーモンド
aAMOndo
almond

カフェテリヤ
kaFETEriya
cafeteria

キャッシュ
KYAsshu
cash

ギャップ
GYAppu
gap

シェークスピア
sheEKUSUPIa
Shakespeare

ティー
TIi
tea

インタヴュー
iNTAvyuu
interview

アクセント
Akusento
accent

ビール
BIiru
beer

ソーセージ
soOSEeji
sausage

マヨネーズ
maYONEezu
mayonnaise

プレーヤー
puREeyaa
player

フォーク
FOoku
fork

ビュッフェ
BYUffe
buffet

コンピューター
koNPYUutaa
computer

ビルディング
biRUDIngu
building

ウェディング
WEdingu
wedding

パーティー
PAatii
party

ベッド
BEddo
bed

パン
PAn
bread

ビル
BIru
building

バス
BAsu
bus

タクシー
TAkushii
taxi

ボタン
boTAN
button

バター
BAtaa
butter

カメラ
KAmera
camera

メートル
meETORU
meter

センチ
SEnchi
centimeter

デパート
dePAato
department

ガス
GAsu
gas

ガラス
gaRASU
glass

グラム
GUramu
gram

ハンカチ
haNKACHI
handkerchief

ホテル
HOteru
hotel

インク
iNKU
ink

キロ
KIro
kilo

ナイフ
NAifu
knife

トイレ
TOire
toilet

マッチ
MAtchi
match

ミリ
MIri
millimeter

ミルク
MIruku
milk

ネクタイ
NEkutai
necktie

ニュース
NYUusu
news

ノート
noOTO
notebook

ズボン
zuBOn
trousers

ペン
PEn
pen

ピアノ
piANO
piano

ラジオ
RAjio
radio

プログラム
puROGUramu
program

スカート
suKAato
skirt

スプーン
suPUun
spoon

スポーツ
suPOotsu
sport

スーツケース
suUTSUKEesu
suitcase

テーブル	テレビ	テニス
teEBURU	TErebi	TEnisu
table	television	tennis
シャツ	ワイシャツ	ゼロ
SHAtsu	waISHATSU	ZEro
shirt	white shirt	zero
イヴ	クォーツ	カンツォーネ
Ivu	KWOotsu	kaNTSOone
eve	quartz	canzone
トゥナイト	レヴュー	チューバ
tuNAito	REvyuu	CHUuba
tonight	revue	tuba

CHAPTER 2 SECTION 3
Kanji

English Words

There are many meaningful components (called “roots,” “prefixes,” “suffixes,” etc.) in English words.
For example:

acrophobia	*acro* = highest, *phobia* = fear
ambivalence	*ambi* = on both sides, *bi* = two, *valence* = value
reimburse	*re* = again, *im* = in, *burse* = purse
philanthropist	*philo* = loving, *anthropo* = mankind, -*ist* = person

Knowledge of these meaningful components helps you to comprehend words and enables you to understand hundreds of new words even if you have never seen them before.

Some words are combined to form a *compound word.*
For example:

fountain-pen	schoolboy	salesman
laughingstock	outlook	pickpocket
homesick	out-of-date	good-for-nothing

Kanji

Meaningful components and compound words are also the fundamentals of constructing kanji characters and Japanese words as you see in the following discussions.

Kanji characters are comprised of pictographs (characters that evolved from pictures) and ideograms (meaningful characters).
Look at the following examples:

木	a character meaning *tree* or *wood* (as a material)
林	two trees meaning *woods*
森	three trees meaning *forest*
本	a mark at the foot of a tree meaning *origin* or *book*
束	a string around woods meaning *bundle*
巣	a bird nest in a tree meaning *nest*
果	a fruit in a tree meaning *fruit*
休	a person by a tree meaning *to rest* or *holiday*
机	wood and a pedestal meaning *desk*

On-readings and Kun-readings

The character 水, when it was developed in China from the shape of flowing water, meant "water" and was read as **sui** in Chinese. When this character was introduced to Japan, it was given another reading, **mizu**, which was the word for "water" in **yamato-kotoba**, the native Japanese language at that time which was spoken only. (**Yamato** is the ancient name for Japan and **kotoba** means "a word" or "language.")

Almost all **kanji** characters have two different readings, an **on**-reading and a **kun**-reading.

The **on**-reading is the reading adapted from the ancient Chinese pronunciation, comparable with Greek or Latin. For example, the reading **sui**, for 水, is equivalent to *hydro* or *aqua*. In general, the **on**-reading is used to read sophisticated compound words of two or more **kanji** characters combined.

The **kun**-reading is the reading of the character's meaning in native Japanese, and is comparable with Anglo-Saxon. **Mizu**, for 水, is equivalent to "water." In general, the **kun**-reading is the reading of a single character, and the first reading that children learn.

Now observe the following:

水力 The second character means "power," and is **chikara** in **kun**-reading. The correct reading of the compound word, however, is **sui-ryoku** in **on**-reading, and it is equivalent to "hydraulic power." It is interesting to note that Japanese children, whose knowledge level is of **kun**-readings only, could still tell (although they cannot read correctly) that 水力 means "water power" by reading it **mizu-no chikara**. On the other hand, English-speaking children would be completely lost when they saw the words "hydraulic power" for the first time, because it is impossible to associate *hydro* with "water."

水族館 Here the second character means "family" or "race" and the third character means "large building." So this compound word is pronounced **sui-zoku-kan**, and means "aquarium."

Superb Features (and Advantages) of Kanji

Knowledge of these meaningful **kanji** and **kanji** components helps you to comprehend words, and enables you to understand hundreds of new words even if you have no knowledge of their **on**-readings, or have never seen them before.

In addition, because of their visually comprehensible nature, the power of **kanji,** unlike **kana** or **rōmaji**, is that it can convey information more quickly to the reader. An understanding of **kanji** can therefore increase your reading speed, and enhance your comprehension of written matter tremendously.

Remember in CHAPTER 1 when I said that, as there are only 101 syllables to compose several hundred thousand Japanese words, we encounter quite a number of homonyms and heteronyms?
Let us examine an example:

はし が おれた。

Hashi ga oreta.

This sentence could have any of these three meanings:
(a) The chopstick was broken.
(b) The bridge was broken.
(c) The edge was broken.

If the sentence is written in **hiragana** only, or in the conventional way of writing in **rōmaji** characters, as shown above, or if the sentence is spoken with no accent, we cannot distinguish between these three. Now carefully observe the difference in **kanji** and accent symbols in the following.

(a) The chopstick was broken.	箸　が HAshi-ga	おれた。 oreta.
(b) The bridge was broken.	橋　が haSHI-ga	おれた。 oreta.
(c) The edge was broken.	端　が haSHI-GA	おれた。 Oreta.

Now you can see that the usage of **kanji** characters, 箸, 橋 or 端, and the correct accent clearly eliminate any ambiguity that exists among the three sentences.

Now I know what you want to ask next—

"How many **kanji** characters do I have to memorize?"

Well, my father, who was a newspaper editor, probably knew more than 20,000 characters. But this was before World War II. At the present time, daily use of **kanji** characters is limited to 1,945.

During the six years in which Japanese students attend elementary school, **kanji** characters are taught as follows

1st year:	80
2nd year:	160
3rd year:	200
4th year:	200
5th year:	185
6th year:	181
Total:	1,006

1,006 characters would cover more than 90% of **kanji** characters that appear in present-day newspapers.

In this book, all **kanji** characters are aligned vertically with the **rōmaji** accent symbols (as shown above) so that you will memorize **kanji** spontaneously while you are reading the romanized version of Japanese. You can test your **kanji** reading ability by covering up the line of **accent symbols** with a piece of paper. Also refer to the List of **Kanji** Radicals (Appendix 2) for further study. (A radical is the key part of a **kanji** which is used when you want to look up a character in a **kanji** dictionary.)

English "to be"

The English verb "to be" (am, are, is, etc.), when it is used as a principal verb in a sentence, has two major usages, namely as a copula and to mean "existence."

Copula

A *copula* (coupler) is the form of the verb "to be" that links the *subject* of a sentence with a *complementary noun* or an *adjective*.
Example:

I am a doctor.
(subject) (copula) (complementary noun)
He is tall.
(subject) (copula) (adjective)

A "to be" verb used as a copula is translated into Japanese as -**desu**, which will be discussed in this chapter.

Existence

In this usage, the "to be" verb means "to exist in a specified place."
For example:

I am in Japan.
(exist)
The park is in New York.
(exists)

A "to be" verb used to mean "existence" is translated into Japanese as either **i-masu** or **ari-masu**, which will be discussed in CHAPTER 4.

CHAPTER 3 SECTION 1
Nouns

A *noun* is a word used to denote or name a person, place, thing, quality, or act.

Below are some nouns to memorize. *Pronouns* (words that function as substitutes for nouns) are also included.

Nouns to Memorize

I	私	waTASHI
you	あなた	aNAta
he	彼	KAre
she	彼女	KAnojo
this (something physically or mentally near the speaker)	これ	koRE
that (something physically or mentally near the listener)	それ	soRE
that (something physically or mentally in the distance)	あれ	aRE
person	人	hiTO
child	子供	koDOMO
friend	友達	toMO-DACHI
name	名前	naMAE
Japan	日本	niHOn
Japanese people	日本人	niHON-JIn
Japanese (language)	日本語	niHON-GO
America	アメリカ	aMERIKA
American	アメリカ人	aMERIKA-jin
English (language)	英語	eI-GO
United Kingdom	イギリス	iGIRISU
Canada	カナダ	KAnada
Australia	オーストラリア	oOSUTORAria
France	フランス	fuRANSU
Germany	ドイツ	DOitsu
Spain	スペイン	suPEin
teacher	先生	seNSEi
student	生徒	SEito
office worker	会社員	kaISHA-in
banker	銀行家	giNKOO-KA
doctor	医者	iSHA

policeman	警官	keIKAN
salesman	セールスマン	seERUSU-man
engineer	エンジニア	eNJINIa
house	家	iE
town	町	maCHI
country	国	kuNI
school	学校	gaKKOO
post office	郵便局	yuUBIn-kyoku
hotel	ホテル	HOteru
department store	デパート	dePAato
train station	駅	Eki
hospital	病院	byoOIN
factory	工場	koOJOo
police station	警察	keISATSU
police box	交番	koOBAN
park	公園	koOEN
shrine	神社	JInja
temple	お寺	o-TERA
money	お金	o-KANE
thing	物	moNO
postage stamp	切手	kiTTE
letter	手紙	teGAMI
clothes	服	fuKU
shirt	シャツ	SHAtsu
hat/cap	帽子	boOSHI
necktie	ネクタイ	NEkutai
shoes	靴	kuTSU
umbrella	傘	KAsa
bread	パン	PAn
meat	肉	niKU
fish	魚	saKANA
egg	卵	taMAgo
apple	りんご	riNGO
banana	バナナ	BAnana
confectionery	お菓子	o-KAshi
coffee	コーヒー	koOHIi
room	部屋	heYA
book	本	HOn
pen	ペン	PEn
pencil	鉛筆	eNPITSU

watch	時計	toKEI
glasses	眼鏡	MEgane
camera	カメラ	KAmera
television	テレビ	TErebi
car	車	kuRUMA
automobile	自動車	jiDOosha
bicycle	自転車	jiTEnsha
bus	バス	BAsu
subway	地下鉄	chiKATETSU
airplane	飛行機	hiKOoki
mountain	山	yaMA
river	川	kaWA
tree	木	KI
water	水	miZU
hot water	お湯	o-YU
dog	犬	iNU
cat	猫	NEko
flower	花	haNA
cherry tree	桜	saKURA
rose	ばら	baRA

Noun and/or Noun

In order to conjoin two or more nouns, the conjunctions **to**, **ya**, and **ka** are used. However their usage is somewhat different from "and" and "or" in English.

"A and B" in English is expressed **A to B** in Japanese.
Examples:

coffee and tea	**kōhii to kōcha**
you and I	**anata to watashi**
a dog and a cat	**inu to neko**

Note the difference in the position of "and" and **to** when three or more nouns are involved.

English	A, B, C, D and E
Japanese	**A to B, C, D, E**

Example:

Bill, Charlie, George, and Tom — **Biru to Chārii, Jōji, Tomu**

Ya also means "and," but it also implies "et cetera" or "among others." In other words, **A ya B** in Japanese means "A, B, and some others."
Examples:

coffee, tea, etc.	**kōhii ya kōcha**
a dog, a cat, etc.	**inu ya neko**

"A or B" in English is expressed **A ka B** in Japanese.
Examples:

coffee or tea	**kōhii ka kōcha**
you or I	**anata ka watashi**
a dog or a cat	**inu ka neko**

CHAPTER 3 SECTION 2
Noun Modifiers (1) : Adjectives

A *noun modifier* is a word, a phrase, or a clause, used to describe or qualify a noun.

Important

In Japanese, unlike English, a noun modifier is always placed before the noun.
Examples:

a red pen	**akai pen**
the pen in my pocket	**poketto-no-naka-no pen**
the pen which I bought yesterday	**kinō katta pen**

In this book, noun modifiers are discussed in the following sections:

CHAPTER 3 Section 2 Noun Modifiers (1): Adjectives
CHAPTER 3 Section 3 Noun Modifiers (2): (Noun)-no
CHAPTER 13 Section 3 Noun Modifiers (3): Adjectival Clause

Adjectives

An *adjective* is a word used to modify a noun by limiting, qualifying, or specifying.
Examples:

young men
something nice
my right hand

There are two kinds of adjectives in Japanese: **i**-adjectives and **na**-adjectives, named after their last syllables.
Examples:

i-adjectives (symbolized as **A-i**)

aka-i	red
furu-i	old
haya-i	fast

na-adjectives (symbolized as **A-na**)

kirei-na	pretty
shizuka-na	quiet
yūmei-na	famous

Adjectives "big" and "small" can be expressed in both **i**-adjective and **na**-adjective forms.

big:	**ooki-i**	**ooki-na**
small:	**chiisa-i**	**chiisa-na**

Some Adjectives to Memorize

a high mountain	高い山 taKAi yaMA
a low tree	低い木 hiKUi KI
an expensive camera	高いカメラ taKAi KAmera
an inexpensive watch	安い時計 yaSUi toKEI
a new hotel	新しいホテル aTARASHIi HOteru
an old temple	古いお寺 fuRUi o TERA
a long river	長い川 naGAi kaWA
a short pencil	短い鉛筆 miJIKAi eNPITSU
a distant country	遠い国 toOI kuNI
a nearby station	近い駅 chiKAi Eki
a quick fox	速いきつね haYAi kiTSUNE
a slow elephant	遅い象 oSOI ZOo
a wide (spacious) room	広い部屋 hiROi heYA
a narrow street	狭い道 seMAi miCHI

an interesting book	おもしろい本 oMOSHIROi HOn
a boring movie	つまらない映画 tsuMARAnai Eiga
a delicious banana	おいしい バナナ oISHII BAnana
an unsavory apple	まずい りんご maZUi riNGO
hot tea	熱いお茶 aTSUi o-CHA
cold water	冷たい水 tsuMETAI miZU
an adorable child	かわいい 子供 kaWAIi koDOMO
a white dog	白い犬 shiROi iNU
a black cat	黒い猫 kuROi NEko
blue sky	青い空 aOi SOra
a yellow flower	黄色い 花 kiIROI haNA
a red rose	赤いばら aKAI baRA
merry Christmas	楽しいクリスマス taNOSHIi kuRISUmasu
a difficult problem	難しい問題 muZUKASHIi moNDAI
easy work	やさしい 仕事 yaSASHIi shiGOTO

a big airplane	大きい(大きな) 飛行機 oOKIi (Ookina) hiKOoki
a small car	小さい(小さな)車 chiISAi (CHIisana) kuRUMA
dirty shoes	汚い靴 kiTANAi kuTSU
a clean shirt	きれいなシャツ KIreina SHAtsu
a pretty flower	きれいな花 KIreina haNA
a convenient store	便利な店 BEnrina miSE
a quiet town	静かな町 SHIzukana maCHI
a famous doctor	有名な医者 yuUMEINA iSHA
a fine school	立派な学校 riPPANA gaKKOO
an honest student	正直な生徒 shoOJIKIna SEito
a kind policeman	親切な警官 SHInsetsuna keIKAN
an important letter	大切な手紙 taISETSUNA teGAMI

CHAPTER 3 SECTION 3

Noun Modifiers (2): (noun) -no

(Noun) -no (Noun)

A noun followed by **no** (hereafter symbolized as **N-no**) behaves just like an adjective, modifying the noun that follows.
Examples:

watashi-no kuruma	my car
Toyota-no kuruma	a **Toyota** car
keisatsu-no kuruma	a police car
Sumisu-san-no Nihon-no kuruma	Mr. Smith's Japanese car
watashi-no tomodachi-no kuruma	my friend's car

In the second-last example, both **Sumisu-san-no** (Mr. Smith's) and **Nihon-no** (Japanese) modify **kuruma** (car), while in the last example, **watashi-no** (my) modifies **tomodachi** (friend), and **tomodachi-no** (friend's) modifies **kuruma**.

Compare these two:

kaisha-no kuruma	a company car (a car owned by the company)
kuruma-no kaisha	a car company (a company that manufactures or sells cars)

When the pronouns **kore**, **sore**, and **are** are used as **N-no** modifiers, they become **ko-no**, **so-no**, and **a-no**, respectively.

Noun	(Noun)-**no**	Examples
kore	**ko-no**	**ko-no kamera** (this camera)
sore	**so- no**	**so-no kamera** (that camera)
are	**a- no**	**a-no kamera** (that camera)

More Examples

this pen	こ の ペン ko-NO PEn
this watch	こ の 時計 ko-NO toKEI
that pencil	そ の 鉛筆 so-NO eNPITSU
that apple	そ の りんご so-NO riNGO
that mountain	あの 山 a-NO yaMA
that airplane	あの 飛行 機 a-NO hiKOoki
my room	私 の 部屋 waTASHI-NO heYA
your country	あなたの 国 aNAta-no kuNI
his house	彼 の 家 KAre-no iE
her letter	彼 女の 手紙 KAnojo-no teGAMI
George's bicycle	ジョージさんの 自転 車 JOoji-san-no jiTEnsha
a new Japanese camera	新 しい 日本 の カメラ aTARASHIi niHON-NO KAmera
a big American car	大きい アメリカ の 車 oOKIi aMERIKA-NO kuRUMA
famous French wine	有 名 な フランス の ワイン yuUMEINA fuRANSU-NO WAin

delicious German bread	おいしいドイツ の パン oISHII DOitsu-no PAn
a kind English policeman	親切 なイギリスの 警官 SHInsetsu-na iGIRISU-NO keIKAN
my Japanese teacher	私 の日本 語の 先生 waTASHI-no niHONGO-NO seNSEi
my friend's house	私 の友 だち の家 waTASHI-NO toMODACHI-NO iE
an old temple in **Kyōto**	京都の古 いお寺 KYOoto-no fuRUi o-TERA
her dog's name	彼女の犬 の名前 KAnojo-no iNU-NO naMAE
research on a new computer	新 しいコンピューターの 研究 aTARASHIi koNPYUutaa-no keNKYUU
a nearby subway station	近 くの地下鉄 の駅 chiKAku-no chiKATETSU-NO Eki
10 o'clock plane to N.Y.	10時 の ニューヨーク行き の 飛行機 JUuji-no nyuUYOOKU-YUKI-NO hiKOoki
a small hotel in an old town	古い町 の小さいホテル fuRUi-machi-no chiISAi HOteru

CHAPTER 3 SECTION 4
Sentence Pattern (1)

Five Sentence Patterns

I have categorized Japanese sentences into five basic sentence patterns, which will be discussed in the following sections:

CHAPTER 3 Section 4 Sentence Pattern (1)
CHAPTER 3 Section 5 Sentence Pattern (2)

CHAPTER 4 Section 3 Sentence Pattern (3)
CHAPTER 4 Section 4 Sentence Pattern (4)
CHAPTER 4 Section 5 Sentence Pattern (5)

Sentence Pattern (1)

Observe the following, and note the word order:

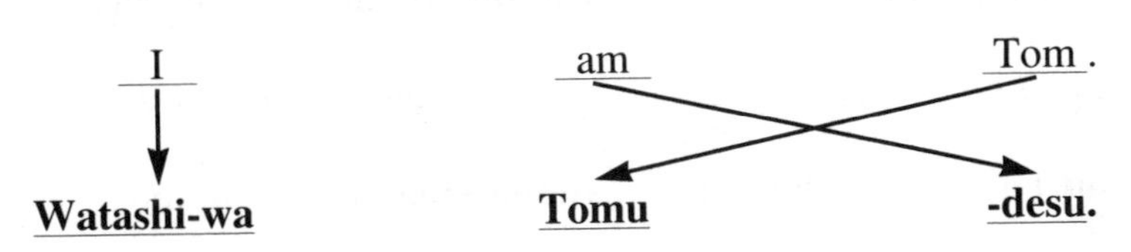

So Sentence Pattern (1) is:

(Theme)**-wa** (Noun)**-desu.**

Breakdown of the Pattern

The postposition **-wa** denotes that the word to which **-wa** is attached is the topic the speaker is going to talk about or the *theme* of the sentence. In the preceding example, the speaker begins with **Watashi-wa**, which indicates that the theme is the speaker himself, and not somebody or something else. (The theme is a significant feature of the Japanese language. Refer to CHAPTER 5 Section 1 for a detailed discussion.)

As discussed in the introduction to CHAPTER 3, **-desu** is equivalent to the English verb "to be" (am, is, etc.).

The (noun)**-desu** part is called the *predicate*. The predicate describes the theme.

Expansion of the Pattern

The noun of (noun)**-desu** can be accompanied by one or more noun modifiers. Examples:

He is a teacher.	**Kare-wa sensei-desu.**
He is a Japanese teacher.	**Kare-wa Nihon-go-no sensei-desu.**
He is our Japanese teacher.	**Kare-wa watashi-tachi-no Nihon-go-no sensei-desu.**

The theme, since it is also a noun, can be accompanied by one or more noun modifiers. Examples:

That building is a hospital.	**Ano-tatemono-wa byōin-desu.**
That big building is a hospital.	**Ano-ookina-tatemono-wa byōin-desu.**
That big, white building is a hospital.	**Ano-ookina-shiroi-tatemono-wa byōin-desu.**
That big, white building on the right is a hospital.	**Ano-migi-no-ookina-shiroi-tatemono-wa byōin-desu.**

Observe this:

This watch is my watch.	**Kono-tokei-wa watashi-no-tokei-desu.**

In both English and Japanese, the second "watch" or **tokei** is redundant and can be omitted as follows:

This watch is mine.	**Kono-tokei-wa watashi-no-desu.**

More Examples

I am Tom Smith.	私はトムスミスです。 waTASHI-WA TOmu SUmisu-desu.
I am an American.	私はアメリカ人です。 waTASHI-WA aMERIKA-jin-desu.
I am a company employee.	私は会社員です。 waTASHI-WA kaISHAin-desu.
I am an employee of the Z Company.	私はZ社の社員です。 waTASHI-WA Z-sha-no SHAin-desu.
He is Mr. **Tanaka**.	彼は田中さんです。 KAre-wa taNAKA-SAN-DEsu.
He is a doctor at this hospital.	彼はこの病院の先生です。 KAre-wa koNO byoOIN-NO seNSEi-desu.
Bill is Tom's friend.	ビルはトムの友達です。 BIru-wa TOmu-no toMODACHI-DEsu.
This is my umbrella.	これは私の傘です。 koRE-WA waTASHI-NO KAsa-desu.

That red umbrella is **Hanako**'s.	あの 赤い 傘 は 花 子さんのです。 a-NO aKAI KAsa-wa HAnako-san-no-desu.
This pretty flower is **sakura**.	こ の きれいな花 は 桜 です。 ko-NO KIreina haNA-wa saKURA-DEsu.
Sakura is a Japanese flower.	桜 は 日本 の 花 です。 saKURA-WA niHON-NO haNA-desu.

CHAPTER 3 SECTION 5
Sentence Pattern (2)

Adjectives

An adjective (both in English and in Japanese!) has two major usages: an *attributive use* and a *predicative use*.

Attributive Use

In this usage an adjective is directly attached to, and modifies, a noun. Example:

Mt. Fuji is a high mountain.

You already have seen examples of this use in CHAPTER 3 Section 2. Note that this is sentence pattern (1).

Predicative Use

In this usage, an adjective acts as a complementary word to a "to be" verb (am, is, are, etc.) to describe the subject. The adjective and the "to be" verb together form the predicate of the sentence.
Example:

Mt. Fuji is high.

And this is sentence pattern (2).

Sentence Pattern (2)

"Mt. Fuji is high" is expressed in Japanese as follows.

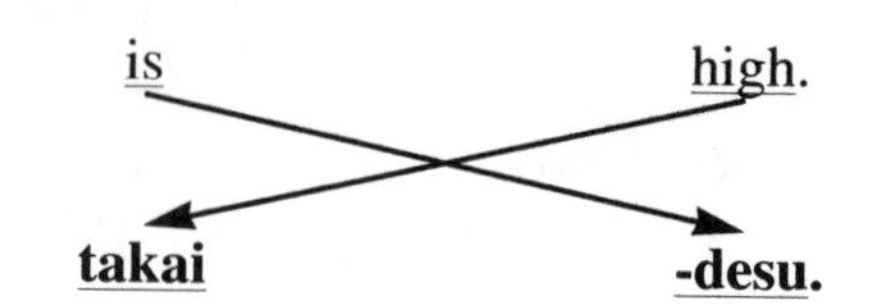

So Sentence Pattern (2) is:

(Theme)**-wa** (Adjective)**-desu.**

Breakdown of the Pattern

Like (noun)**-desu** in the previous section, (adjective)**-desu** is also a predicate.

When a **na**-adjective is used as a predicate, the **-na** part must be dropped.
Examples:

Betty is pretty.	**Betei-san-wa kirei-desu.**
	(not **kirei-na-desu**)
Betty is kind.	**Betei-san-wa shinsetsu-desu.**
	(not **shinsetsu-na-desu**)

As described in Section 2, adjectives "big" and "small" can be expressed in both **i-**adjective and **na-**adjective forms.

big:	**ooki-i**	**ooki-na**
small:	**chiisa-i**	**chiisa-na**

However **ooki-na** and **chiisa-na** cannot be used as a predicate even after the **-na** part is dropped. Observe the following.

An elephant is big.	**Zō-wa ooki-i desu.**	(right)
	Zō-wa ooki-na desu.	(wrong)
	Zō-wa ooki desu.	(wrong)

A mouse is small.	**Nezumi-wa chiisa-i desu.**	(right)
	Nezumi-wa chiisa-na desu.	(wrong)
	Nezumi-wa chiisa desu.	(wrong)

More Examples

This is good.	これ は いいです。 koRE-WA Ii- desu.
That is bad.	それ は 悪 いです。 soRE-WA waRUi-desu.
This camera is expensive.	この カメラは 高 いです。 koNO-KAmera-wa taKAi-desu.
This personal computer is cheap.	この パソコン は 安 いです。 koNO-paSOKON-WA yaSUi-desu.
This big hotel is new.	この 大きな ホテル は 新 しいです。 koNO-Ookina-HOteru-WA aTARASHIi-desu.
That small temple is old.	あの 小さいお寺 は 古 いです。 aNO-chiISAi-o-TERA-WA fuRUi-desu.
This book is interesting.	この 本 は おもしろいです。 koNO-HOn-wa oMOSHIROi-desu.
That movie is boring.	その 映画は つまらないです。 soNO-Eiga-wa tsuMARAnai-desu.
The Japanese pear is delicious.	日本 の 梨 は おいしいです。 niHON-NO naSHI-WA o I SHI i -desu.
This apple is unsavory.	この りんごは まずいです。 koNO-riNGO-WA maZUi-desu.
His shoes are dirty.	彼 の 靴 は 汚 いです。 KAre-no kuTSU-wa kiTANAi-desu.
This shrine is famous.	この 神社は 有 名 です。 koNO-JInja-wa yuUMEI-DEsu.
The subway in **Tōkyō** is convenient.	東京 の 地下鉄 は 便利 です。 toOKYOO-NO chiKATETSU-WA BEnri-desu.

CHAPTER 3 SECTION 6
Questions

Question Form

Observe the following.

Sentence Pattern (1)

He is Tom.	**Kare-wa Tomu-desu.**
Is he Tom?	**Kare-wa Tomu-desu-ka?**

Sentence Pattern (2)

Mt. Fuji is high.	**Fuji-san-wa takai-desu.**
Is Mt. Fuji high?	**Fuji-san-wa takai-desu-ka?**

All you have to do to convert these sentences to question form is add **ka** at the end of the sentence, and pronounce it with a raised intonation. Simple, isn't it?

To Answer

The answer to questions formed from sentence patterns (1) and (2) is either "yes" or "no," or **hai** or **iie**.

Important

"Yes" and "no" in English do not always correspond to **hai** and **iie** in Japanese. There are some cases that you must say **iie** to mean "yes" and **hai** to mean "no."

Carefully observe the following examples:

You speak Japanese, don't you?	**Hai.**	(I do)
	Iie.	(I do not)
You don't speak Japanese, do you?	**Iie.**	(I do)
	Hai.	(I do not)

Hai really means "you are right," or "I agree with you."
Iie really means "you are wrong," or "I disagree with you."

Therefore you must be careful when a question is asked in a negative form like the second example above. To be safe, you should not just say **hai** or **iie**, but you had better complete the sentence to avoid misunderstanding.

Hai and **iie** are formal expressions. In English there are some informal words, like "uh-huh", "yeah", and "nope," that are used only when speaking to close friends or family members. Some of them are (in order of formality):

hai group	**hā, ē, ā, un**
iie group	**ie, iya, uun**

More Examples

Are you Mr. **Tanaka**?	あなた は 田中 さん です か。 aNAta-wa taNAKA-SAN-DEsu-KA?
Is he a policeman?	彼 は 警官 です か。 KAre-wa keIKAN-DEsu-KA?
Is that white car yours?	あの 白 い車 は あなたの です か。 aNO-shiROi-kuRUMA-WA aNAta-no-desu-KA?
Is Japanese difficult?	日本 語 は 難 しいです か。 niHON-GO-WA muZUKASHIi-desu-KA?
Is the subway station nearby?	地下鉄 の 駅 は 近 いですか。 chiKATETSU-NO Eki-wa chiKAi-desu-KA?
Is your neighborhood quiet?	お宅 の あたりは 静 か です か。 o-TAKU-NO Atari-wa SHIzuka-desu-KA?
Is that story true?	その 話 は 本当 です か。 soNO-haNASHI-wa hoNTOO-DEsu-KA?
Is the town of **Tōkyō** clean?	東 京 の 町 は きれいです か。 toOKYOO-NO-maCHI-wa KIrei-desu-KA?

CHAPTER 3 SECTION 7
Interrogatives: Who, What, Which

Interrogative words are discussed as follows.

CHAPTER 3 Section 7 Interrogatives: Who, What, Which
CHAPTER 4 Section 11 Interrogatives: When, Where, Why, How

Who

The English interrogative "who" is **dare** in Japanese, but note the word position:

Is he Tom?	**Kare-wa Tomu-desu-ka?**
Who is he?	**Kare-wa dare-desu-ka?**

The difference between the two Japanese sentences is that only the word **Tomu** is replaced with **dare**. In other words, the Japanese word order for "who is he?" is "is he who?"

What

The English interrogative "what" is **nani** in Japanese, but it becomes **nan** before the consonants **t**, **n**, and **d**, and counting units. (Refer to Appendix 3 for the counting units.)

Is this a pen?	**Kore-wa pen-desu-ka?**
What is this?	**Kore-wa nan-desu-ka?**

Again the Japanese word order for "what is this?" is "is this what?"

Which

The English interrogative "which" is either **dotchi** (selecting one out of two) or **dore** (selecting one out of three or more).

Which (of two) is your umbrella?	**Anata-no-kasa-wa dotchi-desu-ka?**
Which (of three) is your umbrella?	**Anata-no-kasa-wa dore-desu-ka?**

As a Noun Modifier

"Who," "what," and "which" can be used as noun modifiers as follows:

whose flower	**dare-no-hana**
what flower	**nan-no-hana**
which flower (of two)	**dotchi-no-hana**
which flower (of three or more)	**do-no-hana** (not **dore-no**)

More Examples

Who is that gentleman?	あの 男 の 人 は だれ です か。 aNO-oTOKO-NO-HITO-wa DAre-desu-KA?
Who is that beautiful lady?	あの 美 しい 女 の 人 は aNO-uTSUKUSHIi-oNNA-NO-HITO-wa だれ です か。 DAre-desu-KA?
Whose photograph is this?	これ は だれ の 写真 です か。 koRE-WA DAre-no-shaSHIN-DEsu-KA?
What is that tall building?	あの 高 いビルは 何 です か。 aNO-taKAi-biru-wa NAn-desu-KA?
What is your name?	あなたの 名前 は 何 です か。 aNAta-no-naMAE-WA NAn-desu-KA?
What book is this?	これ は 何 の 本 です か。 koRE-WA NAn-no-HOn-desu-KA?
What time is it now?	いま 何 時で す か。 Ima NAn-ji-desu-KA?
Which (of two) is yours?	あなたの は どっち です か。 aNAta-no-wa DOtchi-desu-KA?

CHAPTER 3 SECTION 8

Negative and Past Forms of -Desu

This chapter will show you how to read the N-P (negative-past) triangle and help you to understand its application to **-desu**.

N-P Triangle

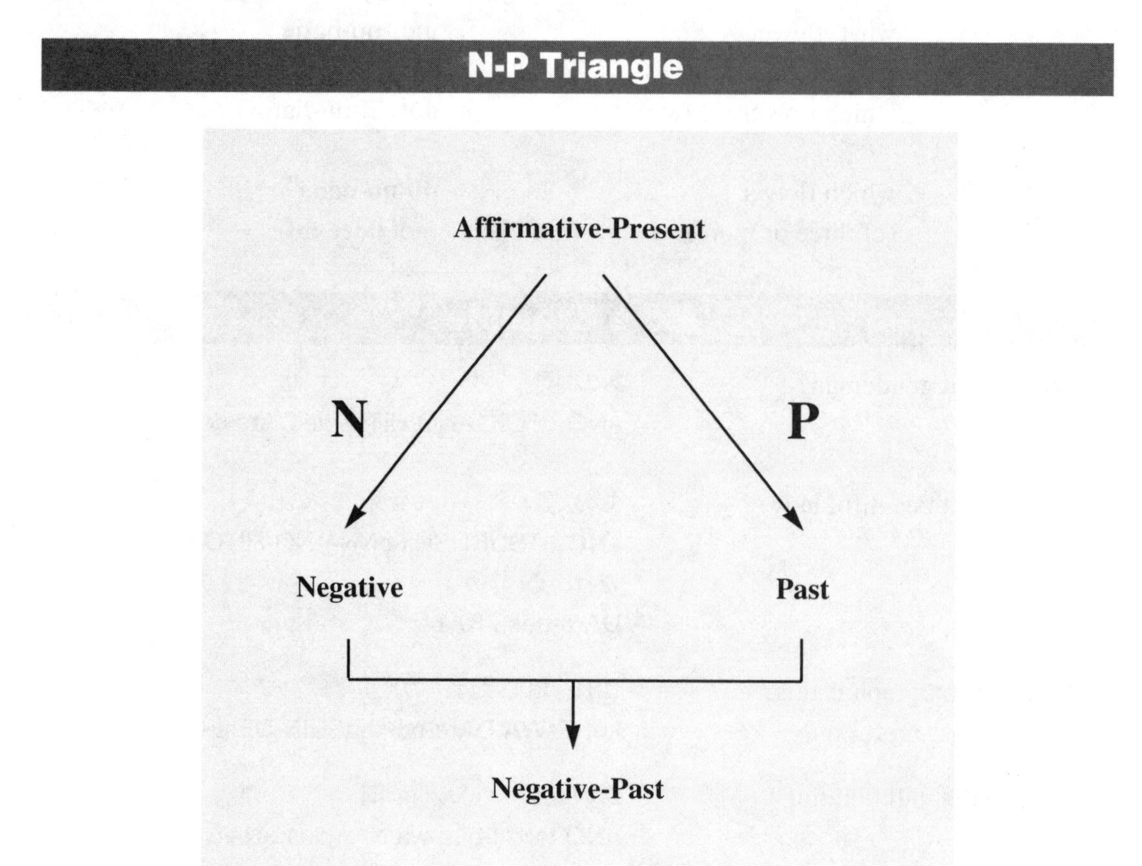

Starting from the *affirmative-present* form (e.g. "he is") at the top, the left arrow leads you to the *negative-present* form (e.g. "he is not"). The right arrow leads you to the *affirmative-past* form (e.g. "he was"), and, at the bottom, you have the combined *negative-past* form (e.g. "he was not").

N-P Triangle for N-desu and A-(na)-desu

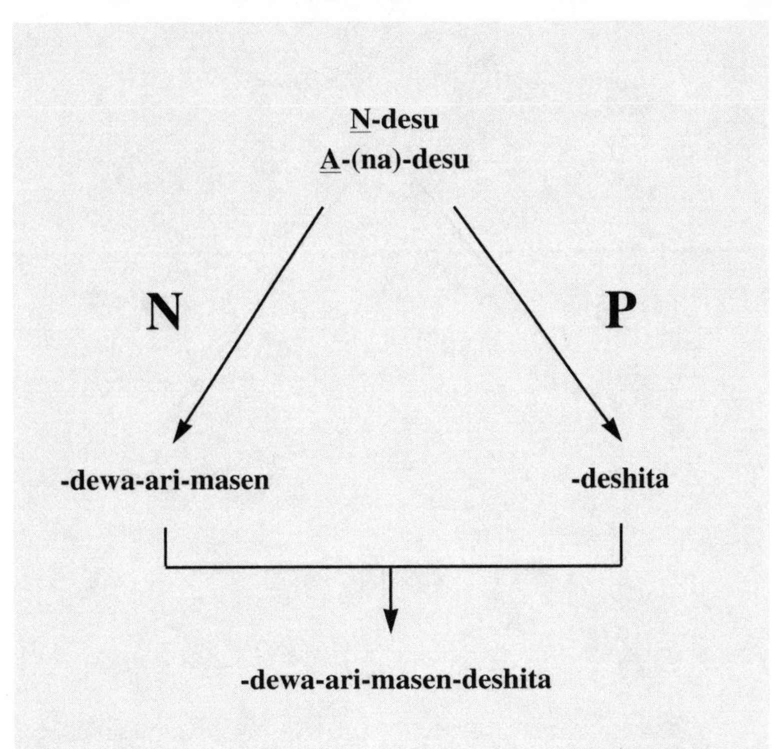

Examples

He is a doctor.	**Kare-wa isha-desu.**
He is not a doctor.	**Kare-wa isha-dewa-ari-masen.**
He was a doctor.	**Kare-wa isha-deshita.**
He was not a doctor.	**Kare-wa isha-dewa-ari-masen-deshita.**
He is famous.	**Kare-wa yūmei-desu.**
He is not famous.	**Kare-wa yūmei-dewa-ari-masen.**
He was famous.	**Kare-wa yūmei-deshita.**
He was not famous.	**Kare-wa yūmei-dewa-ari-masen-deshita.**

Dewa in the negative and negative-past forms is rather formal.
In an informal environment, it becomes **ja**. For example:

He is not a doctor. **Kare-wa isha-ja-ari-masen**.

N-P Triangle for A-i-desu

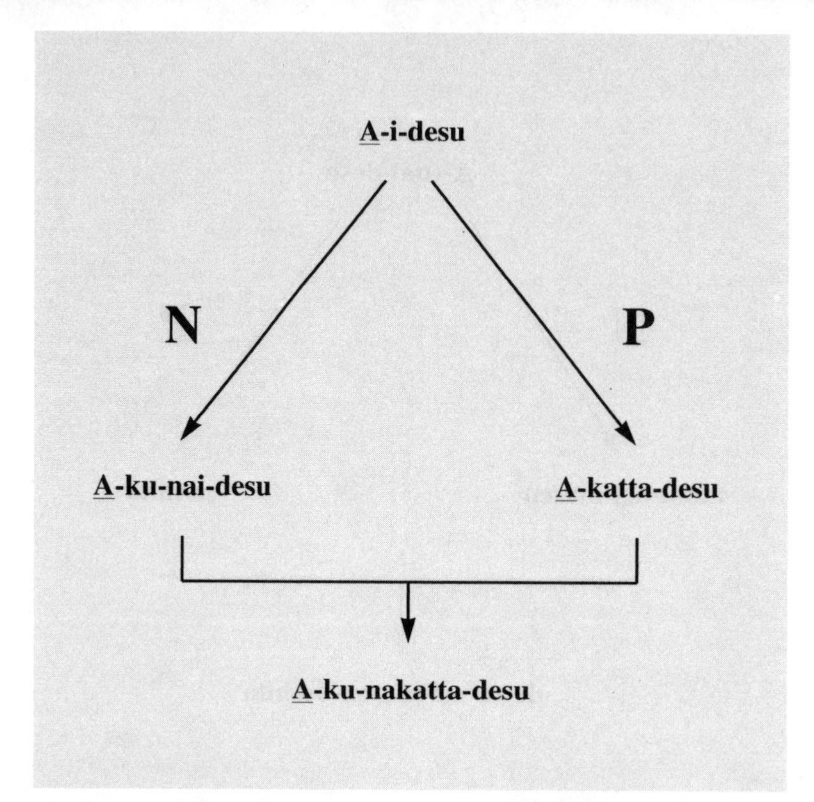

Examples

It is long.	**Sore-wa naga-i-desu.**
It is not long.	**Sore-wa naga-ku-nai-desu.**
It was long.	**Sore-wa naga-katta-desu.**
It was not long.	**Sore-wa naga-ku-nakatta-desu.**

The following forms are also used, but they are rather formal:

negative	**A-ku-ari-masen**
negative-past	**A-ku-ari-masen-deshita**

The original form of an adjective **i-i** (good) is **yo-i**, which is still used in the negative, past, and negative-past forms.

It is good.	**Sore-wa i-i-desu.**
It is not good.	**Sore-wa yo-ku-nai-desu.**
It was good.	**Sore-wa yo-katta-desu.**
It was not good.	**Sore-wa yo-ku-nakatta-desu.**

More Examples

Mr. **Tanaka** is not a salesman. He is a system engineer.	田中 さんは セールス マン では ありません。システム エンジニア です。 taNAKA-SAN-WA seERUSU-man-dewa-aRI-MASEn. shiSUTEMU-ENJINIa-desu.
Rashōmon was an interesting movie.	羅生 門 は おもしろい映画 でした。 raSHOOMON-WA oMOSHIROi-Eiga-deshita.
This neighborhood was quiet.	この あたりは 静 か でした。 koNO-Atari-wa SHIzuka-deshita.
Tarō was not a bad boy.	太郎 は 悪 い子 では ありません でした。 TAroo-wa waRUi-ko-dewa-aRI-MASEn-deshita.
The air in **Tōkyō** was not clean.	東京 の 空気 は きれい では ありません でした。 toOKYOO-NO-KUuki-wa KIrei-dewa-aRI-MASEn-deshita.
It is not cold today.	きょうは 寒 く ないです。 KYOo-wa SAMUku-NAi-desu.
Was the weather good?	お天気 は よかった です か。 oTEnki-wa YOkatta-desu-KA?
This camera was not cheap.	この カメラ は 安 くなかった です。 koNO-KAmera-wa YAsu-ku-NAkatta-desu.

CHAPTER 3 SECTION 9

Comparison

Adjectives

Adjectives, the words of qualitative or quantitative nature, make the comparison possible. Example:

long	longer	longest
Positive	Comparative	Superlative

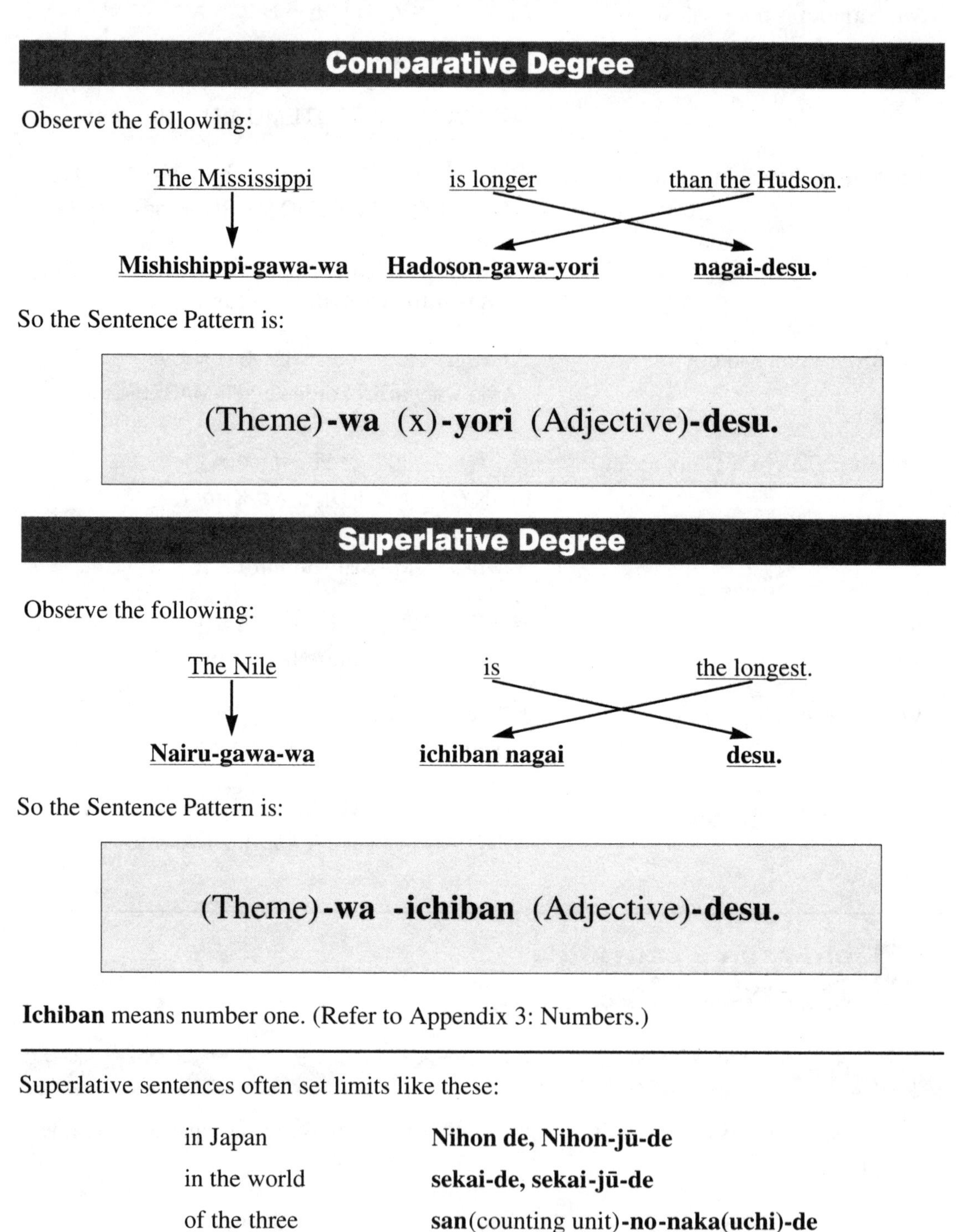

This chapter will discuss the basic sentences of comparison. The sentence patterns shown here are variations of Sentence Pattern (2) ([Theme]**-wa** **A-desu**).

Comparative Degree

Observe the following:

The Mississippi | is longer | than the Hudson.

Mishishippi-gawa-wa **Hadoson-gawa-yori** **nagai-desu.**

So the Sentence Pattern is:

(Theme)**-wa** (x)**-yori** (Adjective)**-desu.**

Superlative Degree

Observe the following:

The Nile | is | the longest.

Nairu-gawa-wa **ichiban nagai** **desu.**

So the Sentence Pattern is:

(Theme)**-wa** **-ichiban** (Adjective)**-desu.**

Ichiban means number one. (Refer to Appendix 3: Numbers.)

Superlative sentences often set limits like these:

in Japan	**Nihon de, Nihon-jū-de**
in the world	**sekai-de, sekai-jū-de**
of the three	**san**(counting unit)**-no-naka(uchi)-de**
of all	**subete(minna)-no-naka(uchi)-de**

More Examples

Mont Blanc is higher than Mt. **Fuji**.	モンブランは富士山より高いです。 moNBURAn-wa FUjisan-yori taKAi-desu.
The earth is bigger than the moon.	地球は月より大きいです。 chiKYUU-WA tsuKI-yori oOKIi-desu.
The bus stop is closer than the subway station.	バス停は地下鉄の駅より baSU-TEI-WA chiKATETSU-NO-Eki-yori 近いです。 chiKAi-desu.
Health is more important than money.	健康はお金より大切です。 keNKOO-WA o-KANE-YOri taISETSU-DEsu.
Sydney is one hour ahead of **Tōkyō**. (**hayai** = early)	シドニーは東京より1時間早いです。 SHIdonii-wa toOKYOO-YOri iCHI-JIkan haYAi-desu.
This store is the most convenient.	この店はいちばん便利です。 koNO-miSE-wa iCHIBAN BEnri-desu.
Mt. Everest is the highest in the world.	エベレスト山は世界でいちばん eBERESUTO-san-wa SEkai-de iCHIBAN 高いです。 taKAi-desu.
This church is the oldest in the town.	この教会は町でいちばん koNO-kyoOKAI-WA maCHI-de iCHIBAN 古いです。 fuRUi-desu.
Bill is the youngest of the three.	ビルは3人のうちでいちばん若いです。 BIru-wa saN-NIn-no-uchi-de iCHIBAN waKAi-desu.
Magic Mirror on the wall, "Who is the fairest one of all?"	壁の魔法の鏡さん。みんなの kaBE-NO maHOO-NO kaGAMI-san. miNNA-no 中でいちばん美しい人は NAka-de iCHIBAN uTSUKUSHIi-hiTO-wa だれですか。 DAre-desu-KA?

CHAPTER 3 SECTION 10

Adjectives that Describe Subjective Feelings

Adjectives that describe subjective feelings, such as **ureshi-i** (glad), **kanashi-i** (sad), **suki-na** (likable), **kirai-na** (dislikable), take (object)-**ga**. For example:

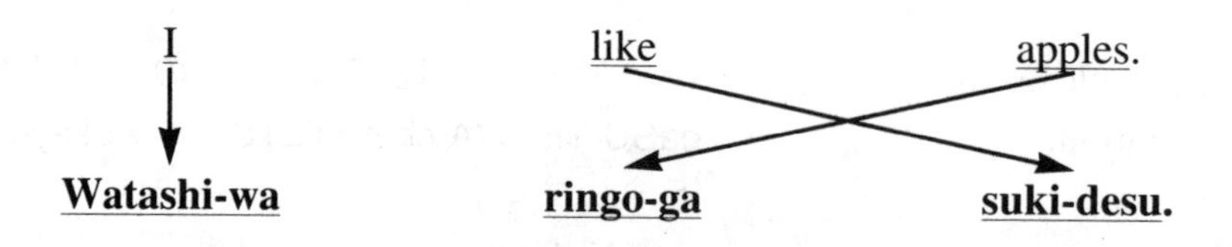

Adjectives that Describe Subjective Feelings

Some of these adjectives are listed below:

want	欲しい	hoSHIi
glad	うれしい	uRESHIi
sad	悲しい	kaNASHIi
delightful	楽しい	taNOSHIi
dear	懐かしい	naTSUKASHIi
hateful	憎い	niKUi
ashamed	恥ずかしい	haZUKASHIi
enviable	うらやましい	uRAYAMASHIi
trying	つらい	tsuRAI
vexing	悔しい	kuYASHIi
regrettable	惜しい	oSHIi
fearful	怖い	koWAi
terrible	恐ろしい	oSOROSHIi
likable	好きな	suKIna
dislikable	嫌いな	kiRAINA
disappointing	残念な	zaNNEnna
anxious	心配な	shiNPAINA
pitiable	気の毒な	kiNODOkuna
incredible	不思議な.	fuSHIGINA
skillful	じょうずな	joOZUna
unskillful	へたな	heTAna

Note

V_2**-tai** forms of a certain verbs (**mi-tai**, "to want to see," **tabe-tai**, "to want to eat," etc.) are verbs that have been turned into adjectives that describe subjective feelings and therefore fall into this category. (See CHAPTER 7 Section 3.)

More Examples

I want some water.
水 が 欲しいです。
miZU-GA hoSHIi-desu.

I long for the days past.
昔 が 懐 かしいです。
muKASHI-GA naTSUKASHIi-desu.

I envy you.
あなた がうら やま しいです。
aNAta-ga uRAYAMASHIi-desu.

I feel pained at parting.
別 れ がつ らいです。
waKARE-ga tsuRAI-DEsu.

I fear a ghost.
お化け が 怖 いです。
oBAke-ga koWAi-desu.

I don't like cigarettes.
タバコ が 嫌 いです。
taBAKO-GA kiRAI-DEsu.

You speak English well,
あなた は 英語 が じょうずです ね。
aNAta-wa eIGO-GA joOZU-desu-NE.

I am poor at Japanese.
私 は 日本 語 が へた です。
waTASHI-WA niHONGO-GA heTA-desu.

CHAPTER 3 SECTION 11

Explanatory -n-desu

Observe the following dialogues:

A: You seem to know Mr. Smith very well.
B: Yes. He is my friend (and that is the reason).

A: You have been reading the book for hours.
B: Yes. This book is very interesting (and that's why).

B's response in each dialogue above is not a simple independent statement, but an explanation about the circumstances—why it is so or why he is acting as such in that context.

Compare a simple independent statement and an explanatory statement in the following.

He is my friend.	**Kare-wa tomodachi-desu.**
He is my friend (and that is the reason).	**Kare-wa tomodachi-nan-desu.**
This book is interesting.	**Kono-hon-wa omoshiroi-desu.**
This book is interesting (and that is why).	**Kono-hon-wa omoshiroi-n-desu.**

In spoken Japanese, this way of speaking is quite common, so I named this form *explanatory -n-desu*, which will be discussed in the following chapters:

CHAPTER 3 Section 11: Explanatory **-n-desu**
CHAPTER 6 Section 7: **V_3-n-desu**

Modifications to Sentence Patterns 1 and 2

To use explanatory **-n-desu**, modifications to sentence patterns (1) and (2) are made as follows:

(Theme)**-wa** (Noun)**-nan-desu.**

(Theme)**-wa** (Adjective)**-n-desu.**

Note

In the case of **na**-adjectives, the **na** is not dropped.

More Examples

He is a banker (and that's why).	彼は銀行家なんです。 KAre-wa giNKOO-KA-NAn-desu.
She is an English teacher (and that's why).	彼女は英語の先生なんです。 KAnojo-wa eIGO-NO-seNSEi-nan-desu.
The bus is slow (and that's why).	バスは遅いんです。 BAsu-wa oSOI-n-desu.
His lecture is boring (and that's why).	彼の講義はつまらないんです。 KAre-no-koOGI-wa tsuMARAnai-n-desu.

This job is important (and that's why).	この 仕事 は 重要 なんです。 koNO-SHIGOTO-WA juUYOO-NA-n-desu.
I am happy (and that's why).	私 は 幸 せ な んです。 waTASHI-WA shiAWASE-NA-n-desu.

CHAPTER 3 SECTION 12

Honorifics (1): Nouns & Adjectives

Honorifics in English

"Yes, sir!"—This is an honorific!

An honorific is a term that conveys respect, used especially when addressing a social superior. Mr., Ms., Dr., Professor, Ladies and Gentlemen, Mr. Chairman, the Honorable Mayor.... are all English honorifics.

Honorifics in Japanese

Due to the old tradition of the class system in Japanese society, the honorifics that educated Japanese people use when they speak or write are complex. Honorifics are an integral part of the Japanese language, so it is important to master them in order to sound natural. A series of discussions on honorifics is given in the following chapters.

CHAPTER 3 Section 12 Honorifics (1): Nouns and Adjectives
CHAPTER 4 Section 12 Honorifics (2): Give and Receive
CHAPTER 4 Section 13 Honorifics (3): Specific Verbs
CHAPTER 7 Section 10 Honorifics (4): **o-V_2** Forms
CHAPTER 8 Section 10 Honorifics (5): **V_2'-te** Forms
CHAPTER 11 Section 2 Honorifics (6): Passive Mode

Japanese honorifics are divided into three categories:

respectful words
humble words
polite words

Respectful Words

Respectful words are used to convey respect when a speaker mentions things or actions of:

(a) the listener, or people related to the listener
(b) a social superior

Humble words

Humble words are used to lower the level of the speaker relative to the level of the listener or a social superior, when the speaker mentions things or actions of the speaker himself or of people who are related to the speaker. The overall effect is the same as that of using respectful words.

Polite Words

Polite words are used when the speaker wants to be polite to the listener and not take the risk of sounding uncouth. The most commonly used polite words are **-desu** and **-masu** endings in a sentence. Some words are embellished just to be polite. This is done more often by women than men.

Honorific Nouns: Family Members

The contrast between respectful words and humble words becomes evident when a speaker talks about a member of either his or her own or the listener's or social superior's family. Observe the following:

	Respectful Word	Humble Word
I		waTASHI
you	aNAta	
wife	Oku-san	KAnai
husband	go-SHUjin	SHUjin
married couple	go-FUsai	FUufu
son	go-SHIsoku	muSUKO
daughter	o-JOo-san	muSUME
child	o-KO-SAN	koDOMO
grandchild	o-MAGO-SAN	maGO
elder brother	o-NIi-san	Ani
elder sister	o-NEe-san	aNE
younger brother	oTOOTO-SAN	oTOOTO
younger sister	iMOOTO-SAN	iMOOTO
sibling	go-KYOodai	KYOodai
father	o-TOo-san	CHIchi
mother	o-KAa-san	HAha
parents	go-RYOoshin	RYOoshin

	Respectful Word	Humble Word
uncle	oJI-SAN	oJI
aunt	oBA-SAN	oBA
grandfather	oJIi-san	SOfu
grandmother	oBAa-san	SObo
cousin	Itoko-san	iTOko
nephew	oI-GO-SAN	oI
niece	meI-GO-SAN	meI

Honorific Nouns: Other Nouns

Respectful words

(a) respectful words per se:

kiMI (used by men only)	you
koCHIRA	this person, this place
DOnata (in place of DAre)	who
kaTA (in place of hiTO)	person
seNSEi	teacher, physician, lawyer, politician

(b) prefixes (**o**, **go**, etc.):

o-HANASHI	your/his/her talk
o-TAKU	your/his/her house
go-Iken	your/his/her opinion
KIsha (in business letters)	your company

(c) suffixes (**san**, **sama** [formal]):

SUmisu-san	Mr./Mrs./Miss/Ms. Smith
o-ISHA-SAn	physician
o-KYAKU-SAma	customer, guest

Humble words

(a) humble words per se:

waTAKUSHI (formal)	I
BOku (men only)	I
SHOosei (men in letters)	I

(b) prefixes (**o**, **go**, etc.):

o-NEGAI	my request
go-Aisatsu	my greeting
SO-cha	humble tea
HEi-sha	our company

Polite words

(a) embellishing prefixes (**o**, **go**):

o-KANE	money
o-KOME	rice
o-SUshi	**sushi**
o-CHA	tea
o-FUro	bath
o-BIiru	beer

(b) words that must always be embellished:

o-MOcha	toy
o-YAtsu	snack
GO-han	steamed rice, meal

(c) words whose meanings change when embellished:

o-NAKA	belly (NAka=inside)
o-SHIROI	face powder (shiROi=white)
o-HIya	cold water (HIya=cold **sake**)
o-NIgiri	rice ball (niGIRI=assorted **sushi**)
go-HASAN	reset to zero (haSAN=bankruptcy)

Honorific Adjectives

Respectful words

o-KIreina	pretty, clean
o-GEnkina	healthy
go-RIPPANA	fine, respectable

Humble words

iTARAnai	incompetent
fuTSUTSUKANA	inexperienced

Polite words

o-ATSUI	hot
o-SAMUI	cold

More Examples

How is your wife?

奥さんはお元気ですか。
Oku-san-wa o-GEnki-desu-KA.

She is fine, thank you.	はい、家内 は 元 気です。ありがとう。 HAi, KAnai-wa GEnki-desu. aRIgatoo.
Is your father a doctor?	お父 さんは お医者 さん です か。 oTOo-san-wa o-ISHA-SAn-desu-KA?
Yes. He is a pediatrician.	はい。父 は 小 児科 の 医者 です。 HAi. CHIchi-wa shoONIKA-NO iSHA-DEsu.

Verbs

A *verb* is a word used to express action or existence.

-desu and -masu

In CHAPTER 3, we learned that the verb "to be," when used as a copula, is translated into Japanese as **-desu**. The suffix-**desu** is attached to either a noun or an adjective.

(Noun)-**desu.**

(Adjective)-**desu.**

The suffix **-masu** is attached to a verb.

(Verb)-**masu.**

-Desu and **-masu** are used as polite endings to a sentence, and should always be used in spoken language among adults who are neither close friends nor family members.

CHAPTER 4 SECTION 1
Verbs

Verbs, both in English and Japanese, conjugate or inflect their forms. For example, the English verb "to go" becomes "goes," "going," "went," "gone," etc. "To go" is called the *root form*.

This chapter will give you a list of some important Japanese verbs. The form shown in the list is the root form, and it is the starting point for all conjugations. (A Conjugation chart is given in Appendix 4.) It is also called the *dictionary form*, because it is the form we can find in a Japanese dictionary. ("H" denotes an "honorific" verb.)

Most of the verbs listed are easy **yamato-kotoba** verbs, and the **kanji** used are read in the **kun**-reading. More sophisticated "do-verbs" (**kanji**-compound action nouns read in the **on**-reading plus "do") are discussed at the end of this chapter.

Because different types of verbs have specific conjugation rules, the verbs listed are grouped as follows:

-iru ending, **-eru** ending
-su ending
-ku ending, **-gu** ending
-tsu ending, **-ru** ending, **-u** ending
-nu ending, **-mu** ending, **-bu** ending
special verbs (**suru**, **kuru**)

The first verb of each group, which is in bold letters, is the representative of the group, and it will be used in the discussion of the conjugations from now.

Important

Let us call the root form "V_3" from now on. Why "3"? The reason is as follows. When you look at the root form verbs in the following list, you will see that their last syllables are always the **u**-row syllables of the syllabary chart (**ru**, **su**, **ku**, **gu**, **tsu**, etc.), and the **u**-row is the 3rd row of the chart.

-iru Ending

to see	**見る**	**MIru**	to get up	起きる	oKIru
to be done	できる	deKIru	to live (subsist)	生きる	iKIru
to believe	信じる	shiNJIru	to lose interest	飽きる	aKIru
to boil (seasoned)	煮る	niRU	to pass	過ぎる	suGIru
to borrow	借りる	kaRIRU	to put on (clothes)	着る	kiRU
to exist (animate)	居る	iRU	to resemble	似る	niRU
to extend	伸びる	noBIru	to shut	閉じる	toJIru
to fall	落ちる	oCHIru	to suffice	足りる	taRIRU
to feel	感じる	kaNJIRU	to use	用いる	moCHIIRU
to get off	降りる	oRIru			

-eru Ending

to sleep	**寝る**	**neRU**	to decide	決める	kiMERU
to add	加える	kuWAERU	to deliver	届ける	toDOKEru
to advance	進める	suSUMERU	to deposit	預ける	aZUKEru
to answer	答える	koTAEru	to disappear	消える	kiERU
to appear	現れる	aRAWAREru	to divide	分ける	waKEru
to arrange	並べる	naRABERU	to eat	食べる	taBEru
to ascertain	確かめる	taSHIKAMEru	to fall down	倒れる	taOREru
to ask	尋ねる	taZUNEru	to find	見つける	miTSUKERU
to attach	付ける	tsuKEru	to finish	終える	oERU
to attack	攻める	seMEru	to flow	流れる	naGAREru
to awaken	覚める	saMEru	to forget	忘れる	waSURERU
to be born	生まれる	uMARERU	to get away	逃げる	niGEru
to be burnt	焼ける	yaKERU	to get used to	慣れる	naREru
to be crushed	つぶれる	tsuBURERU	to get wet	ぬれる	nuRERU
to be defeated	負ける	maKERU	to give	くれる	kuRERU
to be destroyed	壊れる	koWAREru	to give up	あきらめる	aKIRAMEru
to be heard	聞こえる	kiKOERU	to go out	出かける	deKAKERU
to be late	遅れる	oKURERU	to go over	越える	koERU
to be seen	見える	miEru	to grow	生える	haEru
to become clear	晴れる	haREru	to hang	掛ける	kaKEru
to become dirty	汚れる	yoGORERU	to help	助ける	taSUKEru
to become thin	やせる	yaSERU	to hide	隠れる	kaKUREru
to become tired	疲れる	tsuKAREru	to hit	当てる	aTERU
to begin	始める	haJIMERU	to inform	知らせる	shiRASERU
to bend	曲げる	maGERU	to investigate	調べる	shiRABEru
to boil (unseasoned)	ゆでる	yuDEru	to join together	合わせる	aWASEru
to break	折れる	oREru	to look on	眺める	naGAMEru
to bring down	下げる	saGEru	to make even	そろえる	soROEru
to bring up (a child)	育てる	soDATEru	to melt	溶ける	toKEru
to build	建てる	taTEru	to memorize	覚える	oBOEru
to change	変える	kaERU	to mistake	間違える	maCHIGAEru
to close	閉める	shiMEru	to mix	混ぜる	maZEru
to collect	集める	aTSUMEru	to offer (H)	差しあげる	saSHIAGERU
to come out	出る	DEru	to open	開ける	aKERU
to compare	比べる	kuRABERU	to part from	離れる	haNAREru
to continue	続ける	tsuZUKERU	to pile up	重ねる	kaSANERU
to convey	伝える	tsuTAERU	to place on	載せる	noSERU
to count	数える	kaZOEru	to praise	ほめる	hoMEru

to put in	入れる	iRERU
to put in order	片付ける	kaTAZUKEru
to put together	まとめる	maTOMERU
to put up	立てる	taTEru
to quit	辞める	yaMERU
to raise	上げる	aGERU
to receive	受ける	uKEru
to request	求める	moTOMERU
to save	ためる	taMERU
to seize	つかまえる	tsuKAMAERU
to sell	売れる	uRERU
to show	見せる	miSEru
to stop	止める	toMERU
to strive	努める	tsuTOMEru
to sway	揺れる	yuRERU
to take (a person)	連れる	tsuRERU
to teach	教える	oSHIERU
to think	考える	kaNGAeru
to throw	投げる	naGEru
to throw away	捨てる	suTERU
to transfer	乗り換える	noRIKAEru
to warm up	暖める	aTATAMEru

-su Ending

to lend	**貸す**	**kaSU**
to add	足す	taSU
to air	干す	HOsu
to boil water	沸かす	waKASU
to bring down	倒す	taOsu
to cool down	冷やす	hiYAsu
to copy	写す	uTSUsu
to cure	治す	naOsu
to deceive	だます	daMAsu
to destroy	壊す	koWAsu
to detach	はずす	haZUSU
to do (H)	いたす	iTAsu
to drop	落とす	oTOsu
to dry	乾かす	kaWAKAsu
to express	表す	aRAWAsu
to extinguish	消す	keSU
to hand over	渡す	waTASU
to hide	隠す	kaKUsu
to indicate	示す	shiMESU
to kill	殺す	koROSU
to leave behind	残す	noKOsu
to lengthen	伸ばす	noBAsu
to let flow	流す	naGAsu
to let pass	通す	TOosu
to lose	なくす	naKUSU
to make a living	暮らす	kuRAsu
to make dirty	汚す	yoGOSU
to mend	直す	naOsu
to move	動かす	uGOKAsu
to move in/out	引っ越す	hiKKOSU
to permit	許す	yuRUsu
to pierce	刺す	SAsu
to point to	指す	SAsu
to push	押す	oSU
to put out	出す	DAsu
to raise up	起こす	oKOsu
to recollect	思い出す	oMOIDAsu
to repeat	繰り返す	kuRIKAesu
to return	返す	KAesu
to say (H)	申す	MOosu
to search	探す	saGASU
to separate	離す	haNAsu
to speak	話す	haNAsu
to spend time	過ごす	suGOsu
to take down	下ろす	oROsu
to transfer to	移す	uTSUsu
to try	試す	taMEsu
to turn	回す	maWASU

-ku Ending

to put on (shoes)	**履く**	**haKU**
to approach	近づく	chiKAZUku
to arrive at	着く	TSUku
to be surprised	驚く	oDOROku
to beat	たたく	taTAku
to become boiled	沸く	waKU
to become dry	乾く	kaWAku
to become empty	すく	suKU
to bloom	咲く	saKU
to blow	吹く	FUku
to burn	焼く	yaKU
to continue	続く	tsuZUKU
to extract	抜く	nuKU
to float	浮く	uKU
to go	行く	iKU
to hug	抱く	daKU
to incline to	傾く	kaTAMUku
to listen	聞く	kiKU
to move	動く	uGOku
to open	開く	aKU
to play (piano etc.)	弾く	hiKU
to polish	磨く	miGAKU
to pull	引く	hiKU
to put	置く	oKU
to reach	届く	toDOku
to receive (H)	いただく	iTADAKU
to scratch	かく	KAku
to solve	解く	TOku
to spread	敷く	shiKU
to stick to	付く	TSUku
to sweep	掃く	HAku
to thrust	突く	tsuKU
to turn toward	向く	muKU
to unfold	開く	hiRAku
to walk	歩く	aRUku
to wind	巻く	maKU
to wipe	拭く	fuKU
to work	働く	haTARAKU
to write	書く	KAku

-gu Ending

to take off	**脱ぐ**	**NUgu**
to connect	つなぐ	tsuNAGU
to defend	防ぐ	fuSEgu
to hurry	急ぐ	iSOgu
to make a noise	騒ぐ	saWAgu
to sniff	かぐ	kaGU
to swim	泳ぐ	oYOgu

-tsu Ending

to wait	**待つ**	**MAtsu**
to be built	建つ	TAtsu
to elapse	経つ	TAtsu
to grow up	育つ	soDAtsu
to have	持つ	MOtsu
to hit	打つ	Utsu
to stand	立つ	TAtsu
to win	勝つ	KAtsu

-ru Ending

to take	**取る**	**TOru**
to accept	受け取る	uKETORU
to accumulate	たまる	taMARU
to be closed	閉まる	shiMAru
to be decided	決まる	kiMARU
to be found	見つかる	miTSUKARU

-ru Ending (cont.)

to be in excess	余る	aMAru
to be in trouble	困る	koMAru
to be left over	残る	noKOru
to be lost	なくなる	naKUNARU
to be mended	直る	naOru
to be piled up	重なる	kaSANARU
to be popular	はやる	haYAru
to become	なる	NAru
to become cloudy	曇る	kuMOru
to begin	始まる	haJIMARU
to bend	曲がる	maGARU
to break	折る	Oru
to change	変わる	kaWARU
to dance	踊る	oDORU
to decline	断る	koTOWAru
to decorate	飾る	kaZARU
to depend on	よる	yoRU
to dig	掘る	HOru
to distribute	配る	kuBAru
to divide	割る	waRU
to do (H)	なさる	naSAru
to drag	引っ張る	hiPPAru
to draw near	近寄る	chiKAYOru
to drop in	寄る	yoRU
to eat (H)	召し上がる	meSHIAGARU
to end	終わる	oWARU
to exist (H)	おる	oRU
to exist (H)	いらっしゃる	iRASSHAru
to exist (inanimate)	ある	Aru
to fall	降る	FUru
to fatten	太る	fuTOru
to freeze	凍る	koORU
to gather	集まる	aTSUMAru
to get angry	怒る	oKOru
to get back	戻る	moDOru
to get well	治る	naOru
to give (H)	くださる	kuDASAru
to give/do	やる	yaRU
to go across	渡る	waTARU
to go down	下る	kuDARU
to go round	回る	maWARU
to go through	通る	TOoru
to go up	上がる	aGARU
to hang	かかる	kaKAru
to hang down	下がる	saGAru
to happen	起こる	oKOru
to hit	当たる	aTARU
to hold out	頑張る	gaNBAru
to hold tongue	黙る	daMAru
to keep in custody	預かる	aZUKAru
to make	作る	tsuKUru
to measure	計る	haKAru
to move to	移る	uTSUru
to paint	塗る	nuRU
to pray	祈る	iNOru
to present	贈る	oKURU
to protect	守る	maMOru
to put on (a hat)	かぶる	kaBUru
to relieve (a person)	代わる	kaWARU
to remove	取る	TOru
to ride	乗る	noRU
to ring	鳴る	naRU
to rise	上る	noBORU
to rot	腐る	kuSAru
to rub	こする	koSURU
to say (H)	おっしゃる	oSSHAru
to scold	叱る	shiKARU
to scrape off	削る	keZURU
to sell	売る	uRU
to send	送る	oKURU
to shake	振る	fuRU
to shave	そる	SOru
to shine	光る	hiKAru
to sit	座る	suWARU
to sleep	眠る	neMURU
to spread	広がる	hiROGARU
to squeeze	しぼる	shiBOru
to stay overnight	泊まる	toMARU

-ru Ending (cont.)

to stop	止まる	toMARU	to touch	さわる	saWARU
to stretch	張る	haRU	to understand	わかる	waKAru
to tear	破る	yaBUru			

The following are "sham" **-iru/-eru** ending verbs. Treat them as **-ru** ending verbs.

to cut	切る	KIru	to run	走る	haSHIru
to enter	入る	HAiru	to chat	しゃべる	shaBEru
to fall (flowers)	散る	chiRU	to decrease	減る	heRU
to get mixed	混じる	maJIru	to grow thick	茂る	shiGEru
to go/to come (H)	参る	MAiru	to kick	ける	KEru
to grasp	握る	niGIRU	to return	帰る	KAeru
to know	知る	shiRU	to shine	照る	TEru
to limit	限る	kaGIru	to slide	滑る	suBEru

-u Ending (u of wa column in the Syllabary Chart)

to buy	**買う**	**kaU**	to follow suit	ならう	naRAu
to act	行う	oKONAU	to get drunk	酔う	yoU
to ask/to visit (H)	伺う	uKAGAU	to give off a smell	匂う	niOu
to be at a loss	迷う	maYOu	to keep (a dog, etc.)	飼う	KAu
to be complete	そろう	soROu	to learn	習う	naRAu
to be in time	間に合う	maNIAu	to meet	会う	Au
to breathe in	吸う	suU	to mistake	間違う	maCHIGAu
to chase	追う	oU	to pay	払う	haRAu
to commute to	通う	kaYOU	to pick up	拾う	hiROU
to congratulate	祝う	iWAu	to put away	しまう	shiMAU
to deal with	扱う	aTSUKAU	to receive	もらう	moRAU
to differ	違う	chiGAU	to say	言う	iU
to dispute	争う	aRASOu	to sew	縫う	NUu
to doubt	疑う	uTAGAU	to sing	歌う	uTAU
to employ	雇う	yaTOU	to think	思う	oMOu
to face	向かう	muKAU	to use	使う	tsuKAU
to fight	戦う	taTAKAU	to wash	洗う	aRAU
to fit	合う	Au	to wish	願う	neGAu
to follow	従う	shiTAGAu			

-nu Ending

to die	**死ぬ**	**shiNU**

-mu Ending

to read	**読む**	**YOmu**
to advance	進む	suSUMU
to be completed	すむ	SUmu
to be crowded	混む	KOmu
to bite	かむ	KAmu
to cease	やむ	yaMU
to contain	含む	fuKUmu
to desire	望む	noZOMU
to drink	飲む	NOmu
to enclose	囲む	kaKOMU
to enjoy	楽しむ	taNOSHImu
to feel a pain	痛む	iTAmu
to fold	たたむ	taTAMU
to give birth to	産む	uMU
to grab up	つかむ	tsuKAmu
to grieve	悲しむ	kaNASHImu
to live (dwell)	住む	SUmu
to pile up	積む	tsuMU
to put between	挟む	haSAmu
to sink	沈む	shiZUMU
to steal	盗む	nuSUmu
to step on	踏む	fuMU
to suffer	苦しむ	kuRUSHImu
to take a rest	休む	yaSUmu
to wrap	包む	tsuTSUmu

-bu Ending

to fly	**飛ぶ**	**toBU**
to be glad	喜ぶ	yoROKObu
to call	呼ぶ	yoBU
to carry	運ぶ	haKOBU
to choose	選ぶ	eRAbu
to fall down	転ぶ	koROBU
to float	浮かぶ	uKABU
to line up	並ぶ	naRABU
to play (game)	遊ぶ	aSOBU
to tie	結ぶ	muSUBU

Special Verbs

to do	する	suRU
to come	来る	KUru

Do-verbs

The special verb **suru** (to do) can be attached to hundreds of sophisticated **kanji**-compound action nouns in order to convert them into verbs.
For example:

kyōsō is a noun meaning "competition"
kyōsō-suru (competition + to do) means "to compete"

Some of these nouns are listed below:

absence	欠席	keSSEKI
anxiety	心配	shiNPAI
approval	賛成	sanSEI
arrival	到着	toOCHAKU
attendance	出席	shuSSEKI
attention	注意	CHUui
broadcasting	放送	hoO SOO
cleaning	掃除	soOJI

Do-verbs (cont.)

command	命令	meIREI
confidence	信用	shiN'YOO
consent	承知	shoOCHI
consultation	相談	soODAN
conversation	会話	kaIWA
cooking	料理	RYOori
cooperation	協力	kyoORYOKU
departure	出発	shuPPATSU
determination	決心	KEsshin
development	発展	haTTEN
difference	区別	KUbetsu
driving (a car)	運転	uNTEN
experience	経験	keIKEN
export	輸出	yuSHUTSU
fashion	流行	ryuU KOO
greeting	あいさつ	Aisatsu
guidance	案内	aNNAi
handshaking	握手	Akushu
import	輸入	yuNYUU
introduction	紹介	shoOKAI
invitation	招待	SHOotai
job	仕事	shiGOTO
journey	旅行	ryoKOO
laundering	洗濯	seNTAKU
marriage	結婚	keKKON
memory	記憶	kiOKU
misunderstanding	誤解	goKAI
opposition	反対	haNTAI
order	注文	chuUMON
peace of mind	安心	aNSHIN
permission	許可	KYOka
plan	計画	keIKAKU
preparation	用意	YOoi
promise	約束	yaKUSOKU
pronunciation	発音	haTSUON
quarrel	けんか	keNKA
question	質問	shiTSUMON
report	報告	hoOKOKU
requirement	要求	yoO KYUU
research	研究	keNKYUU
satisfaction	満足	MAnzoku
schedule	予定	yoTEI
sightseeing	見物	keNBUTSU
stroll	散歩	saNPO
study	勉強	beNKYOO
studying abroad	留学	ryuUGAKU
success	成功	seIKOO
telephone	電話	deNWA
test	試験	shiKEn
trouble	迷惑	MEiwaku
understanding	理解	RIkai
use	使用	shiYOO
utilization	利用	riYOO
war	戦争	seNSOO

CHAPTER 4 SECTION 2

V_2-masu

In the previous section, we discussed **V_3**, the root form (dictionary form) of verbs.

The polite ending of a sentence, **-masu**, can not be attached to the **V_3** form. It is attached to the form we call **V_2**. Now the question is how we can convert **V_3** to **V_2-masu**. The answer is by utilizing the following chart.

Conversion Chart: V_3 to V_2-masu

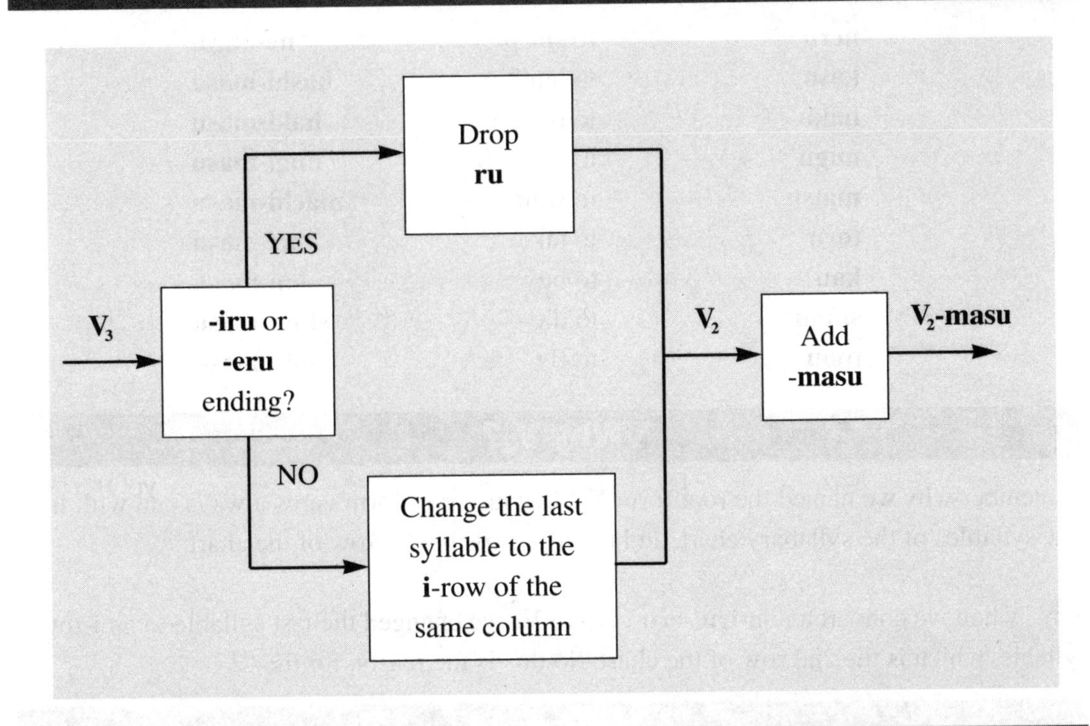

How to Read the Flow Chart

Example 1: Let's start from the left side of the chart.
V_3 (root form) of the verb "to see" is **miru**.
The first box says, "Is the ending **-iru** or **-eru**?"
Miru ends with **iru**, so the answer is "YES."
The next box says, "Drop **ru**."
The result is **mi**. **Mi** is the V_2 form of **miru**.
So the polite ending, **V_2-masu**, is **mi-masu**.

Example 2: V_3 (root form) of the verb "to read" is **yomu**.
The first box says, "Is the ending **-iru** or **-eru**?"
The answer is "NO."
The next box says, "Change the last syllable to the **i**-row syllable of the same column."
The last syllable of **yomu** is **mu**.
In the syllabary chart, **mu** is found in the **ma-mi-mu-me-mo** column.
Therefore the **i**-row syllable is **mi**.
So change **mu** to **mi**. The result is **yomi**.
Yomi is the V_2 form of **yomu**.
So the polite ending, **V_2-masu**, is **yomi-masu**.

Examples for other representative verbs:

neru	to sleep	**ne-masu**
kasu	to lend	**kashi-masu**
haku	to put on	**haki-masu**
nugu	to take off	**nugi-masu**
matsu	to wait	**machi-masu**
toru	to take	**tori-masu**
kau	to buy	**kai-masu**
shinu	to die	**shini-masu**
tobu	to fly	**tobi-masu**

Why V_2?

Remember why we named the root form $\mathbf{V_3}$? Because root form verbs always end with **u**-row syllables of the syllabary chart, and the **u**-row is the 3rd row of the chart.

Now, when we convert a non-**iru/-eru** verb to $\mathbf{V_2}$, we changed the last syllable to an **i**-row syllable, which is the 2nd row of the chart. So this is the reason for the "2."

Important

The flow charts do not apply to the special verbs **suru** (to do) and **kuru** (to come). These verbs are always exceptions.

The $\mathbf{V_2}$**-masu** form of **suru** is **shi-masu**.
The $\mathbf{V_2}$**-masu** form of **kuru** is **ki-masu**.

Practice

Go back to Section 1 and convert the verbs listed to $\mathbf{V_2}$**-masu** forms.

Pay attention to those "sham" **-iru/-eru** ending verbs listed at the end of **-ru** ending group. Also note that some honorific verbs require a slight modification in modern Japanese, as shown in the table on the next page.

V_3		V_2-masu	
		Classical Japanese	Modern Japanese
gozaru	to be	**gozari-masu**	**gozai-masu**
kudasaru	to give	**kudasari-masu**	**kudasai-masu**
nasaru	to do	**nasari-masu**	**nasai-masu**
irassharu	to be	**irasshari-masu**	**irasshai-masu**
ossharu	to say	**osshari-masu**	**osshai-masu**

CHAPTER 4 SECTION 3
Sentence Pattern (3)

Verbs can be categorized as either intransitive or transitive, and as either complete or incomplete.

Intransitive Verbs

An *intransitive verb* is a verb that does not take an *object* (a person or a thing that receives the action). For example, the verb "walk" in the sentence "I walk" is an intransitive verb. This is sentence pattern (3).

Transitive Verbs

A *transitive verb* is a verb that has an object which receives the action. For example, the verb "strike" in the sentence "The hammer strikes the bell" is a transitive verb, and "bell" is the object. This is sentence pattern (4).

Incomplete Verbs

An *incomplete verb* is a verb that requires a complement to complete the predicate. For example, the verb "make" in the sentence "we will make him president of the company" is an incomplete verb and requires a word or words ("president of the company" in this example) to complete the predicate. This is sentence pattern (5).

Sentence Pattern (3)

I	walk.
↓	↓
Watashi-wa	**aruki-masu.**

So sentence pattern (3) is:

(Theme) **-wa** (Intransitive Verb)**-masu.**

More Examples

I will go.	私は行きます。 waTASHI-WA iKI-MAsu.
I will work.	私は働きます。 waTASHI-WA haTARAKI-MAsu.
The dog runs.	犬は走ります。 iNU-wa haSHIRI-MAsu.
The cat sleeps.	猫は寝ます。 NEko-wa NE-MAsu.
The bird sings.	鳥は歌います。 toRI-WA uTAI-MAsu.
We will get married.	私達は結婚します。 waTASHI-tachi-wa keKKON-SHI-MAsu.

CHAPTER 4 SECTION 4

Sentence Pattern (4)

As described in the previous section, sentence pattern (4) is based on the transitive verb.

Sentence Pattern (4)

Observe the following:

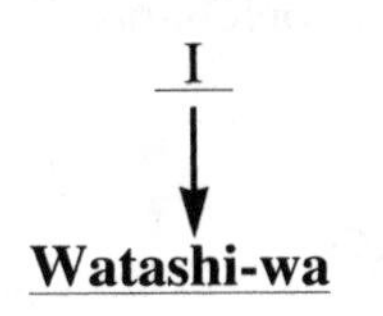

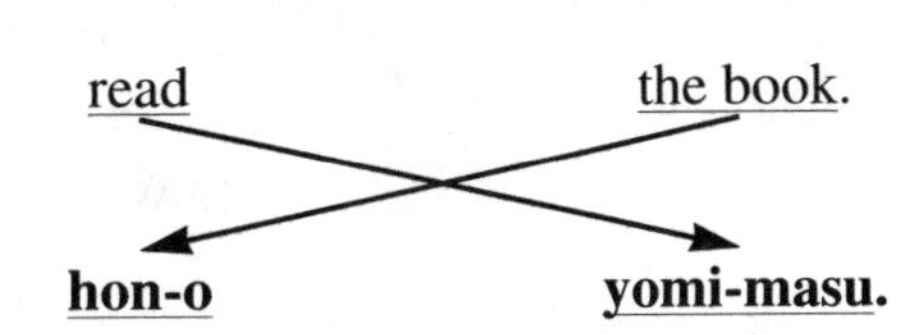

So the sentence pattern is:

> (Verb) **-wa** (Object) **-o** (Transitive Verb) **-masu.**

More Examples

I will open the window.	私は窓を開けます。 waTASHI-WA MAdo-o aKE-MAsu.
She sings a song.	彼女は歌を歌います。 KAnojo-wa uTA-o uTAI-MAsu.
He plays the piano.	彼はピアノを弾きます。 KAre-wa piANO-O hiKI-MAsu.
We study Japanese.	私達は日本語を勉強 waTASHI-tachi-wa niHONGO-O beNKYOO- します。 SHI-MAsu.

Indirect and Direct Objects

Certain verbs (give, send, bring, etc.) sometimes require "to whom" infomation, which is called an indirect object, and "what thing" information which is called a direct object. In Japanese, the indirect objects and the direct object take postpositions such as (person)-**ni** (thing)-**o** respectively.

For example:

I will give him the book.

Watashi-wa kare-ni sono-hon-o age-masu.

More Examples

I will send him the photo.	私　　は　彼　にその　写真　を送り waTASHI-WA KAre-ni soNO-shaSHIN-O oKURI- ます。 MAsu.
I will bring him a chair.	私　　は　彼　にいすを持って　きます。 waTASHI-WA KAre-ni iSU-o moTTE-KI-MAsu.

CHAPTER 4 SECTION 5

Sentence Pattern (5)

As described in Section 3, sentence pattern (5) is based on the incomplete verb.

Incomplete Verbs in English

The verb "am" in the context of the sentence "I am in Japan" is complete as a predicate by itself, meaning "I exist." ("When?" or "where?" kind of information is only additional.) On the other hand, in the sentence "I am a doctor," the part "I am" is incomplete without "I-am-what?" information to complete the predicate—you cannot stop there just by saying "I am." This component of the sentence ("a doctor," in this example) is called a *complement*.

The verb "make" in the sentence "I make a doll" is by itself a complete predicate, meaning "I create." On the other hand, when the verb "make" is used in the context of "they make him president of the company," the part "they make" is incomplete. In order to complete the predicate, we need the complement "president of the company."

Incomplete Verbs in Japanese

There are also a few incomplete verbs in Japanese. For example:

(complement)-**de aru**	copula "to be" (same as the first example in English above)
(complement)-**ni suru**	to make (same as the second example above)
(complement)-**ni naru**	to become
(complement)-**ni erabu**	to elect
(complement)-**ni mieru**	to look
(complement)-**to yobu**	to call
(complement)-**ga dekiru**	to be able to do
(complement)-**ga wakaru**	to understand

For example:

I am a doctor. **Watashi-wa isha-de ari-masu**

Shouldn't this be **watashi-wa isha-desu**?
(The answer is hidden in CHAPTER 4 Section 13.)

They will make him president. **Mina-wa kare-o shachō-ni shi-masu.**

Sentence Pattern (5)

Sentence pattern (5) is:

(Theme)**-wa** (Object)**-o** (Complement)**-x** (Incomplete Verb).

Note
If the verb is intransitive, disregard (object)**-o**. Also note that complements take several different postpositions as shown on the previous page.

More Examples

I will become a lawyer.	私は弁護士になります。 waTASHI-WA beNGOshi-ni naRI-MAsu.
We will elect Mr. **Tanaka** chairman.	私達は田中さんを議長に選びます。 waTASHI-tachi-wa taNAKA-SAN-O GIchoo-ni eRABI-MAsu.
He looks well.	彼は健康に見えます。 KAre-wa keNKOO-NI miE-MAsu.
They call him "Professor."	人々は彼を「教授」と呼びます。 hiTObito-wa KAre-o "kyoOJU"-TO yoBI-MAsu.
Mike can do a handstand.	マイクは逆立ちができます。 MAiku-wa saKADACHI-GA deKI-MAsu.
Kate understands French.	ケイトはフランス語がわかります。 KEito-wa fuRANSU-GO-GA waKARI-MAsu.

CHAPTER 4 SECTION 6
Negative & Past Forms of V_2-masu

N-P Triangle for V_2-masu

(Refer to CHAPTER 3 Section 8 on how to read the N-P [negative-past] triangle.)

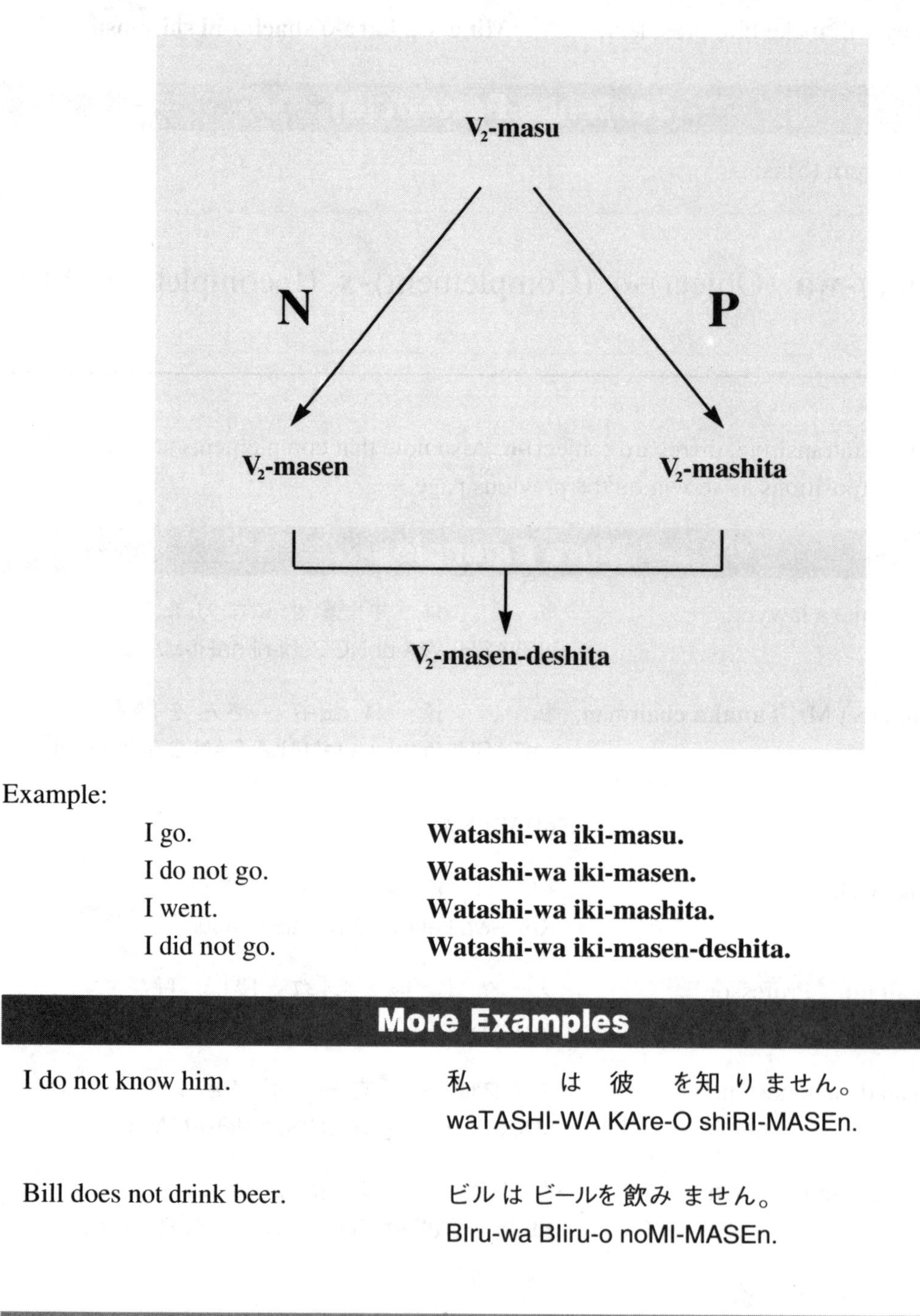

Example:

I go.	**Watashi-wa iki-masu.**
I do not go.	**Watashi-wa iki-masen.**
I went.	**Watashi-wa iki-mashita.**
I did not go.	**Watashi-wa iki-masen-deshita.**

More Examples

I do not know him.	私　は 彼　を知 りません。 waTASHI-WA KAre-O shiRI-MASEn.
Bill does not drink beer.	ビルは ビールを飲み ません。 BIru-wa BIiru-o noMI-MASEn.

My father does not watch TV.
父はテレビを見ません。
CHIchi-wa TErebi-o mi-MASEn.

My mother does not eat raw fish.
母は生の魚を食べません。
HAha-wa NAma-no-saKANA-O taBE-MASEn.

I wrote a letter to my daughter.
娘に手紙を書きました。
muSUME-ni teGAMI-O kaKI-MAshita.

Tom forgot his book.
トムは本を忘れました。
TOmu-wa HOn-o waSURE-MAshita.

I sold my car.
私は車を売りました。
waTASHI-WA kuRUMA-O uRI-MAshita.

I did not read the newspaper.
私は新聞を読みませんでした。
waTASHI-WA shiNBUN-O yoMI-MASEn-deshita

I did not buy the camera.
私はそのカメラを買いませんでした。
waTASHI-WA soNO-KAmera-o kaI-MASEn-deshita.

CHAPTER 4 SECTION 7
Time Definition

Let us discuss various expressions that define the time of action in a sentence. For example:

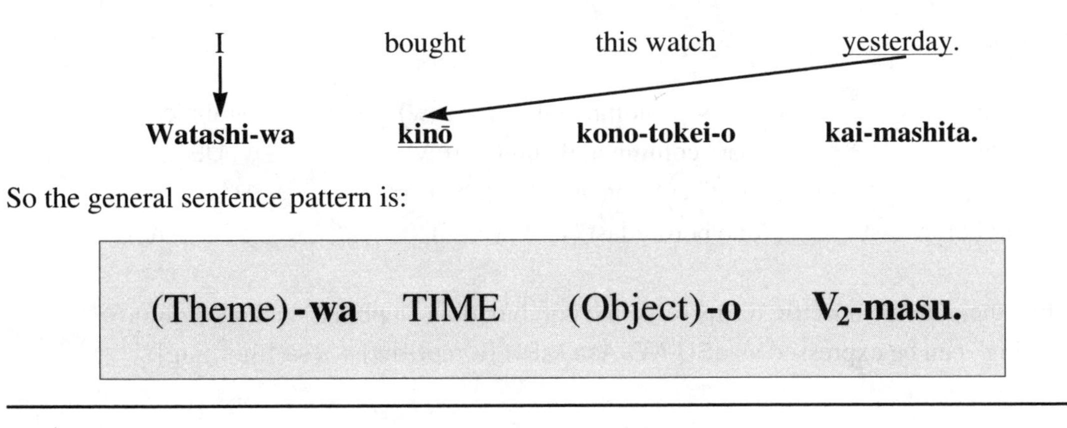

I bought this watch yesterday.
Watashi-wa kinō kono-tokei-o kai-mashita.

So the general sentence pattern is:

(Theme)**-wa** TIME (Object)**-o** **V_2-masu.**

Note
If the verb is intransitive, disregard (object)**-o**.

Time information is normally, but not always, placed after (theme)**-wa** and before (object)**-o**.

If the time information is important, you may bring it out to the beginning of the sentence.

Various Time Definitions

Specific terms

	every	one before last	last	this	next	one after next
day	MAi-nichi	oTOTOI iSSAKU-jitsu	kiNOO saKU-jitsu	KYOo HOn-jitsu KOn-nichi	aSU aSHITA MYOo-nichi	aSAtte myoOGO-nichi
morning	MAi-asa			KEsa		
evening (night)	MAi-ban		yuUBE saKU-ban saKU-ya	KOn-ban KOn-ya	MYOo-ban	
week	maI-SHUU	seNSEn-shuu	seN-SHUU	koN-SHUU	raI-SHUU	saRAI-SHUU
month	maI-TSUKI maI-GETSU	seNSEn getsu	SEn-getsu	koN-GETSU	RAi-getsu	saRAI-GETSU
year	maI-TOSHI maI-NEN	oTOtoshi	KYO-nen	ko-TOSHI	raI-NEN	saRAI-NEN

Examples:

every day	("every" column and "day" row)	MAi-nichi
last night	("last" column and "night" row)	yuUBE
next month	("next" column and "month" row)	RAi-getsu
the year before last	("one before last" and "year")	oTOtoshi

While there are no specific terms for some combinations, a phrase such as "tomorrow morning" can be expressed as aSU-NO-Asa (aSU [tomorrow] + Asa [morning]).

Important

Postpositions are not required for the words above.

Point of Time (in, on, at)

This is expressed as (time) **-ni**.

Examples:

in 2000	(seIREKI) ni-SEN-NEN-NI
on Sunday	niCHIYOo-bi-ni
at 9 o'clock a.m	goZEN KUji-ni
at about 6 o'clock p.m	goGO roKU-JI-GOro-ni

Ago, later

"Ago" and "later" are expressed as **-mae** and **-go** respectively, and the postposition **-ni** is also required.

two years ago	ni-NEN-MAe-ni
two hours later	ni-JIKAN-GO-ni

Last, next

"Last" and "next" are expressed as **kono-mae-no** and **kondo-no** (or **kono-tsugi-no**) respectively, and the postposition **-ni** is also required.

last Sunday	koNO-MAe-no-niCHIYOobi-ni
next Sunday	KOndo (koNO-TSUGI)-no niCHIYOobi-ni

From (time) until (time)

"From (time) until (time)" is expressed as (time)**-kara** (time)**-made**. The postpositions **-kara** and **-made** normally appear as a pair.

from 3 o'clock until 4 o'clock	SAnji-kara YOji-made
from morning until evening	Asa-kara baN-MAde
from January until March	iCHI-GATSU-kara SAn-gatsu made

By (time)

"By (time)" meaning "not later than" is expressed as (time)**-made-ni.**

by 4 o'clock	YO-ji-made-ni

Relative time

There are many ways to express a relative time without mentioning a specific date or time:

a long time ago	muKASHI
sometime before	KAtsute

this time last year	KYOnen-no iMA-GORO
already	MOo, toKKUNI, SUdeni
the other day	koNO-AIDA, koNO-MAe, seNJITSU
a little while ago	SAkki, choTTO-MAe-ni, saKIHODO
after a long while	hiSASHIBURI-ni
these days	koNO-GORO, chiKA-goro
now	Ima, GEnzai
until now	iMA-MAde-ni
still	MAda
soon	SUgu, moOSUgu, jiKINI, chiKAku, maMONAKU
later	Atode
not yet	MAda
no longer	MOo, MOhaya

Frequency

There are many ways to express frequency of action:

always	Itsumo, TSUne-ni
usually	fuTSUU, FUdan, taITEI
often	YOku, taBITABI
many times	NAndomo
every Sunday	maI-NICHIYOobi-ni, niCHIYOOBI-GOTO-ni
every other day	iCHINICHI-oKI-ni
sometimes	toKIDOKI
three times a month	tsuKI-ni-SAn-do
once in a while	taMA-ni
again	maTA, fuTATABI
once more	moO-ICHIDO
for the first time	haJImete
suddenly	kyuU-NI, toTSUZEN
accidentally, unexpectedly	guUzen
seldom	meTTANI
never	zeNZEN, iCHIDOMO, keSSHITE

Examples

I study Japanese every day.

私 は 毎日 日本 語 を
waTASHI-WA MAinichi niHON-GO-O
勉強 します。
beNKYOO-shi-MAsu.

My father takes a walk every morning.	父は毎朝散歩します。 CHIchi-wa MAi-asa saNPO-SHI-MAsu.
Did you read the paper this morning?	けさ新聞を読みましたか。 KEsa shiNBUN-O yoMI-MAshita-KA?
I took a day off yesterday.	きのう会社を休みました。 kiNOO kaISHA-O yaSUMI-MAshita.
I bought this car last year.	去年この車を買いました。 kyoNEN koNO-KURUMA-O kaI-MAshita.
I went to bed at eleven last night.	ゆうべ11時に寝ました。 yuUBE juU-ICHI-ji-ni ne-MAshita.
I was born in 1960.	私は1960年 waTASHI-WA SEn-KYUu-hyaku-roKU-JUu-nen- に生まれました。 ni uMARE-MAshita.
We got married five years ago.	私達は5年前に結婚 waTASHI-tachi-wa go-NEN-MAe-ni keKKON- しました。 SHI-MAshita.
I saw a movie last Saturday.	この前の土曜日に映画を見ました。 koNO-MAe-no doYOobi-ni Eiga-o mi-MAshita.
I waited for my friend from one o'clock until two o'clock.	私は1時から2時まで waTASHI-WA iCHI-ji-kara NI-ji-made 友達を待ちました。 toMODACHI-O maCHI-MAshita.
I work from Monday through Friday.	私は月曜から金曜まで waTASHI-WA geTSUYOo-kara kiN'YOo-made 仕事をします。 shiGOTO-o SHI-MAsu.
I will be back by five o'clock.	5時までに帰ります。 GOji-made-ni kaERI-MAsu.
Our children have already gone to bed.	子供達はもう寝ました。 koDOMO-tachi-wa MOo ne-MAshita.

The bus will come soon.	バス は もうすぐ 来ます。 BAsu-wa moOSUgu ki-MAsu.
He always drinks beer.	彼 は いつもビールを 飲み ます。 KAre-wa Itsumo BIiru-o noMI-MAsu.
I often forget my umbrella.	私 は よく 傘 を忘 れ ます。 waTASHI-WA YOku KAsa-o waSURE-MAsu.
She writes a letter to her mother twice a month.	彼 女は 月 に 2 度 お母 さんに 手紙 KAnojo-wa tsuKI-ni-ni-DO oKAasan-ni teGAMI- を書き ま す。 O kaKI-MAsu.
I sometimes use chopsticks.	私 は ときどき 箸 を使 います。 waTASHI-WA toKIDOKI HAshi-o tsuKAI-MAsu.
We seldom quarrel.	私 達 は めったに けんか し ません。 waTASHI-tachi-wa meTTAni keNKA-SHI-MAsen.

CHAPTER 4 SECTION 8
Place Definition

Let us discuss various expressions that define place of action in a sentence. For example:

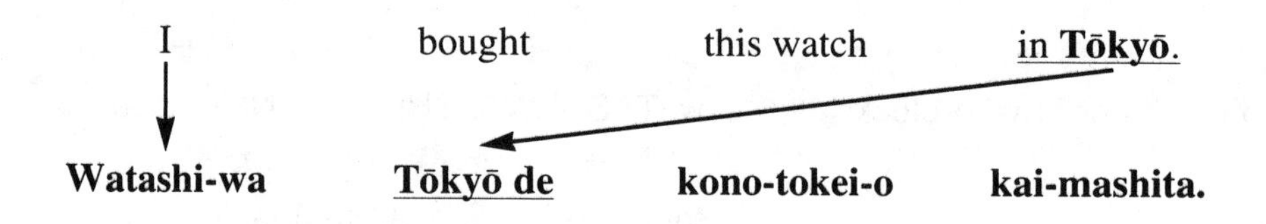
I
bought
this watch
in Tōkyō.
Watashi-wa
Tōkyō de
kono-tokei-o
kai-mashita.

So the general sentence pattern is:

> (Theme)**-wa** (Time) PLACE (Object)**-o** (V_2)**-masu.**

Note

If the verb is intransitive, disregard (object)**-o**.

Place definition is normally, but not always, inserted after time definition (if any) and before (object)**-o**. If the place information is important, it may be placed before the time definition or at the beginning of the sentence.

Various Place Definitions

Place of existence

The verb "to exist" in Japanese is either **aru** for inanimate objects or **iru** for animate beings. Their **V_2-masu** forms are **ari-masu** and **i-masu** respectively.

Place of existence is expressed as (place)**-ni**.
For example:

Central Park is in New York.	セントラル パーク は ニューヨークに seNTORARU-PAaku-wa nyuUYOoku-ni あります。 aRI-MAsu.
My family is in **Tōkyō**.	私 の 家族 は 東京 にいます。 waTASHI-NO KAzoku-wa toOKYOO-NI i-MAsu.

A specific place may be expressed with a group of words.
For example:

on the table	teEBURU-NO-uE-ni
under the table	teEBURU-NO-shiTA-ni
in front of the station	Eki-no-MAe-ni
behind the station	Eki-no-uSHIRO-NI
by the station	Eki-no-yoKO-NI
next to the station	Eki-no toNARI-NI
to the right of the station	Eki-no-miGI-NI
to the left of the station	Eki-no-hiDARI-NI
inside the station	Eki-no-NAka-ni
outside the station	Eki-no-SOto-ni
near the station	Eki-no-SOba (chiKAku)-ni
on the way to the station	Eki-no-toCHUU-NI

The cat is under the table.	猫 は テーブル の 下 にいます。 NEko-wa teEBURU-NO-shiTA-ni i-MAsu.
The bank is in front of the station.	その 銀行 は 駅 の 前 にあります。 soNO-giNKOO-WA Eki-no-MAe-ni aRI-MAsu.

Destination

Destination is expressed as (place)-**ni**.
Examples:

He is going to **Kyōto** tomorrow.
彼はあす京都に行きます。
KAre-wa aSU KYOoto-ni iKI-MAsu.

We will arrive at Kennedy Airport.
私達はケネディ空港に
waTASHI-tachi-wa keNEDII-KUu koo-ni
着きます。
tsuKI-MAsu.

Moving into a place

Moving into a place is expressed as (place)-**ni**.
Examples:

They enter the restaurant.
彼らはレストランに入ります。
KArera-wa REsutoran-ni haIRI-MAsu.

I get on the bus.
私はバスに乗ります。
waTASHI-WA BAsu-ni noRI-MAsu.

Place of action

Place of action is expressed as (place)-**de**.
Examples:

I was born in New York.
私はニューヨークで生まれました。
waTASHI-WA nyuUYOoku-de uMARE-MAshita.

I learned Japanese in America.
私はアメリカで日本語を
waTASHI-WA aMERIKA-DE niHONGO-O
習いました。
naRAI-MAshita.

Direction

Direction (toward ([place]) is expressed as (place)-**no-hō-e**, or simply (place)-**e**.
Examples:

This bus goes toward **Ginza**.
このバスは銀座のほうへ行きます。
koNO-BAsu-wa giNZA-NO-HOo-e iKI-MAsu.

He hurried to the station.
彼は駅のほうへ急ぎました。
KAre-wa Eki-no-HOo-e iSOGI-MAshita.

From (place) to (place)

"From (place) to (place)" is expressed as (place)**-kara** (place)**-made**. This is the same as "from (time) until (time)."

Examples:

I walk from my house to the office.	私 は 家から会社 まで 歩き waTASHI-WA iE-kara kaISHA-MAde aRUKI- ます。 MAsu.
I flew from London to Paris.	私 は ロンドンからパリまで waTASHI-WA ROndon-kara PAri-made 飛びました。 toBI-MAshita.

Moving out of (place)

Moving out of (place) is expressed as (place)**-o**.

Examples:

They left the restaurant.	彼らはレストランを出ました。 KArera-wa REsutoran-o de-MAshita.
She got off the bus.	彼女はバスをおりました。 KAnojo-wa BAsu-o oRI-MAshita.

Through (place)

Through (place) is expressed as (place)**-o**.

Examples:

I take a walk through the park every day.	私 は 毎日 公園を散歩 waTASHI-WA MAinichi koOEN-O saNPO- します。 SHI-MAsu.
I cross the street.	私 は 道 を渡ります。 waTASHI-WA miCHI-O waTARI-MAsu.

More Examples

My house is in **Azabu**, **Tōkyō**.	私の家は東京の麻布 waTASHI-NO-iE-wa toOKYOO-NO-aZABU- にあります。 NI aRI-MAsu.
My son is in **Kyōto** now.	息子はいま京都にいます。 muSUKO-WA Ima KYOoto-NI i-MAsu.
Mr. Smith is not in the room.	スミスさんは部屋にいません。 SUmisu-san-wa heYA-ni i-MASEn.
The post office is next to the bank.	郵便局は銀行の隣 yuUBIn-kyoku-wa giNKOO-NO-toNARI- にあります。 NI aRI-MAsu.
The hotel is near the American Embassy.	その ホテルは アメリカ大使館の soNO-HOteru-wa aMERIKA-taISHIkan-no- 近くにあります。 chiKAku-ni aRI-MAsu.
I am going to **Oosaka** next week.	来週大阪に行きます。 raISHUU oOSAKA-NI iKI-MAsu.
She didn't come to the party last night.	彼女はゆうべのパーティーに来ません KAnojo-wa yuUBE-NO PAatii-ni ki-MASEn- でした。 deshita.
They went into the coffee shop in the park.	彼らは公園の中の喫茶店に KArera-wa koOEN-NO-NAka-no kiSSAten-ni 入りました。 haIRI-MAshita.
I saw many old temples in **Kyōto**.	京都でたくさんの古いお寺を KYOoto-de taKUSAn-no fuRUi-o-TERA-O 見ました。 mi-MAshita.

I bought this camera in **Tōkyō** four years ago.	4年前に東京でこのカメラを yoNEN-MAe-ni toOKYOO-DE koNO-KAmera-o 買いました。 kaI-MAshita.
We will get married in Hawaii next month.	私達は来月ハワイで waTASHI-tachi-wa RAigetsu HAwai-de 結婚します。 keKKON-SHI-MAsu.
We parted in front of the station.	私達は駅の前で別れ waTASHI-tachi-wa Eki-no-MAe-de waKARE- ました。 MAshita.
The conference will be held in **Kyōto** next year.	会議は来年京都で開かれます。 kaIGI-wa raINEN KYOoto-de hiRAKARE-MAsu.
The typhoon is coming toward the **Kantō** area tomorrow.	台風は明日関東のほうへ来ます。 taIFUu-wa aSU KAntoo-no-hoo-e ki-MAsu.
I took the shinkansen from **Tōkyō** to **Oosaka** last year.	去年東京から大阪まで kyoNEN toOKYOO-KARA oOSAKA-MAde 新幹線に乗りました。 shiN-KAnsen-ni noRI-MAshita.
I borrowed money from the bank yesterday.	きのう銀行からお金を借りました。 kiNOO giNKOO-KARA o-KANE-O kaRI-MAshita.
I got off the subway at **Ginza**.	銀座で地下鉄をおりました。 giNZA-DE chiKATETSU-O oRI-MAshita.
I am leaving **Narita** in two hours.	2時間後に成田を立ちます。 niJIKAN-GO-ni NArita-o taCHI-MAsu.
We crossed the street at the signal.	信号で道を渡りました。 shiNGOO-DE miCHI-O waTARI-MAshita.

CHAPTER 4 SECTION 9
Other Definitions

Let us discuss various expressions that define necessary information in a sentence other than "time" and "place."

The general sentence pattern is:

(Theme)-**wa** T P O (Object)-**o** V_2**-masu.**

(T: Time definition; P: Place definition; O: Other definitions)

Note

If the verb is intransitive, disregard (object)-**o**.

Various Definitions

Purpose

Purpose is expressed as (purpose)-**ni**.

Examples:

We went hiking.	私　　達　は ハイキングに行きました。 waTASHI-tachi-wa haIKIngu-ni iKI-MAshita.
She went shopping.	彼　女は 買い物　 に行きました。 KAnojo-wa kaIMONO-NI iKI-MAshita.

Result of change

Result of change is expressed as (result)-**ni**.

Examples:

The signal will change to red.	信 号　 は 赤 に 変 わ り ます。 shiNGOO-WA Aka-ni kaWARI-MAsu.
The population has increased to 10,000.	人 口　は　1　万　に 増えま した。 jiNKOO-WA iCHI-MAn-ni fuE-MAshita

---

Reason

Reason is expressed as (reason)-**ni**.

Examples:

He was surprised by the sound.	彼は物音に驚きました。 KAre-wa moNOOTO-ni oDOROKI-MAshita.
I got wet in the rain.	雨にぬれました。 Ame-ni nuRE-MAshita.

Unilateral approach

A unilateral approach to a person or a thing is expressed as (person or thing)**-ni**.

Examples:

I unexpectedly met him in Ginza yesterday.	きのう銀座で偶然彼に会いました。 KiNOO GiNZA-de guUZEN KAre-ni aI-MAshita.
I bumped into a telephone pole.	電柱にぶつかりました。 deNCHUU-NI buTSUKARI-MAshita.

Bilateral approach

A bilateral approach with someone or an act done together with someone is expressed as (person)**-to**.

Examples:

I will meet with him today at the appointed place.	きょう彼と約束の場所で会います。 KYOo KAre-to yaKUSOKU-NO-baSHO-DE aI-MAsu.
I played tennis with my friend.	友達とテニスをしました。 toMODACHI-TO TEnisu-o shi-MAshita.

Means of transportation or communication

Means of transportation or communication is expressed as (means)**-de**.

Examples:

by bus	BAsu-de
by car	kuRUMA-DE, jiDOosha-de
by bicycle	jiTEnsha-de
by subway	chiKATETSU-DE
by train	DEnsha-de
by bullet train	shiN-KAnsen-de
by taxi	TAkushii-de
by airplane	hiKOoki-de
by ship	FUne-de
by telephone	deNWA-DE
by telegram	deNPOO-DE
by facsimile	FAkkusu-de

I will go home by taxi.	タクシーで帰ります。 TAKUshii-de kaERI-MAsu.
We talked over the telephone.	私達は電話で話しました。 waTASHI-tachi-wa deNWA-DE haNASHI-MAshita.

Tools

Using an object as a tool is expressed as (tool)**-de**.

Examples:

with a pen	PEn-de
with a pencil	eNPITSU-DE
with chopsticks	HAshi-de
with a knife and fork	NAifu-to-FOoku-de
with a hand	TE-de
with eyes	ME-de
with ears	miMI-de

I write a letter with a pen.	私はペンで手紙を書きます。 wa TASHI-WA PEn-de teGAMI-O kaKI-MAsu.
Japanese eat **sushi** with their hands.	日本人は手ですしを食べます。 niHON-JIn-wa TE-de suSHI-o taBE-MAsu.

Materials

The condition of being made using a certain material is expressed as (material)**-de**.

Examples:

using paper	kaMI-de
using gold	KIn-de
using silver	GIn-de
using copper	DOo-de
using iron	teTSU-DE
using glass	gaRASU-DE

She made a doll from paper.	彼女は紙で人形を作りました。 KAnojo-wa kaMI-de niNGYOO-O tsuKURI-MAshita.

Conditions

Various conditions are expressed as (condition)**-de**.

Examples:

in cash	geNKIn-de
with traveller's checks	ryoKOO-koGItte-de
with a credit card	kuREJITTO-KAado-de
for ¥10,000 (price)	iCHI-MAN-EN-DE
in Western clothes	yoOFUKU-DE
in a **kimono**	kiMONO-DE
with shoes on	kuTSU-de
with bare feet	haDASHI-DE
two of us	fuTARI-de

I will pay in cash.
現金で払います。
geNKIn-de haRAI-MAsu.

I bought this camera for ¥20,000.
2万円でこのカメラを買いました。
ni-MAN-EN-DE koNO-KAmera-o kaI-MAshita.

Raw materials

The condition of being made from or out of raw materials is expressed as (raw material) **-kara.**

Example:

Sake is made from rice.
酒は米から造ります。
saKE-WA koME-kara tsuKURI-MAsu.

Source

Source is expressed as (source)**-kara**.

Example:

I heard about you from Bill.
ビルからあなたのことを聞きました。
BIru-kara aNAta-no-koTO-o kiKI-MAshita.

Cause

Cause is expressed as (cause)**-kara**.

Example:

The accident took place because of his carelessness.
事故は彼の不注意から起きました。
JIko-wa KAre-no-fuCHUui-kara oKI-MAshita.

CHAPTER 4 SECTION 10
Adverbs

An *adverb*, a verb modifier, defines how the action is performed. In addition, an adverb can also modify an adjective or another adverb.

For example, the word **hayaku** (quickly) in the following sentence is an adverb modifying the verb **aruku** (to walk).

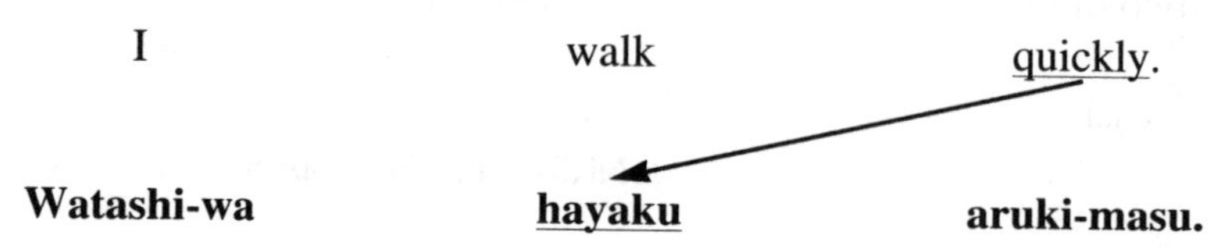
I
walk
quickly.
Watashi-wa
hayaku
aruki-masu.

An adverb is normally placed in a sentence directly before the verb or the object, if one appears. So the general sentence pattern is:

(Theme)**-wa** T P O A (Object)**-o** **V_2-masu**.

(T: Time definition; P: Place definition; O: Other definitions; A: Adverb)

Note
If the verb is intransitive, disregard (object)**-o**.

There are three types of Japanese adverbs:

1. adverbs derived from adjectives
2. nouns with adverbial suffixes
3. adverbs proper

Adverbs Derived from Adjectives

Just like the English words "quick" (adjective) and "quickly" (adverb), Japanese adjectives can also be converted to adverbs by changing their suffixes in the following manner.

Adjective →	Adverb
A-i	**A-ku**
A-na	**A-ni**

Examples:

haya-i	quick	**haya-ku**	quickly
oso-i	slow	**oso-ku**	slowly
atarashi-i	new	**atarashi-ku**	newly
tanoshi-i	merry	**tanoshi-ku**	merrily
shinsetsu-na	kind	**shinsetsu-ni**	kindly
shōjiki-na	honest	**shōjiki-ni**	honestly
shizuka-na	quiet	**shizuka-ni**	quietly

We spent the holiday merrily.

私達は楽しく休日を
waTASHI-tachi-wa taNOSHI-ku kyuUJITSU-O
過ごしました。
suGOSHI-MAshita.

She read the book quietly.

彼女は静かに本を読みました。
KAnojo-wa SHIzuka-ni HOn-o yoMI-MAshita.

Nouns with Adverbial Suffixes

Nouns with the following adverbial suffixes can function as adverbs:

about	**-gurai**
to the extent of	**-hodo**
only	**-dake**
nothing but	**-bakari**
or something like that	**-demo, -nado**
even	**-demo, -datte, -desae**
such as	**-nanka**

Examples:

I spent about ¥50,000.

私は5万円ぐらい使いました。
waTASHI-WA go-MAN-EN-GUrai tsuKAI-MAshita.

It will cost almost ¥5,000 more.

それは5,000円ほど多くかかります。
soRE-WA go-SEN-EN-HODO Ooku kaKARI-MAsu.

I learned only English.

私は英語だけ習いました。
waTASHI-WA eIGO-DAKE naRAI-MAshita.

He does nothing but work.

彼は仕事ばかりします。
KAre-wa shiGOTO-BAkari shi-MAsu.

Shall we have tea or something?	お茶　でも　飲みますか。 o-CHA-DEmo noMI-MAsu-KA?
I can even sing Japanese songs.	日本　の　歌　だって　歌います。 niHON-NO uTA-datte uTAI-MAsu.
I don't need anything like money.	お金　なんて要りません。 o-KANE-NAnte iRI-MASEn.

Adverbs Proper

Adverbs of degree

fully	iPPAI, juUBUn-ni, ZEnbu, suKKAri
all, every	miNA, miNNA
very much, extremely	toTEMO, taIHEN, hiJOO-NI
by far	zuTTO, daNZEN
by all means	ZEhi, ZEhitomo
quite	maTTAKU, naKANAKA, soOTOO
many, much	taKUSAn, oOZEi (people only)
almost	hoTOndo, daITAI
generally	fuTSUU, taITEI
mainly	Omo-ni, SHU-to-shite
considerably	daIBU, KAnari
especially	TOku-ni, toKUBETSU
variously	iROIRO
tentatively	iCHIOO, toRIAEZU
more	MOtto, iSSOO
surely	kiTTO, kaNARAZU
probably, may be	TAbun, oSOraku
as...as possible	naRUBEKU, deKIRUDAKE
well	YOku, uMAku
a few, a little	CHOtto, suKOshi
unexpectedly	aNGAI
not much, not quite	aMARI
not a bit	chiTTOmo, suKOSHIMO
never	keSSHITE, zeTTAI-NI

Adverbs of manner

rapidly	DOndon, suMIyaka-ni
suddenly	kyuU-NI, toTSUZEN

gradually	daNDAN, shiDAI-NI
slowly	yuKKUri
properly	chaNTO
truly	hoNTOO-NI
exactly	choODO, piTTAri
firmly	shiKKAri-to
clearly	haKKIRI-to
utterly	maRUDE
after all	yaHAri, keKKYOKU
anyhow	TOnikaku
rather	MUshiro, KAette

Examples:

I am very tired.	私はたいへん疲れました。 waTASHI-WA taIHEN tsuKARE-MAshita.
I had a little **sake** last night.	ゆうべお酒を少し飲みました。 yuUBE o-SAKE-O suKOshi noMI-MAshita.
She will surely keep her promise.	彼女はきっと約束を守ります。 KAnojo-wa kiTTO yaKUSOKU-O maMORI-MAsu.
He will probably not come.	彼はたぶん来ません。 KAre-wa TAbun ki-MASEn.
I don't drink much.	私はあまり飲みません。 waTASHI-WA aMARI noMI-MASEn.
I never tell a lie.	私は決してうそをつきません。 waTASHI-WA keSSHITE Uso-o tsuKI-MASEn.
He suddenly stood up.	彼は突然立ち上がりました。 KAre-wa toTSUZEN taCHI-AGARI-MAshita.
She held my arm firmly.	彼女はしっかりと私の腕を KAnojo-wa shiKKARI-to waTASHI-NO-uDE-o つかみました。 tsuKAMI-MAshita.
The dream did not come true after all.	夢はやはり実現しませんでした。 yuME-wa yaHAri jiTSUGEN-shi-MASEn-deshita.

CHAPTER 4 SECTION 11

Interrogatives: When, Where, Why, How

In sections 7 through 10, we looked at how to add various information (time, place, reason, etc.) to the basic sentences. In this section, we will discuss the interrogatives related to this information, namely "when," "where," "why," and "how."

When

"When" is **itsu** in Japanese. For example:

When did you come to Japan?	**Itsu Nihon-ni ki-mashita-ka?**

As with the other time definitions, various postpositions may accompany **itsu**. For example:

from when	**itsu-kara**
till when	**itsu-made**
by when	**itsu-made-ni**

To be more precise, the following may be used instead of "when."

on what day	**nan-nichi-ni**
on what day of the week	**nan-yōbi-ni**
in what month	**nan-gatsu-ni**
in what year	**nan-nen-ni**

Where

"Where" is **doko** in Japanese. For example:

Where am I?	**Koko-wa doko-desu-ka?** (Literally "where is this place")

As with the other place definitions, various postpositions may accompany **doko**. For example:

place of existence	**doko-ni**
place of action	**doko-de**
direction	**doko-e**
from where	**doko-kara**

to where	**doko-made**
through where	**doko-o**

Why

"Why" is **naze** (formal) or **dō-shite** (more colloquial) in Japanese. For example:

Why did you do that?	**Naze sonna-koto-o shi-mashita-ka**?

How

"How" is expressed in many ways, but two major ones are the following.

(1) in what state or manner: **dō**, **dono-yō-ni**, or **donna-fū-ni**
Example:

How do you write this **kanji**?	**Kono-kanji-wa dō kaki-masu-ka**?
How do I get to **Ginza**?	**Ginza-wa dono-yō-ni iki-masu-ka**?
How do I look?	**Watashi-wa donna-fū-ni mie-masu-ka**?

(2) to what extent or amount: **dono-kurai**
This "how" is often combined with adjectives or adverbs.
For example:

how far	**dono-kurai tooi**
how long	**dono-kurai nagai, itsu-made**
how many	**dono-kurai ooi, ikutsu**
how much	**dono-kurai ooi, ikura** (price)
how fast	**dono-kurai hayai**
how old	**dono-kurai furui, or nan-sai** (age)
how often	**nan-do-gurai**

More Examples

When and where were you born?	あなたは いつどこ で 生まれ ました か。 aNAta-wa Itsu DOko-de uMARE-MAshita-KA?
How long (until when) will you stay in Japan?	あなた は いつまで 日本 にい ます か。 aNAta-wa Itsu-made niHOn-ni i-MAsu-KA?
Where is your school?	あなたの 学 校 は どこ にあり ます か。 aNAta-no-gaKKOO-WA DOko-ni aRI-MAsu-KA?

Where did you go last Sunday?	この前の日曜日にどこへ koNO-MAe-no-niCHIYOobi-ni DOko-e 行きましたか。 iKI-MAshita-KA?
Where did you buy the ticket?	どこでその券を買いましたか。 DOko-de soNO-KEn-o kaI-MAshita-KA?
Why do you study Japanese?	どうして日本語を勉強するん DOoshite niHON-GO-O beNKYOO-suRU-n- ですか。 desu-KA?
How do I put on this **kimono**?	この着物はどのように着るん koNO-KIMONO-WA DOno-yoo-ni kiRU-n- ですか。 desu-KA?

CHAPTER 4 SECTION 12
Honorifics (2): Giving & Receiving

Refer to CHAPTER 3 Section 12 for the definition of honorifics.

Giving and Receiving a Gift

Different verbs are used in giving and receiving a gift depending on the relationship between the donor and the donee. Look carefully at the following chart. The arrows indicate the direction in which the gift moves and the corresponding verbs in the plain style and honorific styles. (P: plain style; R: respectful style; H: humble style.)

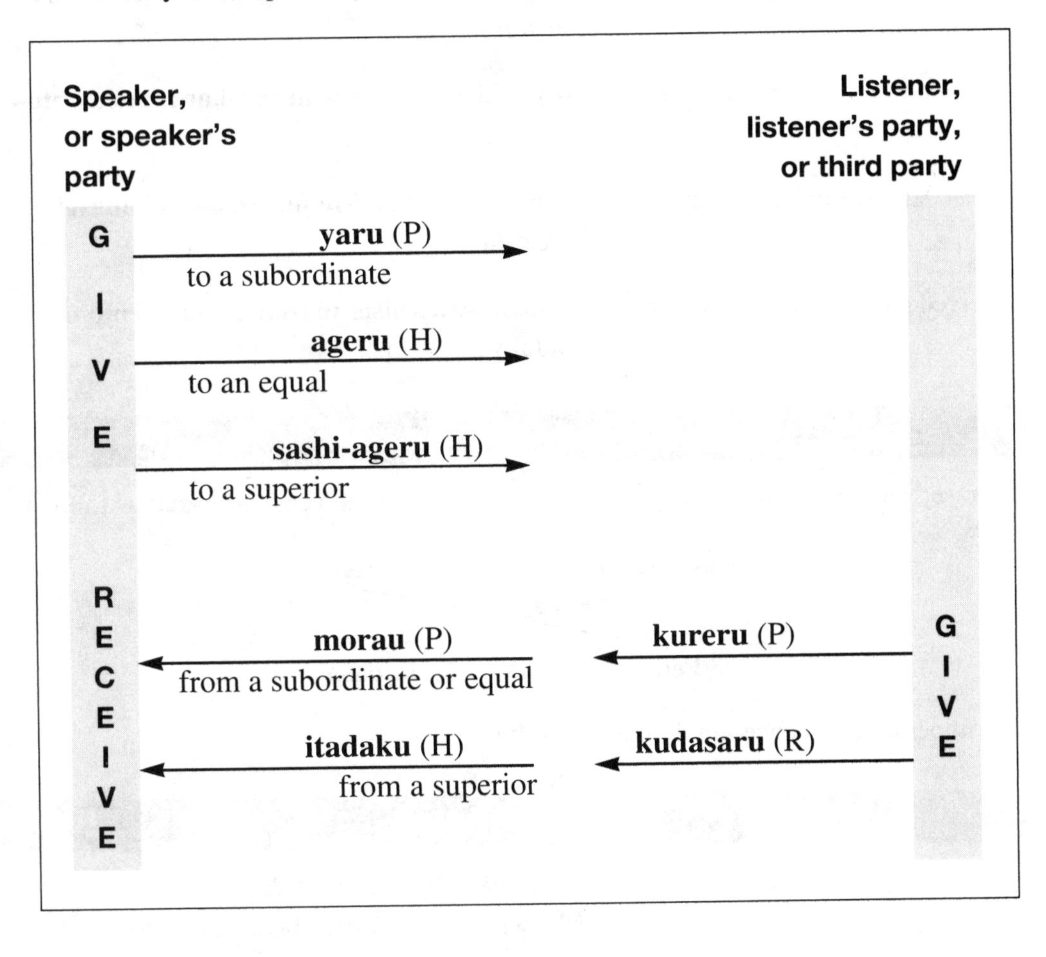

Examples

I gave a present to my son.	**Watashi-wa musuko-ni purezento-o yari-mashita.**
I gave a present to my friend.	**Watashi-wa tomodachi-ni purezento-o age-mashita.**
I gave a present to my teacher.	**Watashi-wa sensei-ni purezento-o sashi-age-mashita.**
My friend gave me a present.	**Tomodachi-wa watashi-ni purezento-o kure-mashita.**
I received a present from my friend.	**Watashi-wa tomodachi-ni (-kara) purezento-o morai-mashita.**
My teacher gave me a present.	**Sensei-wa watashi-ni purezento-o kudasai-mashita.**
I received a present from my teacher.	**Watashi-wa sensei-ni (-kara) purezento-o itadaki-mashita.**

Please Give Me...

The phrase "please give me" is expressed as a variation of the verb **kudasaru** as follows.

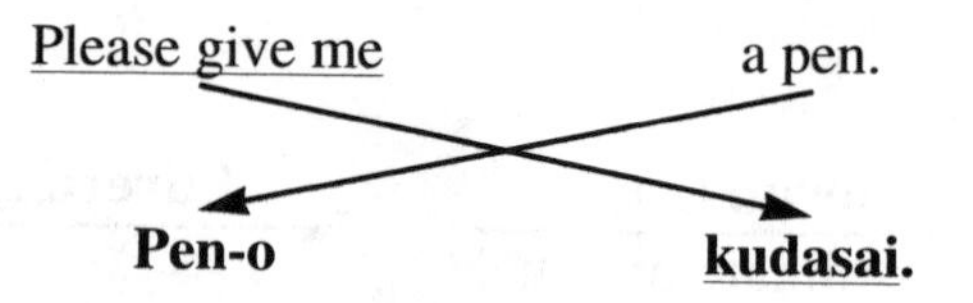

It is an imperative sentence, but in the respectful style.

More Examples

I gave the dog some meat.	犬に肉をやりました。 iNU-ni niKU-o yaRI-MAshita.
I will give you a cake. (to a child)	お菓子をあげます。 oKAshi-o aGE-MAsu.

My daughter gave a bouquet to the guest.	娘はお客様に花束をさしあげました。 muSUME-wa oKYAKU-SAMA-ni haNAtaba-o saSHI-AGE-MAshita.
My father received a winning cup from the mayor.	父は市長さんから優勝盃をいただきました CHIchi-wa SHIchoo-san-kara yuUSHOo-hai-o iTADAKI-MAshita.
The company president gave me a letter of introduction.	社長さんは私に紹介状をくださいました。 shaCHOO-SAN-WA waTASHI-NI shoOKAI-JOO-O kuDASAI-MAshita.
Please give me five apples.	りんごを 5 つください。 riNGO-O iTSUtsu kuDASAi.
Please give me three bottles of beer.	ビールを 3 本ください。 BIiru-o SAn-bon kuDASAi.
Please give me ten ¥100 stamps.`	100 円切手を 10 枚ください。 hyaKU-EN-KItte-o JUu-mai kuDASAi.

Note

A series of discussions on honorifics is given in the following sections. CHAPTER 3 Section 12 gives an overall definition of honorifics in the Japanese language.

CHAPTER 3 Section 12 Honorifics (1): Nouns and Adjectives
CHAPTER 4 Section 12 Honorifics (2): Giving and Receiving
CHAPTER 4 Section 13 Honorifics (3): Specific Verbs
CHAPTER 7 Section 10 Honorifics (4): **o-V_2** Forms
CHAPTER 8 Section 10 Honorifics (5): **V_2'-te** Forms
CHAPTER 11 Section 2 Honorifics (6): Passive Mode

CHAPTER 4 SECTION 13

Honorifics (3) : Specific Verbs

In this section, we will look at specific verbs used as honorifics other than "to give" and "to receive." (Those in parentheses are related to the forms that we will study in CHAPTER 7 Section 10.)

Verb	Plain	Respectful	Humble
to be (exist)	iRU	iRASSHAru (o-IDE-NI-NAru)	oRU
to go	iKU		MAiru
to come	KUru		
to hear, to ask	kiKU		uKAGAU
to ask, to visit	taZUNEru		
to be told	kiKU		uKE-TAMAWAru
to do	suRU	naSAru	iTAsu
to kowtow			kaSHIKOMAru
to say	iU	oSSHAru	MOosu
to eat	taBEru	(meSHI)-aGARU	iTADAKU
to borrow	kaRIRU		haISHAKU-SURU
to know	shiRU		zoNJI-AGEru
to see	MIru	(go-RAN-NI-NAru)	haIKEN-SURU
to meet	Au		o-ME-NI-KAKAru
to show	miSEru		o-ME-NI-KAKEru

English "to be"

As explained in the introduction to CHAPTER 3, the English verb "to be" has two usages: as a term to mean existence and as a copula.

Existence "to be"

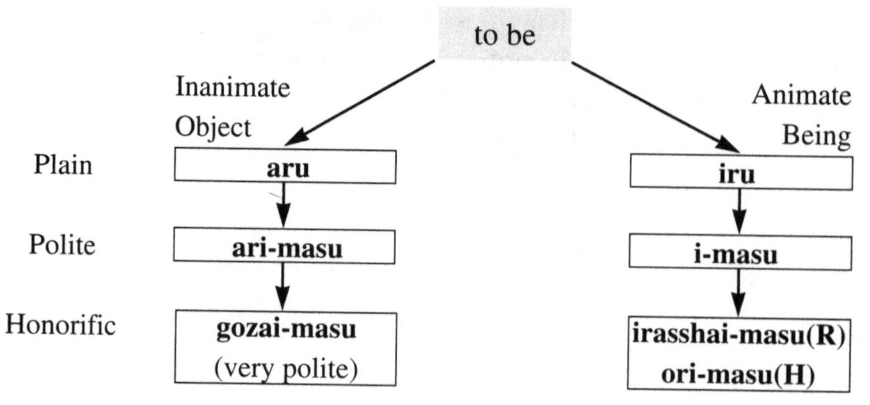

Irasshai-masu is a respectful word, and **ori-masu** is a humble word.

Gozai-masu is the **V_2-masu** form of a word **gozaru** (old Japanese "to be"), and it is still used in some greetings and "very polite" expressions with customers or social superiors. Examples:

Good morning	**O-hayō gozai-masu.**
Thank you	**Arigatō gozai-masu.**
Our head office is in**Tōkyō**.	**Watakushi-domo-no honsha-wa Tōkyō-ni gozai-masu.**
The mens wear department is on the 3rd floor.	**Shinshi-fuku-uriba-wa san-gai-ni gozai-masu.**

Copula "to be" and -Desu derivation

When used as a copula, the verb "to be" couples a subject (a theme) with a complementary word in a sentence, for example "I (subject/theme) am (verb/copula) a doctor (complementary noun)." The origin of the Japanese copula, (complement)**-de aru**, is found in sentence pattern (5). All the other copula forms including **-desu** shown below stem from **-de aru**.

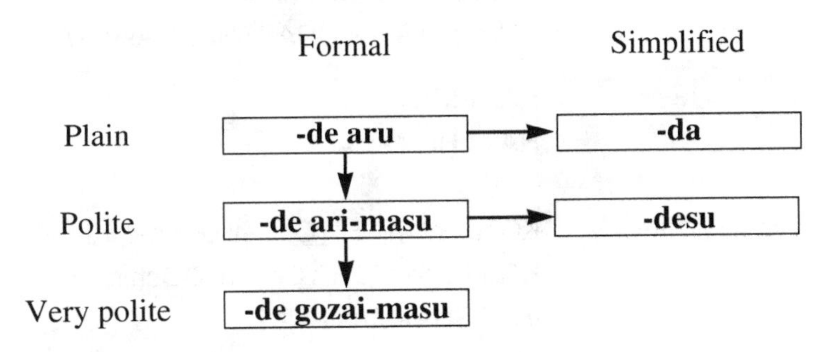

The simplified copula forms are used in casual language.

The plain form **-de aru** and its simplified form **-da** (the first letters of **-de** and **-aru**) are used mostly in the written language such as in books, newspapers, diaries. The **-da** form is also used in spoken language among close friends and family members. (See CHAPTER 13 Section 1 for a more detailed discussion.)

The **-de ari-masu** form is the **V_2-masu** form of **-de aru**. It is a formal expression used in public speeches or in official letters.

The simplified form, **-desu** (the first and the last syllables of **-de ari-masu**), is polite but not too formal, and therefore widely used in everyday conversation among adults who are neither close friends nor family members. Remember that sentence patterns (1) and (2) are based on **-desu**.

De gozai-masu is a very polite expression, also used in the spoken language with customers and social superiors.

Important

Once you have selected the most appropriate copula for what you want to say or write, consistency is very important. The following, for example, is bad Japanese.

Watashi-wa inu-ga suki-desu. Shikashi neko-wa kirai-da.
(I like dogs. But I don't like cats.)

If you have begun by using the copula **-desu**, DO NOT swap **-desu** for **-da** in midstream.

Examples

Compare the polite style (marked "P") and honorific style (marked "R" for respectful style or "H" for humble style) in the following examples.

Is Mr. Smith in?	SUmisu-san-wa i-MAsu-KA?	P
	SUmisu-san-wa iRASSHAI-MAsu-KA?	R
Yes, he is.	HAi, i-MAsu.	P
	HAi, oRI-MAsu.	H
Where will you go next Sunday?	KOndo-no-niCHIYOobi-ni DOko-e iKI-MAsu-KA?	P
	KOndo-no-niCHIYOobi-ni DOchira-e iRASSHAI-MAsu-KA?	R
I will go to **Hakone**.	haKONE-NI iKI-MAsu.	P
	haKONE-NI maIRI-MAsu.	H
Where did you come from?	aNAta-wa DOko-kara ki-MAshita-KA?	P
	aNAta-wa DOchira-kara iRASSHAI-MAshita-KA?	R
I came from **Tōkyō**.	toOKYOO-KARA ki-MAshita.	P
	toOKYOO-KARA maIRI-MAshita.	H
When will you come to my house?	Itsu waTASHI-NO-uCHI-NI ki-MAsu-KA?	P
	Itsu waTASHI-NO-uCHI-NI iRASSHAI-MAsu-KA?	R
I will come tomorrow.	aSU iKI-MAsu.	P
	aSU uKAGAI-MAsu.	H

What did you say?	NAn-to iI-MAshita-KA?	P
	NAn-to oSSHAI-MAshita-KA?	R
I said, "Good morning."	"oHAYOO"-to iI-MAshita.	P
	"oHAYOO-goZAI-MAsu"-to moOSHI-MAshita.	H
What will you eat?	NAni-o taBE-MAsu-KA?	P
	NANI-o meSHI-AGARI-MAsu-KA?	R
I will eat **sushi**.	waTASHI-WA suSHI-o taBE-MAsu.	P
	waTASHI-WA o-SUshi-o iTADAKI-MAsu.	H
Will you take a look at your room now?	Ima heYA-o mi-MAsu-KA?	P
	Ima o-HEYA-o go-RAN-NI-naRI-MAsu-KA?	R
Yes, I will.	HAi, mi-MAsu.	P
	HAi, haIKEN-SHI-MAsu.	H
I will take your order.	chuUMON-O kiKI-MAsu.	P
	go-CHUUMON-O uKE-TAMAWARI-MAsu.	H
I will do so.	soO SHI-MAsu.	P
	kaSHIKOMARI-MAshita. (Certainly, sir.)	H
I will borrow your pen.	PEn-o kaRI-MAsu.	P
	PEn-o haISHAKU-SHI-MAsu.	H
I don't know him.	waTASHI-WA aNO-hito-o shiRI-MASEn.	P
	waTASHI-WA aNO-KATA-o zoNJI-aGE-MASEn.	H
I will see you tomorrow.	aSU aI-MAsu.	P
	aSU o-ME-NI-kaKARI-MAsu.	H
I will show you something nice.	Ii-moNO-o miSE-MAsu.	P
	Ii-moNO-o o-ME-NI-KAKE-MAsu.	H

Chapter 5

Postpositions -wa and -ga

Up to this point, we have always begun a sentence with (theme-**wa**), and the theme has always been the subject (a word that denotes the doer of the action) in a sentence.
For example:

Watashi-wa Nihon-go-o hanashi-masu. (I speak Japanese.)

Watashi is the theme denoted by the postposition **-wa**, and it is also the subject (doer) of the action "speak."

But we will soon find out that:
(1) the theme is not always the subject of a sentence
(2) the subject may sometimes take the postposition **-ga** instead of **-wa**.

In this chapter, we will study the difference between the theme and the subject and the uses of postpositions **-wa** and **-ga**.

CHAPTER 5 SECTION 1
Postposition -wa

In this section, we will discuss eight uses of the postposition **-wa**. They are:

(1) (theme)**-wa** in contrast to something else
(2) eternal truth or known facts
(3) existence of a specific person or thing
(4) interrogatives used as predicates
(5) negative sentence
(6) partial negation
(7) at least, at most
(8) repetition

1. (Theme)-wa in contrast to something else

The theme or topic of a sentence is a unique feature of the Japanese language. The speaker presents a theme or topic that the speaker wants to talk about in contrast to or in comparison with something else. The speaker then gives a judgement or description of the theme. The theme denoted by the postposition **-wa** is normally placed at the beginning of a sentence.

Important

The theme is not always the subject in a sentence. An object, time definition or place definition can be used as the theme of a sentence. Carefully observe the following examples.

(a) **Watashi-wa sono-hon-o yomi-mashita.** (I read the book.)

Here, as denoted by **-wa**, **watashi** has been introduced as the theme in order to express a contrast to other people. The implication is "I don't know about other people, but, as far as I am concerned, I havc read the book." In this example, the theme is also the subject of the sentence.

(b) **Sono-hon-wa yomi-mashita.** (I read that book.)

Here, as again denoted by **-wa**, **sono-hon** (that book) is used as the theme in order to present it in contrast to other books. The implication is, "I haven't read some other books, but as far as that book is concerned, I read it." In this example, the object of the verb "to read" is used as the theme. The subject of the sentence, **watashi**, is known and was therefore omitted.

(c) **Nichiyō-bi-ni-wa gorufu-o shi-masu.** (I play golf on Sundays.)

Nichiyō-bi-ni (on Sundays) is here introduced as the theme, as denoted by **-wa**, in order to express a contrast between Sundays and other days. The implication is, "on Sundays, yes, but not on any other day." In this example, the time definition is the theme. The subject of the sentence, **watashi**, is known and was therefore omitted.

(d) **Oosaka-de-wa "arigatō"-o "ooki-ni"-to ii-masu**. (In **Oosaka**, they say "**ooki-ni**" for "thank you.")

Here, denoted by **-wa**, **Oosaka-de** (In **Oosaka**) has been introduced as the theme in order to express a comparison with other cities. The implication is, "in **Oosaka**, as opposed to **Tōkyō**." In this example, the place definition is the theme. The subject of the sentence, "they (the people in **Oosaka**)," was omitted.

2. Eternal Truths or Known Facts

The postposition **-wa** can be used to describe eternal truths or know facts. In this usage, **-wa** implies "always" or "as a rule." (The postposition **-ga** is used to describe a phenomenon. See Section 2.)
Examples:

The sun always rises in the east.	**Taiyō-wa higashi-ni nobori-masu.**
Brass is an alloy of copper and zinc.	**Shinchū-wa dō-to aen-no gōkin-desu.**
An egg is easy to break.	**Tamago-wa ware-yasui-desu.**

3. Existence of a Specific Person or Thing

The postposition **-wa** can be used to describe the existence of a specific person or thing. (The postposition **-ga** is used to describe existence of a non-specific person or thing. See Section 2.)
Examples:

My elder brother is in New York.	**Ani-wa Nyū-yōku-ni i-masu.**
The Arc de Triomphe is in Paris.	**Gaisen-mon-wa Pari-ni ari-masu.**

4. Interrogatives Used as Predicates

When the interrogatives **dare** (who), **nani** (what), **dotchi** (which), and **dore** (which) are used as predicates, their subjects take the postposition **-wa**. It is more natural for answers to questions of this type to take the (subject)**-wa** construction. (When interrogatives are used as subjects, the subjects take the postposition **-ga**. See section 2 and compare them.)
Examples:

Who is the president?	**Shachō-wa dare-desu-ka?**
The president is Mr. Tanaka.	**Shachō-wa Tanaka-san-desu.**
What is the problem?	**Mondai-wa nan-desu-ka?**
The problem is money.	**Mondai-wa o-kane-desu.**
Which is your pen?	**Anata-no-pen-wa dotchi-desu-ka?**
My pen is this one.	**Watashi-no-pen-wa kotchi-desu.**

5. Negative Sentences

The postposition **-wa** is also used in negative sentences.
Examples:

He is not a doctor.	**Kare-wa isha-de-wa ari-masen.**
He is not in Tōkyō	**Kare-wa Tōkyō-ni-wa i-masen.**

6. Partial Negation

The postposition **-wa** can be used to negate part (but not all) of the main word to which **-wa** is attached.
Examples:

I did not eat them all. (I left some.)	**Zenbu-wa tabe-masen-deshita.**
I do not drink every night. (I drink some nights.)	**Maiban-wa nomi-masen.**

7. At Least, at Most

The postposition **-wa** can also be used to mean "at least" in a positive sentence, or "at most" in a negative sentence.
Examples:

I waited at least one hour.	**Ichi-jikan-wa machi-mashita.**
It did not cost ¥1,000 at most.	**Sen-en-wa shi-masen-deshita.**

8. Repetition

The postposition **-wa** can be used to express repetition.
Examples:

Every time I wrote a letter, I tore it up.	**Tegami-o kaite-wa yaburi-mashita.**
The child sobbed "Mama" over and over.	**Sono-ko-wa "Mama"-to itte-wa nakijakuri-mashita.**

CHAPTER 5 SECTION 2

Postposition -ga

In this section, we will discuss eight uses of the postposition **-ga**. They are:

(1) phenomenon
(2) existence of a non-specific person or thing
(3) interrogatives used as subjects
(4) (object)-**ga** for adjectives describing subjective feelings
(5) (complement)-**ga** in sentence pattern (5)
(6) (subject)-**ga** in the subordinate sentence
(7) **-no** equivalent
(8) conjunctive **-ga**

1. Phenomenon

The (subject)-**ga** construction can be used to describe a phenomenon as it occurs. (The postposition **-wa** construction is used to describe eternal truths or known facts. See Section 1.)
Examples:

The sun is rising now in the east.	**Taiyō-ga higashi-ni nobori-masu.**
The egg is broken	**Tamago-ga ware-mashita.**

2. Existence of a Non-specific Person or Thing

The postposition **-ga** can also be used to describe the existence of a non-specific person or thing. (The postposition **-wa** is used to describe the existence of a specific person or thing. See Section 1.)
Examples:

There is a policeman at the corner.	**Machi-kado-ni keikan-ga i-masu.**
There is a bank in front of the station.	**Eki-no-mae-ni ginkō-ga ari-masu.**

3. Interrogatives Used as Subjects

When interrogatives **dare** (who), **nani** (what), **dotchi** (which), and **dore** (which) are used as subjects, the subjects take the postposition **-ga**. It is more natural for answers to questions of this type to take the (subject)-**ga** construction. (When interrogatives are used as predicates, the subjects take the postposition **-wa**. See section 1, and compare them carefully.)

Examples:

Who is the president?	**Dare-ga shachō-desu-ka?**
Mr. Tanaka is the president.	**Tanaka-san-ga shachō-desu.**
What is the problem?	**Nani-ga mondai-desu-ka?**
Money is the problem.	**O-kane-ga mondai-desu.**
Which is your pen?	**Dotchi-ga anata-no pen-desu-ka?**
This is my pen.	**Kotchi-ga watashi-no pen-desu.**

4. (Object)-ga for Adjectives Describing Subjective Feelings

Adjectives that describe subjective feelings take (object)**-ga**. (See CHAPTER 3 Section 10.)
Examples:

I like apples.	**Watashi-wa ringo-ga suki-desu.**
I want some water.	**Watashi-wa mizu-ga hoshii-desu.**

5. (Complement)-ga in Sentence Pattern 5

Certain complements take the postposition **-ga**. (See CHAPTER 4 Section 5.)
Examples:

Mike can play **go**.	**Maiku-wa go-ga deki-masu.**
Our dog understands Japanese.	**Uchi-no-inu-wa Nihon-go-ga wakari-masu.**

6. (Subject)-ga in the Subordinate Sentence

The subject in the subordinate sentence takes the postposition**-ga**. (Refer to the introduction to CHAPTER 13.)
Examples:

I didn't know that brass was an alloy of copper and zinc.	**Shinchū-ga dō-to aen-no gōkin-da-to-wa shiri-masen-deshita.**
An elephant has a long trunk	**Zō-wa hana-ga nagai-desu.**

7. -no Equivalent

The postposition **-ga** is used in place of the postposition **-no** of a "(noun)**-no**" modifier in some specific terms.

For example:

wa-ga-ko	my child (**wa-ga-ko = ware-no-ko** **Ware** is an old Japanese word for "I.")
wa-ga-ya	my house
wa-ga-kuni	our country
oni-ga-shima	The Ogres' Island (from a Japanese fairy tale)

8. Conjunctive -ga

Used on its own, **-ga** can mean "but" or "and," and can be used to conjoin two sentences. (Refer to CHAPTER 12 Section 2.)
Examples:

He came but she did not.	**Kare-wa ki-mashita-ga, kanojo-wa ki-masen-deshita.**
I saw the movie last night, and it was very interesting.	**Yūbe sono-eiga-o mi-mashita-ga, taihen omoshiro-katta-desu.**

Chapter 6

The Uses of V_3

V_3 is the root form or the dictionary form of a verb. (Refer to CHAPTER 4 Section 1.)

In CHAPTER 6, we will discuss the uses of V_3 as follows:

Section 1 **V_3-tsumori-desu**
Section 2 **V_3-hazu-desu**
Section 3 **V_3-tokoro-desu**
Section 4 **V_3-sō-desu**
Section 5 **V_3-yō-desu**
Section 6 **V_3-rashii-desu**
Section 7 **V_3-n-desu**
Section 8 **V_3-deshō**
Section 9 **V_3-koto-ga-deki-masu**
Section 10 **V_3-koto-ga-ari-masu**
Section 11 **V_3-koto-ni-shi-mashita**
Section 12 **V_3-koto-ni-nari-mashita**
Section 13 **V_3-kamo-shire-masen**

CHAPTER 6 SECTION 1
V_3-tsumori-desu

Tsumori expresses an intention, belief, or expectation. Therefore **V_3-tsumori-desu** means "to intend to do something."

Examples

I intend to buy a car.	車 を買うつ もり です。 kuRUMA-O kaU-TSUMORI-DEsu.
I intend to get up early tomorrow morning.	あすの 朝 は 早 く起きるつもり です。 aSU-NO-Asa-wa HAyaku oKIru-tsuMORI-DEsu.

I intend to quit smoking starting tomorrow	あしたからタバコをやめるつもりです。 aSHITA-kara taBAKO-O yaMERU-tsuMORI-DEsu.
I intend to live in Japan for one year.	日本に一年住むつもりです。 niHOn-ni iCHINEn SUmu-tsuMORI-DEsu.
I intend to consult my friend later.	あとで友達に相談する Ato-de toMODACHI-NI soODAN-SURU- つもりです。 tsuMORI-DEsu.
I intended to come back earlier.	もっと早く帰るつもりでした。 MOtto-HAyaku KAeru-tsuMORI-DEshita.
What do you intend to do today?	きょう何をするつもりですか。 KYOo NAni-o suRU-TSUMORI-DEsu-KA?
I have no intention of meeting Mr. **Tanaka** today.	きょう田中さんに会うつもりは KYOo taNAKA-SAN-NI Au-tsuMORI-WA ありません。 aRI-MASEn.

CHAPTER 6 SECTION 2
V_3-hazu-desu

Hazu means "ought to" or "supposed to," Therefore **V_3-hazu-desu** means "ought to do something" or "supposed to do something."

Examples

She is supposed to come.	彼女は来るはずです。 KAnojo-wa KUru-hazu-desu.
He should be home today.	彼はきょう家にいるはずです。 KAre-wa KYOo iE-ni iRU-HAZU-DEsu.
We should be arriving in New York around 9 o'clock.	9時ごろにはニューヨークに着くはずです。 ku-JI-GOro-ni-wa nyuUYOoku-ni TSUku-hazu-desu.
The meeting is supposed to be over before 4.	会議は4時前に終わるはずです。 kaIGI-wa yoJI-MAe-ni oWARU-HAZU-DEsu.

The department store is supposed to be open at 10.	デパートは 10 時に開く はず です。 dePAato-wa JUu-ji-ni aKU-HAZU-DEsu.
He was supposed to be back by noon.	彼 は昼 までに戻 るはずでした。 KAre-wa HIru-made-ni moDOru-haZU-DEshita.
He surely has not forgotten our promise.	彼 が約 束 を忘 れる はずは KAre-ga yaKUSOKU-O waSURERU-haZU-WA- ありません。 aRI-MASEn.

CHAPTER 6 SECTION 3

V_3-tokoro-desu

Tokoro by itself means "a place" or "a point." Therefore **V_3-tokoro-desu** means "to be on the point of doing something" or "to be about to do something."

Examples

I am about to return.	帰 るところ です。 KAeru-toKORO-desu.
I am about to have my breakfast.	朝 ご飯 を食べるところ です。 aSA-GOhan-o taBEru-toKORO-desu.
The movie is just about to begin.	映画 はちょうど 始 まる ところ です。 EIga-wa choODO haJIMARU-toKORO-desu.
I am leaving for school.	学 校 に行くところ です。 gaKKOO-NI iKU-TOKORO-desu.
The sun is about to set.	陽が沈 む ところ です。 hi-GA shiZUMU-toKORO-desu.
I was about to call you on the telephone.	あなたに電 話 する ところ でした。 aNAta-ni deNWA-SURU-toKORO-deshita.
I almost had an accident.	事故を 起こす ところ でした。 JIko-o oKOsu-toKORO-deshita.

CHAPTER 6 SECTION 4
V_3-sō-desu

Sō means "so I hear" or "so they say," and expresses hearsay. Therefore **V_3-sō-desu** means "they say that he or she does or will do something." (Do not mix this up with **V_2-sō-desu** which will be discussed in CHAPTER 7 Section 2.)

Examples

They say she is coming.	彼　女は 来るそうです。 KAnojo-wa KUru-soo-desu.
I understand that he speaks Japanese.	彼　は 日本　語を話　すそうです。 KAre-wa niHON-GO-O haNAsu-soo-desu.
They say that it will rain today.	きょう雨　が 降るそうです。 KYOo Ame-ga FUru-soo-desu.
People say that Kate is going to get married this fall.	ケイトは この　秋に結婚　する　そうです。 KEito-wa koNO-Aki-ni keKKON-SURU-SOo-desu.
You understand French, I hear.	あなたは フランス 語 が わかるそうですね。 aNAta-wa fuRANSU-GO-GA waKAru-soo-desu-NE.
They say that the Prime Minister is going to visit the U.S. next month.	首相　　は 来 月　アメリカを訪 問 shuSHOO-WA RAigetsu aMERIKA-O hoOMON- する そう です。 suRU-SOo-desu.
I understand that the ABC Company is going to announce a new product soon.	ABC社 は 近　く 新　製品を発 表 ABC-sha-wa chiKAku shiN-SEihin-o haPPYOO- する そう です。 suRU-SOo-desu.

(Nouns), (Adjectives)-sō-desu

-Sō-desu, meaning "they say," can be attached to nouns and adjectives after they are modified as follows:

N-da-sō-desu
A-i-sō-desu
A-(na)-da-sō-desu

Examples

They say that **Rashōmon** is a good movie.	羅生門はいい映画だそうです。 raSHOO-MON-WA Ii-Eiga-da-soo-desu.
They say that this book is interesting.	この本はおもしろいそうです。 koNO-HOn-wa oMOSHIROi-soo-desu.
They say that this temple is famous.	このお寺は有名だそうです。 koNO-O-TERA-WA yuUMEI-DA-SOo-desu.

CHAPTER 6 SECTION 5

V_3-yō-desu

Yō means "an appearance" or "a sign." Therefore **V_3-yō-desu** means that "it seems that he or she does or will do something."

Examples

He seems to study hard.	彼はよく勉強するようです。 KAre-wa YOku beNKYOO-suRU-YOo-desu.
She seems to go to the movies often.	彼女はよく映画に行くようです。 KAnojo-wa YOku Eiga-ni iKU-YOo-desu.
They seem to quarrel sometimes.	彼らはときどきけんかするようです。 KArera-wa toKIDOKI keNKA-SURU-YOo-desu.
This dog seems to understand words.	この犬は言葉がわかるようです。 koNO-INU-wa koTOBA-ga waKAru-yoo-desu.
There seems to be somebody in the house.	家の中にだれかいるようです。 iE-NO-NAka-ni DAre-ka iRU-YOo-desu.

CHAPTER 6 SECTION 6

V_3-rashii-desu

Rashii means "likely" or "apparently." Therefore **V_3-rashii-desu** means "he or she is likely to do something."

Examples

The typhoon is likely to come to the **Tōkyō** area.	台風 は 東 京　地 方 に 来るらしいです。 taIFUu-wa toOKYOO-CHIhoo-ni KUru-raSHIi-desu.
Our departure is likely to be delayed for about one hour.	出　発　は　1　時間 ぐらい 遅 れる shuPPATSU-WA iCHI-JIKAN-GUrai oKURERU- らしい です。 raSHIi-desu.
Mr. Smith is likely to return to his country next year.	スミス さんは 来年　帰国　する らしい SUmisu-san-wa raINEN kiKOKU-SURU-raSHIi- です。 desu.

(Nouns), (Adjectives)-rashii-desu

-Rashii-desu can also be attached to nouns and adjectives as follows:

N-rashii-desu
A-i-rashii-desu
A-(na)-rashii-desu

Examples

Apparently that is the cause.	それ が 原 因らしいです。 soRE-GA geN'IN-raSHIi-desu.
It looks cold in New York.	ニューヨーク は 寒　いらしいです。 nyuUYOoku-wa saMUi-raSHIi-desu.
He seems to be ill.	彼　は 病　気らしい です。 KAre-wa byoOKI-raSHIi-desu

CHAPTER 6 SECTION 7
V_3-n-desu

Refer to the related discussion in CHAPTER 3 Section 11:Explanatory **-n-desu**.

V_3-n-desu

V_2-masu is simply a statement of an action. If you replace **V_2-masu** with **V_3-n-desu**, you can add a nuance of explaining the reason or the circumstances. The **V_3-n-desu** form is often used in a colloquial environment, particularly if the speaker is asking for an explanation from the listener.

Examples for comparison (Arbitrary reason is added in parenthesis):

V_2-masu	**Kanojo-to ai-masu.**	I am going to meet with her.
V_3-n-desu	**Kanojo-to au-n-desu.**	I am going to meet with her, and that is the reason (that I look so happy today).
V_2-masu	**Doko-e iki-masu-ka?**	Where are you going?
V_3-n-desu	**Doko-e iku-n-desu-ka?**	Tell me where you are going (in such a hurry).

More Examples

I won't drink coffee now. I am going to bed soon, and that's why.	いまはコーヒーを飲みません。 もう すぐ 寝るんです。 Ima-wa koOHIi-o noMI-MASEn. moO-SUgu neRU-n-desu.
I borrowed some money from the bank. I am going to buy a car, and that's why.	銀行 でお金 を借りました。 giNKOO-DE o-KANE-O kaRI-MAshita. 車 を買うんです。 kuRUMA-O kaU-n-desu.
Tell me where you are now.	いまどこにいるんですか。 Ima DOko-ni iRU-n-desu-KA?
What time does the meeting begin?	会議は何 時に始 まるんですか。 kaIGI-wa NAn-ji-ni haJIMARU-n-desu-KA?
When is the rainy season over?	梅雨は いつ終わる んですか。 tsuYU-WA Itsu oWARU-n-desu-KA?

Who is going to attach a bell to the cat?	だれがあの猫に鈴を付けるんですか。 DAre-ga aNO-NEko-ni suZU-O tsuKEru-n-desu-KA?

CHAPTER 6 SECTION 8
V_3-deshō

Deshō means "I think" or "I suppose." Therefore **V_3-deshō** means "I think he or she does or will do something," or "I think something will happen."

Examples

I think that spring will come soon.	春はもうすぐ来るでしょう。 HAru-wa moO-SUgu KUru-deshoo.
I think it will snow today.	きょうは雪が降るでしょう。 KYOo-wa yuKI-ga FUru-deshoo.
I hope that the Giants will win the game.	ジャイアンツが勝つでしょう。 JAiantsu-ga KAtsu-deshoo.
I think she will be glad.	彼女は喜ぶでしょう。 KAnojo-wa yoROKObu-deshoo.
I am afraid that your mother will be worried.	お母さんが心配するでしょう。 oKAasan-ga shiNPAI-SURU-DEshoo.
I think my father will be surprised with the news.	父はその知らせに驚くでしょう。 CHIchi-wa soNO-SHIRASE-NI oDOROku-deshoo.
I am sure that we will be in time for the 10:00 train.	10時の列車にきっと間にあうでしょう。 JUu-ji-no reSSHA-NI kiTTO ma-NI-Au-deshoo.

(Noun)-deshō, (Adjective)-deshō

Deshō can also be attached to nouns and adjectives.

N-deshō
A-i-deshō
A-(na)-deshō

Examples

I think Mr. **Tanaka** will be the next company president.	田中 さんが 次 の 社長 でしょう。 taNAKA-SAN-GA tsuGI-no shaCHOO-DEshoo.
I am afraid that it is probably a mistake.	それ は たぶん 間違 いでしょう。 soRE-WA TAbun maCHIGAi-deshoo.
I think the subway is faster than the bus.	地下鉄 の ほうが バスより 速 い chiKATETSU-NO-HOo-ga BAsu-yori haYAi- でしょう。 deshoo.
I think the **shinkansen** is the most convenient.	新 幹 線 が いちばん 便 利でしょう。 shiN-KAnsen-ga iCHIBAN BENri-deshoo.

CHAPTER 6 SECTION 9
V_3-koto-ga-deki-masu

Koto is a general term meaning a thing, a matter, an affair, a fact, an incident, a set of circumstances, etc. **Deki-masu** (root form: **dekiru**) means "to be able to do." Therefore **V_3-koto-ga-deki-masu** is, as a whole, equivalent to "can + verb" in English.

Refer to CHAPTER 11 Section 3 Potential Mode which has the same function.

Examples

I can speak Japanese.	私 は 日本 語を 話 すことが waTASHI-WA niHON-GO-O haNAsu-koTO-ga- でき ます。 deKI-MAsu.
I can read **kanji**.	私 は 漢字を 読む ことが できます。 waTASHI-WA kaNJI-O YOmu-koTO-ga-deKI-MAsu.
Can you write your name in **katakana**?	あなたは 自分 の 名前 をカタカナ で aNAta-wa jiBUN-NO-naMAE-O kaTAkana-de 書く こと が でき ます か。 KAku-koTO-ga-deKI-MAsu-KA?
We can see Mt. **Fuji** from our house.	うち から 富士 山 を 見ること が できます。 uCHI-KARA FUji-san-o MIru-koTO-ga-deKI-MAsu.

I cannot drive a car.

私 は 自動 車 を 運転 する
waTASHI-WA jiDOosha-o uNTEN-SURU-
こと が でき ません。
KOTO-ga deKI-MASEn.

CHAPTER 6 SECTION 10
V_3-koto-ga-ari-masu

Koto, as described in the previous section, means a matter, a fact, or a set of circumstances. **Ari-masu** means "there is." Therefore **V_3-koto-ga-ari-masu** means that "there are situations in which he or she does something," or "there are situations when something happens."

Examples

He sometimes comes late for school.

彼 は 学校 に 遅刻 する こと
KAre-wa gaKKOO-NI chiKOKU-SURU-koTO-
が あります。
ga-aRI-MAsu.

I watch movies once in a while.

私 は たまに 映画 を 見る こと が
waTASHI-WA taMANI Eiga-o MIru-koTO-ga-
あり ます。
aRI-MAsu.

This clock sometimes stops.

この 時計 は 止まる こと があり ます。
koNO-toKEI-WA toMARU-KOTO-ga-aRI-MAsu.

I sometimes get lost in **Tōkyō**.

東京 で 道 に 迷 うこと が
toOKYOO-DE miCHI-NI maYOu-koTO-ga-
あり ます。
aRI-MAsu.

In **Tōkyō** it sometimes snows in April.

東京 では 4月 に 雪 の 降る
toOKYOO-DE-wa shiGATSU-ni yuKI-NO FUru-
こと があり ます。
koTO-ga-aRI-MAsu.

Do you occasionally meet Mr. **Itō**?

伊藤 さん に 会うこと が あり ます か。
iTOO-SAN-NI Au-koTO-ga-aRI-MAsu-KA?

CHAPTER 6 SECTION 11
V_3-koto-ni-shi-mashita

Koto means, as described in Section 9, a thing, a matter or a fact. **Shi-mashita** is the past tense of **shi-masu** (root form: **suru** meaning "to do" or "to make"). Therefore **V_3-koto-ni-shi-mashita** means "I have made up my mind to do something" or "I have decided to do something."

Examples

I have decided to go to Japan.

日本 へ行く こと に しまし た。
niHOn-e iKU-KOTO-ni-shi-MAshita.

I have decided to live in **Tōkyō**.

東 京 に 住む こと に し ま し た。
toOKYOO-NI SUmu-koTO-ni-shi-MAshita.

I have decided to quit smoking.

タバコ を やめ る こと に し ま し た。
taBAKO-O yaMERU-KOTO-ni-shi-MAshita.

I have decided to buy a new car.

新 車 を 買うこと に し ま し た。
shiNSHA-O kaU-KOTO-ni-shi-MAshita.

I have decided to take a vacation for a week.

1 週 間 休 暇 を とる こと にし
iSSHUu-kan kyuUKA-O TOru-koTO-ni-shi-
ま し た。
MAshita.

I have decided to take Japanese lessons Monday through Friday.

月 曜 から 金 曜 まで 日本 語 を
geTSUYOo-kara kiNYOo-made niHON-GO-O
習 うこと に し ま し た。
naRAu-koTO-ni-shi-MAshita.

I have decided to forget about her.

彼 女を 忘 れる こと に し ま し た。
KAnojo-o waSURERU-koTO-ni-shi-MAshita.

CHAPTER 6 SECTION 12
V_3-koto-ni-nari-mashita

Koto, as described in Section 9, means a thing, a matter or a set of circumstances. **Nari-mashita** is the past tense of **nari-masu**, and its root form, **naru**, means "to become." Therefore **V_3-koto-ni-nari-mashita** means "things have become so that he or she does something," or "circumstances have turned out to be as such that he or she does something."

Examples

As it turns out, Mr. **Satō** is going to quit the company	佐藤さんは会社を辞めることに SAtoo-san-wa kaISHA-O yaMERU-KOTO-ni- なりました。 naRI-MAshita.
The result is that we will hold the next meeting in **Kyōto**.	次の会議は京都で開く tsuGI-no-kaIGI-wa KYOoto-de hiRAku- ことになりました。 koTO-ni-naRI-MAshita.
It has been decided that we will announce the new product on May 10.	新製品は5月10日に shiN-SEihin-wa GO-gatsu-toO-KA-NI 発表することになりました。 haPPYOO-suRU-KOTO-ni-naRI-MAshita.
It has been decided that my mother will enter the hospital tomorrow.	母はあす入院することになり HAha-wa aSU nyuUIN-suRU-KOTO-ni-naRI- ました。 MAshita.
It has been decided that Mr. **Tanaka** will be transferred to the **Oosaka** branch.	田中さんは大阪支店に転勤 taNAKA-SAN-WA oOSAKA-SHIten-ni teNKIN- することになりました。 suRU-koTO-ni-naRI-MAshita.

CHAPTER 6 SECTION 13
V_3-kamo-shire-masen

Kamo means “whether or not,” and **shire-masen** is the negative form of **shire-masu**, whose root form **shireru** means “to become known.” Therefore **kamo-shire-masen** means “whether or not is not known,” and it is, as a whole, equivalent to the English word “may.”

Examples

He may come.	彼は来るかもしれません。 KAre-wa KUru-kamo-shiRE-MASEn.
She may be home.	彼女は家にいるかもしれません。 KAnojo-wa iE-ni iRU-kamo-shiRE-MASEn.
It may rain.	雨が降るかもしれません。 Ame-ga FUru-kamo-shiRE-MASEn.
He may say so.	彼はそう言うかもしれません。 KAre-wa <u>soO</u> iU-kamo-shiRE-MASEn.
This machine may sell well.	この機械はよく売れるかもしれ koNO-KIKAi-wa YOku uRERU-kamo-shiRE- ません。 MASEn.

(Noun), (Adjective)-kamo-shire-masen

The **kamo-shire-masen** structure can also be attached to nouns and adjectives with the forms shown below.

<u>N</u>-kamo-shire-masen
<u>A</u>-i-kamo-shire-masen
<u>A</u>-(na)-kamo-shire-masen

Examples

Drinking may be the cause.	飲酒が原因かもしれません。 iNSHU-GA geN'IN-KAmo-shiRE-MASEn.
That might be the right answer.	それが正解かもしれません。 soRE-GA seIKAI-KAmo-shiRE-MASEn

It may be cold tomorrow.	あすは寒いかもしれません。 aSU-wa saMUi-kamo-shiRE-MASEn.
The novel may be interesting.	その小説はおもしろいかもしれません。 soNO-shoOSETSU-WA oMOSHIROi-kamo-shiRE-MASEn.
She may be fond of music.	彼女は音楽が好きかもしれません。 KAnojo-wa Ongaku-ga suKI-kamo-shiRE-MASEn.
The job may be easy.	その仕事は楽かもしれません。 soNO-SHIGOTO-WA raKU-kamo-shiRE-MASEn.

Chapter 7

The Uses of V_2

(Refer to CHAPTER 4 Section 2 for the definition and conjugation of the V_2 form.)

The most important usage of V_2 is the **V_2-masu** form that we discussed in CHAPTER 4.

Some Other Uses of V_2

In this chapter we will discuss some other uses of V_2 in the following Sections:

Section 1 **V_2-yasui (-nikui)-desu**
Section 2 **V_2-sō-desu**
Section 3 **V_2-tai-desu**
Section 4 **V_2-mashō, V_2-mashō-ka?**
Section 5 **V_2-nasai**
Section 6 **V_2-ni-iki (-ki,-kaeri)-masu**
Section 7 **V_2-mono** and **V_2-kata**
Section 8 Compound Verbs **V_2-V_3**
Section 9 **V_2** used as a noun
Section 10 Honorifics (4): **o-V_2** Forms

As you go through some of these uses, you will notice that the V_2 form in Japanese has the same function as the English *gerund*, that is a verbal form used as a noun. For example: "seeing is believing."

CHAPTER 7 SECTION 1
V_2-yasui (nikui) -desu

Yasui means "easy," and **nikui** means "difficult." Therefore:

V_2-yasui means "to be easy to do something" and
V_2-nikui means "to be difficult to do something"

Both **V_2-yasui** and **V_2-nikui** are treated as **i**-Adjectives, and their Negative and Past forms are derived accordingly.

Examples

This pen is easy to write with.	この ペンは 書きやすい です。 koNO-PEn-wa kaKI-YASUi-desu.
These shoes are easy to wear.	この 靴 は 履きやすいです。 koNO-KUTSU-wa haKI-YASUi-desu.
This camera is easy to use.	この カメラ は 使 いやすい です。 koNO-KAmera-wa tsuKAI-YASUi-desu.
This medicine is difficult to take.	この 薬 は 飲み にくいです。 koNO-KUSURI-WA noMI-NIKUi-desu.
His story was difficult to understand.	彼 の 話 は わかりにくかったです。 KAre-no-haNASHI-wa waKARI-NIKU-katta-desu.
His handwriting is difficult to read.	彼 の 字は 読みにくいです KAre-no-JI-wa yoMI-NIKUi-desu.
Is **Tōkyō** easy to live in or difficult to live in?	東京 は 住み やすいです か 住み にくい toOKYOO-WA suMI-YASUi-desu-KA suMI-NIKUi- です か。 desu-KA?

CHAPTER 7 SECTION 2

V_2-sō-desu

This **sō** means "it looks" or "it seems," and is used to express a speaker's observation. Therefore **V_2-sō-desu** means "it looks like he or she does or will do something." It is almost the same as **V_3-rashii-desu** (Chapter 6 Section 6). Pay attention to the difference between **V_3-sō-desu** (Chapter 6 Section 4) and **V_2-sō-desu**.
For example:

V_3-sō-desu
Taifū-ga kuru-sō-desu. (They say that a typhoon is coming.)

V_2-sō-desu
Taifū-ga ki-sō-desu. (It looks like a typhoon is coming.)

Examples

It looks like rain.	雨　が降りそうです。 Ame-ga fuRI-SOo-desu.
He seems to be rich.	彼　はお金　がありそうです。 KAre-wa o-KANE-GA aRI-SOo-desu.
It looks as if that old tree is about to fall down.	その古い木はいまにも倒れそうです。 soNO-FURUi-KI-wa Ima-nimo taORE-SOo-desu.
Everything seems to be going all right.	すべてうまく行きそうです。 SUbete Umaku iKI-SOO-DEsu.
It looks like even I can do it.	私　にもできそうです。 waTASHI-NI-mo deKI-SOo-desu.

(Adjective)-sō-desu

Sō-desu meaning "it looks" or "it seems" can also be attached to adjectives with the following forms:

A-(i)-sō-desu
Example: **taka-i** (high) becomes **taka-sō-desu** (seems high)

A-(na)-sō-desu
Example: **genki-na** (healthy) becomes **genki-sō-desu** (seems healthy)

I-i (good) and **na-i** (not existing), although they are **A-i**, are exceptions to the above forms and are expressed as follows:

I-i or **yo-i** (good) becomes **yo-sa-sō-desu** (seems good), not **i-sō-desu** or **yo-sō-desu**.

Na-i (not existing) becomes **na-sa-sō-desu** (does not seem to be existing), not **na-sō-desu**.

Examples

This pie looks delicious.	この パイは おいしそう です。 koNO-PAi-wa oISHI-SOO-DEsu.
She seems to be very delighted.	彼 女はとても 嬉 し そうです。 KAnojo-wa toTEMO uRESHI-SOo-desu.
The new car seems to be quite good.	新 しい車 は なか なか よさ aTARASHIi-kuRUMA-WA naKANAKA yo-SA- そう です。 SOo-desu.
There seems to be no problem.	問 題 は な さ そう です。 moNDAI-WA na-SA-SOo-desu.
They seem to be very happy.	あの 人 達 は 大変 幸 せ そう です。 aNO-hiTOtachi-wa taIHEN shiAWASE-SOO-DEsu.

CHAPTER 7 SECTION 3

V_2-tai-desu

Tai means "I want to," so **V_2-tai-desu** means "I want to do something." The subject is always the first person (I). For example, **tabe-tai-desu** always means. "I want to eat."

In order to express the desire of a third person (he or she), you can use the verb form **V_2-tagaru**, or you could use **V_2-tai** in a quoted sentence. For example:

He wants to eat.	**Kare-wa tabe-tagari-masu.**
He says, "I want to eat."	**Kare-wa tabe-tai-to ii-masu.**

(Refer to CHAPTER 13 Section 2 for an explanation of the quoted sentence.)

In a question to a second person (you), **V_2-tai** is used. Therefore, "Do you want to eat?" is **Anata-wa tabe-tai-desu-ka?**

Important

A **V_2-tai** form is treated as an **i-**adjective of subjective feelings. Therefore it takes an "(Object)**-ga**." (See CHAPTER 3, Section 10)

"I want to eat an apple" is **Ringo-ga tabe-tai-desu**.

More Examples

I want to go to Japan.	日本に行きたいです。 niHOn-ni iKI-TAi-desu.
I want to live in **Tōkyō**.	東京に住みたいです。 toOKYOO-NI suMI-TAi-desu.
I want to see **kabuki**.	歌舞伎が見たいです。 kaBUKI-GA mi-TAi-desu.
I want to meet my old friend in **Tōkyō**.	東京の古い友達に会いたいです。 toOKYOO-NO fuRUi-toMODACHI-NI aI-TAi-desu.
I want to work for the ABC company.	ABC社で働きたいです。 eI-BII-SHIi-sha-de haTARAKI-TAi-desu.
I want to go back to America.	アメリカに帰りたいです。 aMERIKA-NI kaERI-TAi-desu.
I want to drink some water.	水が飲みたいです。 miZU-GA noMI-TAi-desu.
What do you want to eat?	何が食べたいですか。 NAni-ga taBE-TAi-desu-KA?
I do not want to eat fish.	魚は食べたくないです。 saKANA-wa taBE-TAku-NAi-desu.
I want to read a Japanese history book.	日本の歴史の本が読みたいです。 niHON-NO reKISHI-NO-HOn-ga yoMI-TAi-desu.
I want to buy a **kimono** and a belt for a lady.	女の人の着物と帯を買いたいです。 oNNA-NO-hiTO-NO kiMONO-TO Obi-o kaI-TAi-desu.

CHAPTER 7 SECTION 4

V_2-mashō, V_2-mashō-ka?

Mashō, when used as a suffix appended to a **V_2** verb, can mean either "let us," in suggesting to the listener to do something together, or "let me" in offering a service to the listener.

Mashō-ka? is the question form of the above, meaning "shall we?" or "shall I?"

Examples

Let's go and eat.	食　事に行きましょう。 shoKUJI-NI IKI-MASHOo.
Let's meet again tomorrow.	あす また 会いましょう。 aSU maTA al-MASHOo.
Let's play tennis.	テニス を し ましょう。 TEnisu-o shi-MASHOo.
Let's speak in Japanese.	日本　語 で 話　し ましょう。 niHON-GO-DE haNASHI-MASHOo.
Let me help you.	お手伝 いし ましょう。 o-TEtsudai-shi-MASHOo.
Let me show you the way.	ご 案内　し ましょう。 go-ANNAI-shi-MASHOo.
Shall we dance?	踊　り ましょう か。 oDORI-MASHOo-ka?
Shall we take a walk?	散　歩 し ましょう か。 saNPO-shi-MASHOo-ka?
Shall I open the window?	窓　を 開け ましょう か。 MAdo-o aKE-MASHOo-ka?

CHAPTER 7 SECTION 5

V_2-nasai

Nasai is an imperative or a command verb form derived from the verb **suru** (to do) as shown below:

suru	——→	**nasaru**	——→	**nasai**
to do		honorific (respectful style)		imperative style

The compound **V_2-nasai**, even though it is derived from the honorific verb, is a straightforward command used only by, for example, a father to his son, or a teacher to his or her pupil. It should not be used with superiors, equals, or strangers, except the customary expressions of **gomen-nasai** (I beg your pardon), **oyasumi-nasai** (good night) and **okaeri-nasai** (welcome home.)

With superiors, equals, or strangers, the honorific request style discussed in CHAPTER 7 Section 10 and CHAPTER 8 Section 10 should be used instead of **V_2-nasai**.

Examples

Go!	行きなさい。 iKI-NASAi!
Come here!	ここ へ来なさい。 koKO-E ki-NASAi!
Get up!	起きなさい。 oKI-NASAi!
Walk quickly!	速 く 歩 き なさい。 HAyaku aRUKI-NASAi!
Sit down!	座 りなさい。 suWARI-NASAi!
Be quiet!	静 かにし なさい。 SHIzukani shi-NASAi!

CHAPTER 7 SECTION 6

V_2-ni-iki (-ki, -kaeri) -masu

Ni is a versatile postposition which, when used in this sequence, indicates purpose, and can be translated effectively as "in order to."

V_2-ni-iki-masu	(to go in order to do something)
V_2-ni-ki-masu	(to come in order to do something)
V_2-ni-kaeri-masu	(to return in order to do something)

Examples

I am going to the post office to buy some stamps.	郵便局へ切手を買いにいきます。 yuUBIn-kyoku-e kiTTE-O kaI-NI-iKI-MAsu.
I went to the station to see my friend off.	駅へ友達を見送りにいきました。 Eki-e toMODACHI-O miOKURI-NI-iKI-MAshita
My wife will come to the airport to meet me.	家内が空港に迎えにきます。 KAnai-ga kuUKOO-NI muKAE-NI-ki-MAsu.
An old friend came to see me from **Kyōto**.	昔の友人が京都から会いに muKASHI-NO-yuUJIN-GA KYOoto-kara Ai-ni- きました。 ki-MAshita.
I went back for the umbrella.	傘を取りに帰りました。 KAsa-o TOri-ni-kaERI-MAshita.
My son comes home to have lunch every day.	息子は毎日昼ご飯を食べに muSUKO-WA MAinichi hiRU-GOhan-o TAbe-ni- 帰ります。 kaERI-MAsu.

CHAPTER 7 SECTION 7
V_2-mono and V_2-kata

V_2-mono-

物 (**mono**) is a noun which literally means "thing," and 者 (also **mono**) means "person" or "fellow." When attached to the V_2 form, **V_2-mono** expresses the literal meaning of "a thing (things) or a person (persons) for a certain function." As you will see, this rather complex-sounding expression usually equates to rather simple English nouns.

Examples

Japanese	Literal Meaning	English Equivalent
tabe-mono	thing to eat	food
nomi-mono	thing to drink	liquors, beverages
ki-mono	thing to wear	(Japanese) clothing
kai-mono	thing to buy	shopping, good buy
uri-mono	thing to sell	for sale
okuri-mono	thing to present	gift
nori-mono	thing to ride	vehicle
mi-mono	thing to see	highlight
yomi-mono	thing to read	literature
iki-mono	living thing	creature
tate-mono	thing to be built	building
koware-mono	thing that is easily broken	fragile
hataraki-mono	person who works hard	hard worker
namake-mono	person who dawdles	lazy person

V_2-kata

The suffix **kata**, when attached to a V_2 form of a verb, expresses the way or manner to do something.

Examples:

tsukai-kata	how to use	**iki-kata**	the way of living
tsukuri-kata	how to make	**hanashi-kata**	the way of speaking
oyogi-kata	how to swim	**kangae-kata**	the way of thinking
ake-kata	how to open	**mi-kata**	the way of looking at
susume-kata	how to proceed	**aruki-kata**	the manner of walking
sodate-kata	how to bring up	**oshie-kata**	the method of teaching

CHAPTER 7 SECTION 8
Compound Verbs V_2-V_3

In certain cases, combining two verbs, the first in V_2 form and the second in V_3 form, can produce a meaningful *compound verb*. For example:

to see: V_3 is **miru**, V_2 is **mi**.
to learn: V_3 is **narau**.

The compound verb in V_2-V_3 form, **mi-narau**, means "to learn by observation," or even "to follow suit."

The above V_2-V_3 compound is considered to be a root form or dictionary form. In conjugation, the V_2 part remains unchanged; only the V_3 part conjugates just like any other single V_3 verb. For example, the polite **V_2-masu** form for a V_2-V_3 is V_2-V_2-masu. So **mi-narau** becomes **mi-narai-masu**.

More Examples

Japanese	Literal Meaning	English Equivalent
mi-naosu	to see and mend	to give it a second look; to discover new merits
mi-wakeru	to see and separate	to distinguish; to identify
mi-yaburu	to see and break	to see through another's plot
mi-nogasu	to see and let go	to overlook; to wink an eye at
nusumi-miru	to steal and see	to cast a furtive glance at
kaki-naosu	to write and mend	to rewrite
hanashi-hajimeru	to talk and begin	to begin talking
aruki-tsuzukeru	to walk and continue	to continue walking
yomi-owaru	to read and finish	to finish reading
nomi-akasu	to drink and sit up all night	to drink the night away
tobi-okiru	to jump and get up	to jump out of bed
ne-sugosu	to sleep and pass	to oversleep
oki-wasureru	to put and forget	to mislay
nori-kaeru	to ride and change	to transfer (to another train, plane, etc.)
tabe-sugiru	to eat and exceed	to eat too much

(Adjective)-sugiru

By following the format below, the verb **sugiru** (to exceed), seen in the last example above, can also be attached to adjectives to describe a degree of excess:

A-(i) -sugiru
A-(na)-sugiru

too expensive	**taka-sugiru**
too big	**ooki-sugiru**
too small	**chiisa-sugiru**
too much	**oo-sugiru**
too little	**sukuna-sugiru**
too quiet	**shizuka-sugiru**

CHAPTER 7 SECTION 9

V_2 Used as a Noun

In most cases, the V_2 form of a verb can be used as an everyday noun either by itself or as a compound word combined with another noun or adjective. (This function is very much like that of the *gerund* in English, as stated in the introduction to CHAPTER 7.)

Examples

V_3		V_2 used as a noun	
hanasu	to speak, to tell	**hanashi**	speech, story
kangaeru	to think	**kangae**	thought, idea, opinion
oshieru	to teach	**oshie**	instruction, doctrine
nagameru	to look on	**nagame**	view
tooru	to pass through	**toori**	street
okonau	to act	**okonai**	behavior
umareru	to be born	**umare**	lineage
kawaru	to replace	**o-kawari**	second helping

More Examples

V_3		V_2 used as a noun	
kasu	to lend	**kashi**	loan
		kashi-kata	credit side
kariru	to borrow	**kari**	debt
		kari-kata	debit side
tetsudau	to help	**tetsudai**	helping hand
		o-tetsudai-san	maid
neru	to sleep	**hiru-ne**	nap
		(combined with **hiru** [daytime])	
nigeru	to run away	**yo-nige**	flight by night
		(combined with **yoru** [night])	
miru	to see	**hana-mi**	cherry blossom viewing
		(combined with **hana** [flower])	
kaku	to write, draw	**e-kaki**	painter
		(combined with **e** [picture])	
shiru	to know	**mono-shiri**	knowledgeable person
		(combined with **mono** [things])	
nomu	to drink	**sake-nomi**	heavy drinker
		(combined with **sake** [rice wine])	
yasumu	to rest	**yasumi**	day off, holiday
		natsu-yasumi	summer vacation
		zuru-yasumi	truancy
		(combined with **zurui** [sly])	
okiru	to get up	**haya-oki**	early riser
		(combined with **hayai** [early])	
uru	to sell	**yasu-uri**	bargain sale
		(combined with **yasui** [cheap])	
ikiru	to live, subsist	**naga-iki**	longevity
		(combined with **nagai** [long])	

CHAPTER 7 SECTION 10
Honorifics (4) : o-V_2 Forms

o-V_2 Forms

The **o-V_2** form, (**V_2** verb used as a noun with prefix **o**, for example **hanasu** (to speak) becomes **o-hanashi**) plays an important role in honorifics in the following forms. (Each form has tentatively been numbered R1 through H4.)

Respectful Forms	doer of V_2
(R1) **o-V_2-desu**	second or third person
(R2) **o-V_2-nasai-masu**	second or third person
(R3) **o-V_2-ni-nari-masu**	second or third person
(R4) **o-V_2-kudasai-masu**	second or third person

Humble Forms	doer of V_2
(H1) **o-V_2-shi-masu**	first person
(H2) **o-V_2-itashi-masu**	first person
(H3) **o-V_2-mōshi-age-masu**	first person
(H4) **o-V_2-itadaki-masu**	second or third person

Important

Pay attention to who is actually doing the action of the **V_2** verb. For example in **o-hanashi** (to talk), pay attention to the person who is doing the talking. In all respectful forms, it is easy to assume that the action of the **V_2** verb is being performed by the second person (you) or the third person (he, she, they). For the forms (H1) through (H3), it is also understandable, by the use of the plain or humble suffixes (**shi-masu, itashi-masu, mōshi-age-masu**) that the doer of **V_2** is the first person (I, we) or the speaker. In (H4), the suffix **itadaki-masu** is the humble form meaning "I receive a favor (from the second or third person)." Therefore the true doer of the action **V_2** is the originator of the favor.

Since the **V_2** of **o-V_2** functions as a verb that has turned into a noun, (as we studied in the previous section) the two-kanji-character action nouns listed on pages 83 and 84 can easily be used in place of the **V_2**. In such cases, however, the prefix **go** is generally used instead of **o**. For example: **go-aisatsu, go-kekkon, go-hatten.**

(R1) o-V_2-desu

This is the simplified form of (R2) or (R3) forms, and is often used in practical conversation.
Examples:

Mr. **Tanaka** is here.
(Mr. **Tanaka** shows up.)
田中さんがお見えです。
taNAKA-SAN-GA o-MIE-DEsu.

The President is calling you.
社長がお呼びです。
shaCHOO-GA o-YOBI-DEsu.

What are you looking for?
何をお探しですか。
NAni-o o-SAGASHI-DEsu-KA?

(R2) o-V_2-nasai-masu and (R3) o-V_2-ni-nari-masu

Both (R2) and (R3) forms indicate a very high degree of respect.
Examples:

Have you talked with Mr. **Tanaka**?
田中さんとお話しなさいましたか。
taNAKA-SAN-TO o-HANASHI-naSAI-MAshita-KA?

Have you ordered already?
もうご注文なさいましたか。
MOo go-CHUUMON-naSAI-MAshita-KA?

Do you often meet with Mr. **Tanaka**?
田中さんとよくお会いになりますか。
taNAKA-SAN-TO YOku o-AI-NI-naRI-MAsu-KA?

Mr. **Satō** was very glad.
佐藤さんはたいへんお喜びになりました。
SAtoo-san-wa taIHEN o-YOROKOBI-NI-naRI-MAshita.

A prince was born.
王子様がお生まれになりました。
Ooji-sama-ga o-UMARE-NI-naRI-MAshita.

You seem to have lost a little weight, haven't you?
少しおやせになりましたね。
suKOshi o-YASE-NI-naRI-MAshita-NE.

Miss **Katō** will graduate from university this year.
加藤さんは今年大学をご卒業になります。
KAtoo-san-wa koTOSHI daIGAKU-O go-SOTSUGYOO-NI-naRI-MAsu.

(H1) o-V_2-shi-masu, (H2) o-V_2-itashi-masu and (H3) o-V_2-mōshi-age-masu

These three forms all mean "I will do" in order of humbleness. (H3 is the most humble form.)
Examples:

I will send it right away.

(H1) すぐにお送りします。
SUguni o-OKURI-SHI-MAsu.

(H2) すぐにお送りいたします。
Suguni o-OKURI-iTASHI-MAsu.

(H3) すぐにお送り申し上げます。
SUguni o-OKURI-moOSHI-aGE-MAsu.

I will call you on the telephone tomorrow.

(H1) あしたお電話します。
aSHITA o-DEnwa-shi-masu.

(H2) あすお電話いたします。
aSU o-DEnwa-itashi-masu.

(H3) あすお電話申し上げます。
Asu o-DEnwa-moOSHI-AGE-MAsu.

I will give you a tour of the factory.

(H1) 工場をご案内します。
koOJOo-o go-ANNAI-SHI-MAsu.

(H2) 工場をご案内致します。
koOJOo-o go-ANNAI-iTASHI-MAsu.

(H3) 工場をご案内申し上げます。
koOJOo-o go-ANNAI-moOSHI-AGE-MAsu.

(R4) o-V_2-kudasai-masu and (H4) o-V_2-itadaki-masu

Kudasaru is a respectful word meaning "to give" and **itadaku** is a humble word meaning "to receive." (See CHAPTER 4 Section 12.) The meaning conveyed here is that the second or the third person is taking the trouble to do the action of the V_2 verb as a favor to the speaker. This can be expressed in two ways: (R4) from the favor-giving side and (H4) from the favor-receiving side.

Examples:

Mr. **Itō** told us the story	伊藤さんが (私達に) お話しくださいました。 iTOO-SAN-GA (waTASHI-tachi-ni) o-HANASHI-kuDASAI-MAshita. (R4)
	(私達は) 伊藤さんにお話しいただきました。 (waTASHI-tachi-wa) iTOO-SAN-NI o-HANASHI-iTADAKI-MAshita. (H4)
Mr. **Itō** informed me of the news.	伊藤さんが (私に) そのニュースをお知らせくださいました。 iTOO-SAN-GA (waTASHI-NI) soNO-NYUusu-o o-SHIRASE-kuDASAI-MAshita. (R4)
	(私は) 伊藤さんにそのニュースをお知らせいただきました。 (waTASHI-WA) iTOO-SAN-NI soNO-NYUusu-o o-SHIRASE-iTADAKI-MAshita. (H4)
Mr. **Satō** invited me to the party.	佐藤さんは私をパーティーにご招待くださいました。 SAtoo-san-wa waTASHI-O PAa tii-ni go-SHOotai-kuDASAI-MAshita. (R4)
	私は佐藤さんからパーティーにご招待いただきました。 waTASHI-WA SAtoo-san-kara PAa tii-ni go-SHOotai-iTADAKI-MAshita (H4)

o-V_2-kudasai

The **O-V_2-kudasai** form is a variation of (R4). This is used in making a respectful request to the listener, and literally means "would you please do me a favor?"
Examples:

Would you please wait a moment?	どうぞしばらくお待ちください。 DOozo shiBAraku o-MACHI-KUDASAi.
Would you please come this way?	どうぞこちらにおいでください。 DOozo koCHIRA-NI o-IDE-KUDASAi.

Please forgive my rudeness.	どうぞ失礼をお許しください。 DOozo shiTSUrei-o o-YURUSHI-KUDASAi.
Please take good care of your health.	どうぞお元気にお過ごしください。 DOozo o-GEnki-ni o-SUGOSHI-KUDASAi.
Kindly refrain from smoking.	おタバコはご遠慮ください。 o-TAbako-wa go-ENRYO-KUDASAi.

Chapter 8

The Uses of "V_2'-te"

V_2 with suffix **-te** is another important form, and as we continue you will notice that some of its uses are similar to the *present participle* form in English like the word "walking" in "I am walking."

However the **V_2-te** form which was used in classical Japanese has been somewhat modified in modern Japanese for easier pronunciation. We call this modified **V_2-te** form "**V_2'-te**."

Observe the differences in the following chart:

V_3		V_2-te Classical Japanese	V_2'-te Modern Japanese
haku	to put on	**haki-te**	**hai-te**
toru	to take	**tori-te**	**tot-te**
yomu	to read	**yomi-te**	**yon-de**

Conversion Flow Chart

(Refer to CHAPTER 4 Section 2, "How to Read a Flow Chart.")

The flow chart for converting **V_3** to **V_2'-te** form is shown on the next page. Examples are shown for representative verbs and the two special verbs, "do" and "come."

The verb **iku** (to go) is an exception. Its **V_2'-te** form is **it-te**.

Also pay attention to those "sham" **-iru/-eru** ending verbs that should be treated as **-ru** ending verbs. (They are listed at the end of **-ru** ending group in the CHAPTER 4 Section 1.)

Conversion Chart: V_3 to V_2'-te

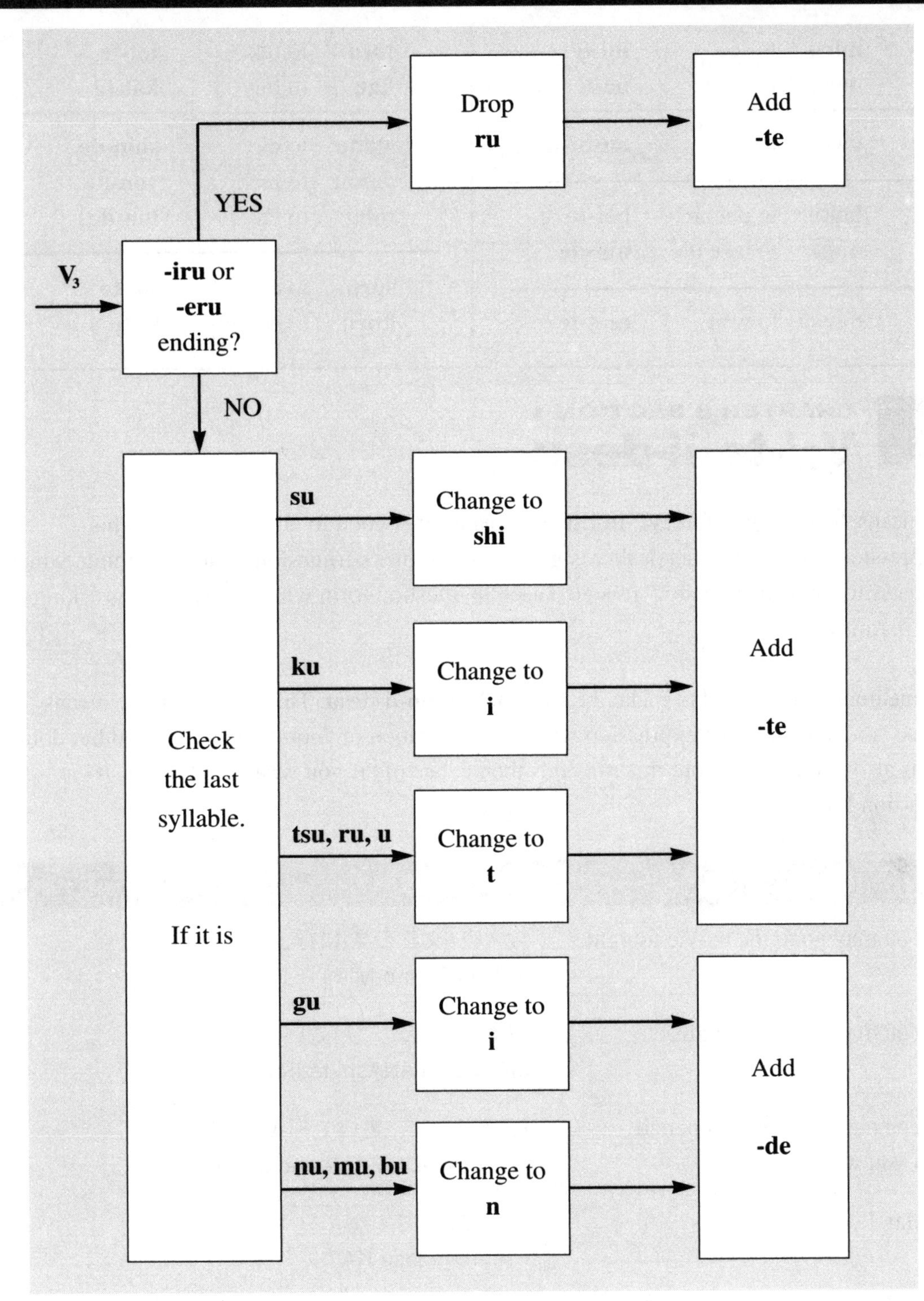

V_3 to V_2'-te (Representative and Special Verbs)

miru	to see	**mi-te**	**toru**	to take	**tot-te**
neru	to sleep	**ne-te**	**kau**	to buy	**kat-te**
kasu	to lend	**kashi-te**	**shinu**	to die	**shin-de**
			yomu	to read	**yon-de**
haku	to put on	**hai-te**	**tobu**	to fly	**ton-de**
nugu	to take off	**nui-de**			
			suru	to do	**shi-te**
matsu	to wait	**mat-te**	**kuru**	to come	**ki-te**

CHAPTER 8 SECTION 1

V_2'-te-ii-desu

Ii means "good," therefore **V_2'-te-ii-desu** means "it is good to do something." This expression is used when a speaker is giving the listener permission to do something, which equates to English "may do." It is also used in question form when the speaker is asking for permission.

Sometimes **mo** is added to make the form **V_2'-te-mo-ii-desu**. This **mo** originally means "also" and it softens the expression with the implication of "not doing so is good but doing so is also good." Therefore this **mo** adds the nuance of "if you wish," or "if I wish" in question form.

Examples

You may go to the movie tonight.	今夜映画を見に行っていいです。 KOnya Eiga-o-MI-ni iT-TE-Ii-desu.
You may speak in English.	英語で話していいです。 eIGO-DE haNAshi-te-Ii-desu.
You may write with a pencil, if you wish.	鉛筆で書いてもいいです。 eNPITSU-DE KAi-te-mo-Ii-desu.
May I come in?	入っていいですか。 HAit-te-Ii-desu-KA?
May I smoke, if I wish?	タバコを吸ってもいいですか taBAKO-O suT-TE-mo-Ii-desu-KA?

May I open the box now?

いま箱を開けていいですか。
Ima haKO-O aKE-TE-Ii-desu-KA?

May I ask you a few questions?

二三質問していいですか。
NI-san shiTSUMON-SHI-TE-Ii-desu-KA?

CHAPTER 8 SECTION 2
V_2'-te-wa-ike-masen

Ike-masen means "must not." Therefore, when **ike-masen** is appended to **V_2'-te**, the result is "you must not do something." **-Wa** is added as this is a negative sentence. (See CHAPTER 5 Section 1: [5])

Examples

You must not come with us.

一緒に来てはいけません。
iSSHO-NI KI-te-wa-iKE-MASEn.

You must not write with a pencil.

鉛筆で書いてはいけません。
eNPITSU-DE KAi-te-wa-iKE-MASEn.

You must not run in the house.

家の中で走ってはいけません。
iE-NO-NAka-de haSHIt-te-wa-iKE-MASEn.

You must not read such a book.

そんな本を読んではいけません。
soNNA-HOn-o YOn-de-wa iKE-MASEn.

You must not watch television until late at night.

夜遅くまでテレビを見てはいけません。
YOru-oSOKU-made TErebi-o MI-te-wa-iKE-MASEn.

You must not ride a bicycle in the park.

公園の中で自転車に乗っては
koOEN-NO-NAka-de jiTENSHA-NI noT-TE-wa-
いけません。
iKE-MASEn.

Children must not drink **sake**.

子供はお酒を飲んではいけません。
koDOMO-WA o-SAKE-O NOn-de-wa-iKE-MASEn.

CHAPTER 8 SECTION 3
V_2'-te-i-masu

Four usages of **V_2'-te-i-masu** will be discussed in this section. Each usage is characterized by the nature of the verbs used:

(1) an action in progress
(2) a habitual or repeated action
(3) the state of being
(4) the result of an autonomous action

(1) An Action in Progress

When used with verbs that describe an action that continues over a certain period of time, **V_2'-te-i-masu** describes an action in progress.

As stated in the introduction to CHAPTER 8, the **V_2'-te** form includes the same function as that of the *present participle* in English. **I-masu** means "to be." Therefore **V_2'-te-i-masu** represents exactly the same pattern of the *progressive* form (to be + verb-ing) in English, for example "I am reading."

Examples:

Tarō is having breakfast.	太郎は朝ご飯を食べています。 TAroo-wa aSA-GOhan-o TAbe-te-i-masu.
Hanako is walking.	花子は歩いています。 HAnako-wa aRUi-te-i-masu.
The baby is sleeping.	赤ん坊は寝ています。 aKANBOO-WA ne-TE-I-MAsu.
My father is reading a paper.	父は新聞を読んでいます。 CHIchi-wa shiNBUN-O YOn-de-i-masu.
My mother is writing a letter.	母は手紙を書いています。 HAha-wa teGAMI-O KAi-te-i-masu.
It is raining.	雨が降っています。 Ame-ga FUt-te-i-masu.

(2) A Habitual or Repeated Action

V_2'-te-i-masu is used to describe a habitual or repeated action when it is used with verbs of that nature.

Examples:

I collect stamps.	私は切手を集めています。 waTASHI-WA kiTTE-O aTSUme-te-i-masu.
I take Japanese lessons every day.	毎日日本語を習っています。 MAinichi niHON-GO-O naRAt-te-i-masu.
My father commutes to his office by subway.	父は地下鉄で会社に通っ CHIchi-wa chiKATETSU-DE kaISHA-NI kaYOT- ています。 TE-I-MAsu.
My mother takes medicine every morning.	母は毎朝薬を飲んでいます。 HAha-wa MAiasa kuSURI-O NOn-de-i-masu.
We subscribe to the **Asahi Shinbun**.	うちは朝日新聞をとっています。 uCHI-WA aSAHI-SHINbun-o TOt-te-i-masu.

(3) State of Being

V_2'-te-i-masu is used to describe the state of being when used with verbs that describe a continuous state.

Examples:

I live in **Tōkyō**.	私は東京に住んでいます。 waTASHI-WA toOKYOO-NI SUn-de-i-masu.
I have a car.	私は車を持っています。 waTASHI-WA kuRUMA-O MOt-te-i-masu.
I know him very well.	彼をよく知っています。 KAre-o YOku shiT-TE-I-MAsu.
I love you.	私はあなたを愛しています。 waTASHI-WA aNAta-o Ai-shi-te-i-masu.
She is thin.	彼女はやせています。 KAnojo-wa yaSE-TE-I-MAsu.
My son resembles me.	息子は私に似ています。 MUsuko-wa watashi-NI niTE-I-MAsu.

(4) The Result of an Autonomous Action

Let's look at an example.

Mado-ga ai-te i-masu. (The window is open.)

Remember that **i-masu** is supposed to have an animate being as its subject. In addition, the verb **ai-te** (to open; root form: **aku**) is an intransitive verb that denotes an autonomous action by the subject, despite the fact that the subject is an inanimate window!

This means that **V_2'-te-i-masu**, when used with an inanimate subject, personifies it and gives a vivid description of the existing result of an action. (Compare this usage with the result of a heteronomous action discussed in Section 4.)
More examples:

The light is on.	電 気が つ いています。 DEnki-ga TSUi-te-i-masu.
The light is off.	電 気が消えて いま す。 DEnki-ga kiE-TE-I-MAsu.
A car is parked.	車 が 止 まっています。 kuRUMA-GA toMAT-TE-I-MAsu.
The door is locked.	ドアの 鍵 がかかっています。 DOa-no kaGI-ga kaKAt-te-i-masu.
Sugar has already been put in.	砂糖 は もう 入っていま す。 saTOo-wa MOo HAitte-i-MAsu.
The clock is five minutes fast.	その 時計 は 5 分 進 んでいま す。 soNO-TOKEI-WA GO-fun suSUN-DE-I-MAsu.

CHAPTER 8 SECTION 4
V_2'-te-ari-masu

V_2'-te-ari-masu is used to describe the result of a heteronomous action. (Compare this usage with the result of an autonomous action discussed in Section 3 (4).)

The Result of a Heteronomous Action

Let's look at an example.

Mado-ga ake-te ari-masu. (Somebody has opened the window.)

Remember that **ari-masu** is supposed to have an inanimate subject. The window is inanimate. Nothing is wrong with this statement, but **ari-masu** is a rather static expression compared with **i-masu** as used in the previous section.

Furthermore the verb **ake-te** (to open; root form: **akeru**) is a transitive verb and **mado** is its object. Although who opened the window is not mentioned in the sentence, the verb **ake-te** is still describing a heteronomous action, and the window is merely the recipient of the action, rather than the doer of the action.

This means that the form **V_2'-te-ari-masu** is a static expression that describes the result of somebody's action.

More Examples

Somebody has turned on the light.	電気が つけ て あり ます。 DEnki-ga tsuKE-te-aRI-MAsu.
Somebody has turned off the light.	電気が 消し て あり ます。 DEnki-ga keSHI-TE-aRI-MAsu.
Somebody has parked a car.	車が 止め て あり ます。 kuRUMA-GA toME-TE-aRI-MAsu.
Somebody has locked the door.	ドアの 鍵が かけて あり ます。 DOa-no kaGI-ga KAke-te-aRI-MAsu.
I have put sugar in already.	砂糖は もう 入れ て あり ます。 saTOo-wa MOo iRE-TE-aRI-MAsu.
I set the clock forward five minutes.	その 時計は 5 分 進め て あります。 soNO-TOKEI-WA GO-fun suSUME-TE-aRI-MAsu.

CHAPTER 8 SECTION 5

V_2'-te-oki-masu

Preparatory Action

Let's look at an example.

Mado-o ake-te-oki-masu. (I open the window and leave it as it is.)

Mado-o ake-te means "to open the window." **Oki-masu** (root form: **oku**) means "to put," "to leave something as it is," or "to do something beforehand." **V_2'-te-oki-masu** is used to describe a preparatory or planned action that has been done in anticipation of a possible occasion for use in the future.

More Examples

I have bought a ticket in advance.
切符を買っておきました。
kiPPU-O kaT-TE-oKI-MAshita.

I will check it beforehand.
調べておきます。
shiRAbe-te-oKI-MAsu.

I will put it in the safe.
金庫にしまっておきます。
KInko-ni shiMAT-TE-oKI-MAsu.

I will fix it by Friday.
金曜までに直しておきます。
kiN'YOo-MAde-ni naOshi-te-oKI-MAsu.

I will leave a message.
メッセージを残しておきます。
MEsseiji-o noKOshi-te-oKI-MAsu.

I have reserved a table in the restaurant.
レストランのテーブルを予約し
REsutoran-no teEBURU-O yoYAKU-SHI-
ておきました。
TE-oKI-MAshita.

CHAPTER 8 SECTION 6
V_2'-te-shimai-masu

Shimai-masu (root form: **shimau**) means "to conclude." Therefore **V_2'-te-shimai-masu** means "to finish doing something." This expression sometimes means "to end up in an awkward situation" or "to end up in doing what should not be done."

Examples

I will have written a letter by noon.	昼までに手紙を書いてしまいます。 hiRU-made-ni teGAMI-O KAi-te-shiMAI-MAsu.
I ate them all.	全部食べてしまいました。 ZEnbu TAbe-te-shiMAI-MAshita.
He is gone.	彼は行ってしまいました。 KAre-wa iT-TE-shiMAI-MAshita.
I have finished reading the book.	その本を読んでしまいました。 soNO-HOn-o YOn-de-shiMAI-MAshita.
I (inadvertently) found out his secret.	彼の秘密を知ってしまいました。 KAre-no hiMITSU-O shiT-TE-shiMAI-MAshita.
I (accidentally) broke the vase.	花瓶を壊してしまいました。 KAbin-o koWAshi-te-shiMAI-MAshita.
I quarreled with her on the spur of the moment.	つい彼女とけんかしてしまいました。 TSUi KAnojo-to keNKA-SHI-TE-shiMAI-MAshita.

CHAPTER 8 SECTION 7
V_2'-te-mi-masu, V_2'-te-mitai-desu

V_2'-te-mi-masu (do **V_2** and see) means "I will try to do something." **V_2'-te-mi-tai-desu** is often used to mean "I would like to try doing something."

Examples

I will try a new coat on.	新しいコートを着てみます。 aTARASHIi KOoto-o ki-TE-MI-MAsu.
May I try the shoes on?	靴を履いてみていいですか。 kuTSU-o haI-TE-MI-te- Ii- desu-KA?
I will think it over.	よく考えてみます。 YOku kaNGAe-te-mi-masu.
I tried to use the new machine.	新しい機械を使ってみました。 aTARASHIi-kiKAi-o tsuKAT-TE-mi-MAshita.
Let's try to call him by telephone.	彼に電話してみましょう。 KAre-ni deNWA-SHI-TE-mi-MASHOo.
I would like to try **sushi**.	おすしを食べてみたいです。 o-SUshi-o TAbe-te-mi-TAi-desu.
I would like to see **kabuki**.	歌舞伎を見てみたいです。 kaBUKI-O MI-te-mi-TAi-desu.
I would like to ride on the **shinkansen**.	新幹線に乗ってみたいです。 shiN-KAnsen-ni noT-TE-mi-TAi-desu.

CHAPTER 8 SECTION 8
V_2'-te-mise-masu

Mise-masu (root form: **miseru**) means "to show" or "to display." Therefore **V_2'-te-mise-masu** (to do **V_2** and show) means "I will show you how to do something".

V_2'-te-mise-masu is sometimes used to express one's firm resolve to do something.

Examples

I will show you a trick.	手品をしてみせましょう。 TEjina-o shi-TE-miSE-MASHOo.
I showed them how to write my name in **katakana**.	私の名前をカタカナで書いてみせました。 waTASHI-NO naMAE-O kaTAkana-de KAi-te-miSE-MAshita.

I showed them how to fold **origami**.
折り紙 を折ってみ せ ま し た。
oRIgami-o Ot-te-miSE-MAshita.

I will quit smoking without fail.
きっとタバコ を やめ て み せ ま す。
kiTTO taBAKO-O yaME-TE-miSE-MAsu.

We will definitely win the game.
絶対 試合に 勝って み せ ます。
zetTAI shiAI-NI KAt-te-miSE-MAsu.

I will certainly become a doctor in the future.
将 来必 ず 医者 になってみ せ ます。
SHOorai kaNARAZU iSHA-NI NAt-te-miSE-MAsu.

CHAPTER 8 SECTION 9

V_2'-te-iki (-ki) -masu

Iki-masu (to go) adds the nuance of going away to the verb **V_2'-te**. On the other hand, **ki-masu** (to come) adds the nuance of coming near.

Examples

He walked to the station in the rain.
彼 は 雨 の 中 を駅 まで 歩いていき
KAre-wa Ame-no-naka-o Eki-made aRUi-te-iKI-
ま し た。
MAshita.

I will take my umbrella with me.
私 は 傘 を 持っていきま す。
waTASHI-WA KAsa-o MOt-te-iKI-MAsu.

The thief ran away at full pelt.
泥 棒 は 一 目 散 に 逃 げていき
doROBOO-WA iCHIMOkusan-ni NIge-te-iKI-
ま し た。
MAshita.

He moved to **Oosaka** last month.
彼 は 先 月 大 阪 に 越 し ていき
KAre-wa SEngetsu oOSAKA-NI koSHI-TE-iKI-
ま し た。
MAshita.

He left some furniture behind.
彼 は 家具 を 少 し置いていきました。
KAre-wa KAgu-o suKOshi oI-TE-iKI-MAshita.

Time has passed like an arrow.	時が矢のように過ぎていきました。 toKI-ga YA-no-YOo-ni SUgi-te-iKI-MAshita.
It is getting cold.	寒くなってきました。 SAmuku NAt-te-ki-MAshita.
Christmas is just around the corner.	クリスマスが近づいてきました。 kuRISUmasu-ga chiKAZUi-te-ki-MAshita.
I hear the sound of a piano from out of nowhere.	ピアノの音がどこからともなく piANO-NO-oTO-ga DOko-kara-TO-mo-naku 聞こえてきます。 kiKOE-TE-ki-MAsu.
It suddenly began to rain.	突然雨が降ってきました。 toTSUZEN Ame-ga FUt-te-ki-MAshita.
I will fetch my hat.	帽子を取ってきます。 boOSHI-O TOt-te-ki-masu.
I will go out to buy cigarettes.	タバコを買ってきます。 taBAKO-O kaT-TE-KI-MAsu.
He rushed into my room.	彼が私の部屋に飛び込んでき KAre-ga waTASHI-NO-heYA-ni toBIKOn-de ki- ました。 mashita.

CHAPTER 8 SECTION 10
Honorifics (5) : V_2'-te Forms

Favor Giving and Receiving V_2'-te Forms

Those verbs for "to give" and "to receive" (**yaru, ageru, sashi-ageru, kureru, morau, kudasaru, itadaku**) (CHAPTER 4 Section 12) can be attached to the **V_2'-te** form to create both plain and honorific compound verbs that mean "to give or receive a favor by doing something." Carefully observe the chart on the opposite page.

Important

Pay attention to the true doer of the action of the **V_2'-te** verb. For example in **hanashi-te** (to talk), pay attention to the person who is actually doing the talking.

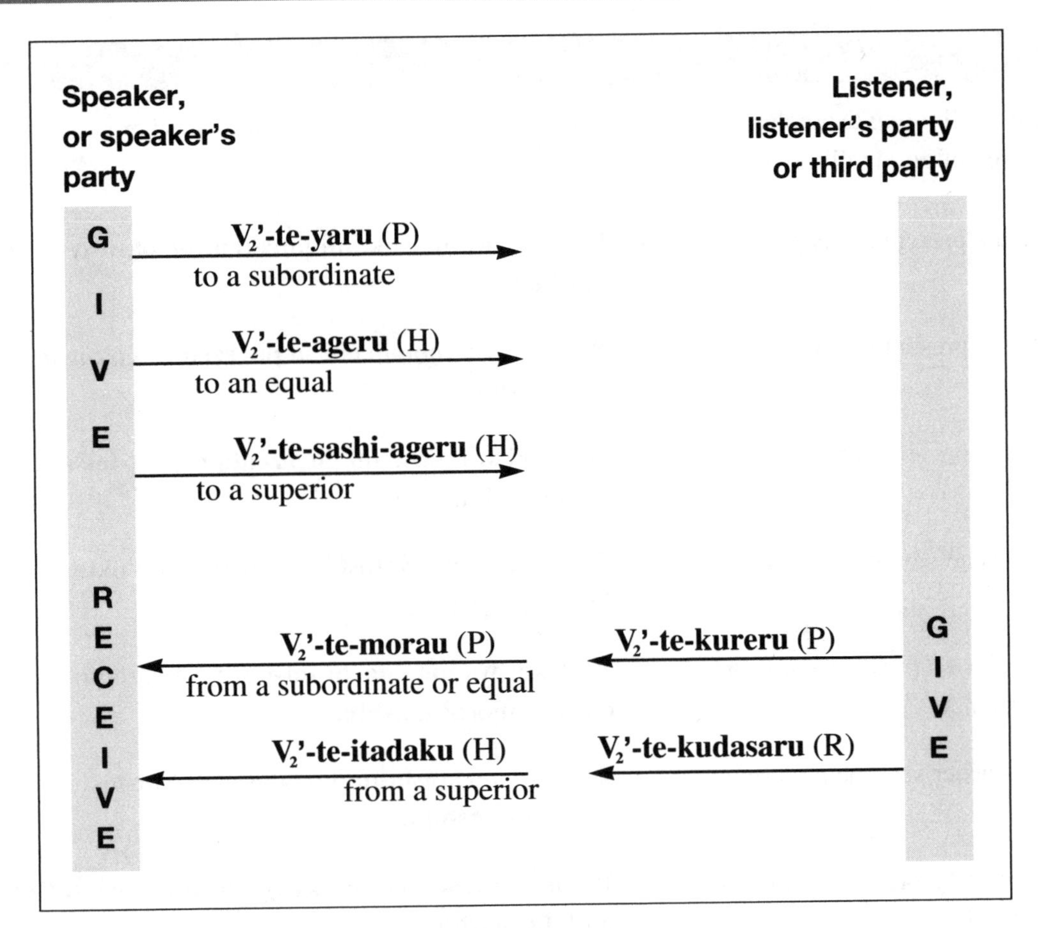

(P) Plain style; (R) Respectful style; (H) Humble style

Favor-Giving-Receiving		doer of V_2'-te
V_2'-te-yari-masu	Plain-give	first person
V_2'-te-age-masu	Humble-give	first person
V_2'-te-sashi-age-masu	Humble-give	first person
V_2'-te-kure-masu	Plain-give	second or third person
V_2'-te-morai-masu	Plain-receive	second or third person
V_2'-te-kudasai-masu	Respectful-give	second or third person
V_2'-te-itadaki-masu	Humble-receive	second or third person

The top three imply "I (we) do **V_2'-te** for you (him, her, them)." Therefore the doer of **V_2'-te** is the first person (I, we). In the case of the bottom four, the second (you) or the third person (he, she, they) is taking the trouble to do **V_2'-te** as a service to the speaker. This fact can be expressed in two ways, from the favor-giving side or from the favor-receiving side.

Examples

In the following examples, a person sent (root form: **okuru**) a present to another person as a token of good will or as a favor.

I sent a present to my son.	**Watashi-wa musuko-ni purezento-o okut-te-yari-mashita.**
I sent a present to my friend.	**Watashi-wa tomodachi-ni purezento-o okut-te-age-mashita.**
I sent a present to my teacher.	**Watashi-wa sensei-ni purezento-o okut-te-sashi-age-mashita.**
My friend sent me a present.	**Tomodachi-wa watashi-ni purezento-o okut-te-kure-mashita.**
I received a present sent from my friend.	**Watashi-wa tomodachi-ni(-kara) purezento-o okut-te morai-mashita.**
My teacher sent me a present.	**Sensei-wa watashi-ni purezento-o okut-te-kudasai-mashita.**
I received a present sent from my teacher.	**Watashi-wa sensei-ni(-kara) purezento-o okut-te-itadaki-mashita.**

More Examples

I bought a doll for my daughter.	娘に人形を買ってやりました。 muSUME-ni niNGYOO-O kaT-TE-yaRI-MAshita.
I will read a book for you.	本を読んであげましょう。 HOn-o YOn-de-aGE-MASHOo.
I showed the way to a stranger.	よその人に道を教えてあげ yoSO-no-hiTO-ni miCHI-O oSHIE-TE-aGE- ました。 MAshita.
I helped a lady to get out of the car.	ご婦人が車からおりるのを go-FUJIN-GA kuRUMA-KARA oRI-ru-no-o 助けてさしあげました。 taSUke-te saSHI-AGE-MAshita.

My teacher praised my picture.	先生が私の絵をほめてくださいました。 seNSEI-ga waTASHI-NO-E-o HOme-te-kuDASAI-MAshita.
I asked Tom to draw a map for me.	トムに地図をかいてもらいました。 TOmu-ni CHIzu-o KAi-te-moRAI-MAshita.
We asked Mrs. Smith to play the piano for us.	スミス夫人にピアノを弾いていただきました。 SUmisu-fujin-ni piANO-O <u>hiI</u>-TE- iTADAKI-MAshita.

V_2'-te-kudasai

V_2'-te-kudasai is used in making a respectful request to the listener literally saying "please do me a favor."

Examples:

Please lend me your pen.	ペンを貸してください。 PEn-o kaSHI-TE-KUDASAi.
Please show me your driver's license.	免許証を見せてください。 meNKYO<u>shoo</u>-o MIse-te-kudasai.
Please speak slowly in Japanese.	日本語でゆっくり話してください。 niHON-GO-DE yuKKUri haNAshi-te-kudasai.
Please marry me.	私と結婚してください。 waTASHI-TO keKKON-SHI-TE-KUDASAi.
Please take me to Disneyland.	ディズニーランドに連れていってください。 diZU<u>NII</u>RAndo-ni tsuRE-TE-IT-TE-KUDASAi.

Comparison of o-V_2 and V_2'-te

The honorific degree of the **o-V_2** form (Chapter 7 Section 11) is higher than that of the **V_2'-te** form. That is to say:

o-V_2-kudasai-masu	is more respectful than	**V_2'-te-kudasai-masu.**
o-V_2-kudasai	is more respectful than	**V_2'-te-kudasai.**
o-V_2-itadaki-masu	is more humble than	**V_2'-te-itdaki-masu**.

Compare the following:

Would you please wait a while?	**Shibaraku o-machi-kudasai.**
Wait a minute.	**Chotto matte-kudasai.**

Chapter 9

The Uses of "V_2'-ta"

V_2'-ta is the plain-past style of a verb, in contrast to **V_2-mashita**, which is the polite-past style. (Refer to CHAPTER 13 Section 1 for detailed discussion on plain styles.)

	Present	Past
Plain	V_3 (Root Form)	V_2'-ta
Polite	V_2-masu	V_2-mashita

Conversion Flow Chart

The flow chart for converting V_3 to **V_2'-ta** form shown on the next page is the same as the V_3 to **V_2'-te** conversion chart shown in CHAPTER 8, with the only difference being suffix changes, **-te** to **-ta** and **-de** to **-da**.

Examples are shown for the representative verbs and the two special verbs, "to do" and "to come."

The verb **iku** (to go) is an exception. Its **V_2'-ta** form is **it-ta**.

Also pay attention to those "sham" **-iru/-eru** ending verbs that should be treated as **-ru** ending verbs. (They are listed at the end of **-ru** ending verb groups in CHAPTER 4 Section 1.)

Conversion Chart: V_3 to V_2'-ta

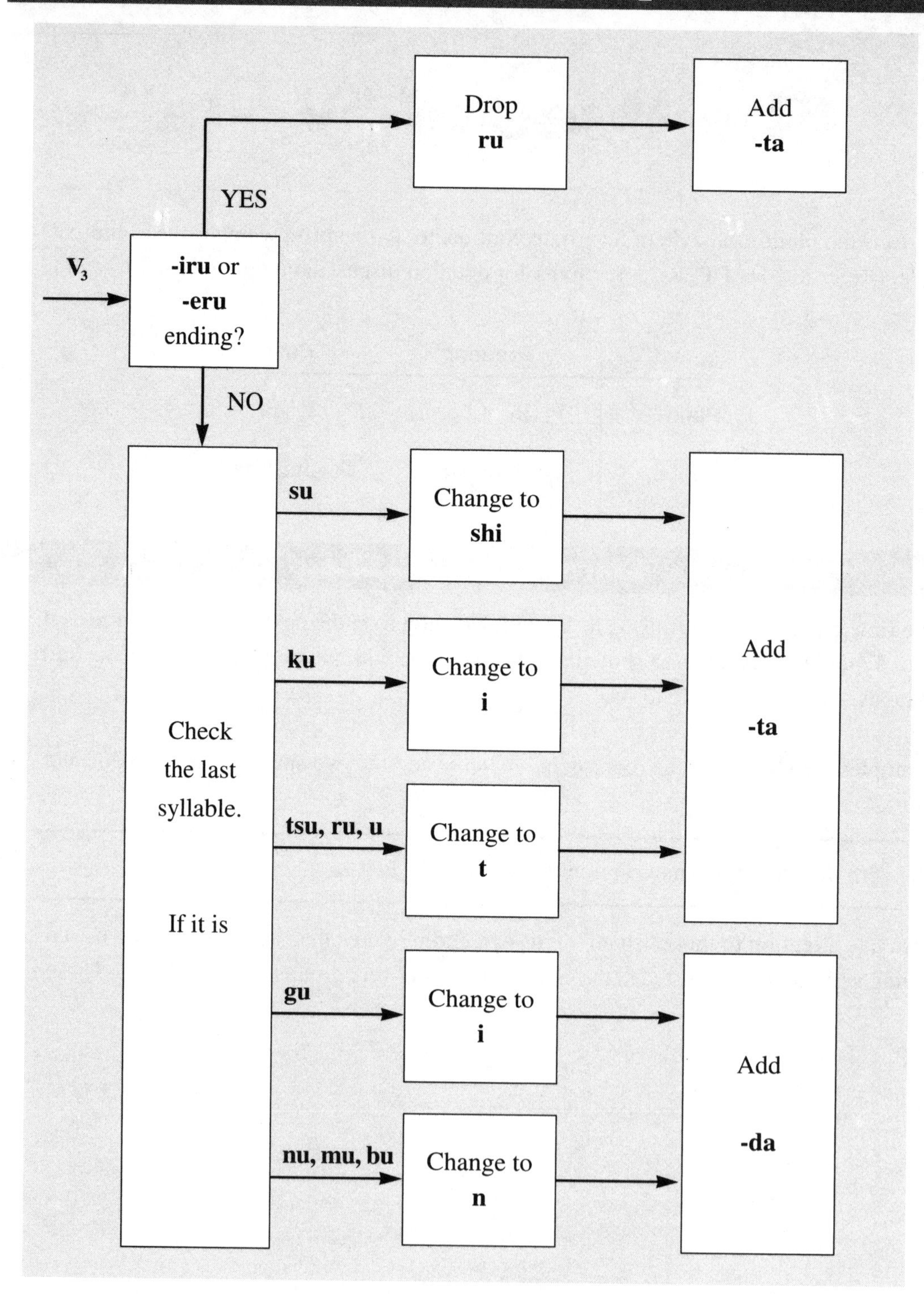

V_3 to V_2'-ta (Representative and Special Verbs)

miru	to see	**mi-ta**
neru	to sleep	**ne-ta**
kasu	to lend	**kashi-ta**
haku	to put on	**hai-ta**
nugu	to take off	**nui-da**
matsu	to wait	**mat-ta**
toru	to take	**tot-ta**
kau	to buy	**kat-ta**
shinu	to die	**shin-da**
yomu	to read	**yon-da**
tobu	to fly	**ton-da**
suru	to do	**shi-ta**
kuru	to come	**ki-ta**

The Uses of V_2'-ta

The suffixes **-hazu-desu, -tokoro-desu, -sō-desu, -yō-desu, -rashii-desu, -n-desu, -deshō, -kamo-shire-masen**, which we discussed as attachments to V_3, can also be attached to **V_2'-ta**, and add the same meanings expressed by the suffixes.

In CHAPTER 9 we will discuss the following uses, which are specific to **V_2'-ta**:

Section 1 **V_2'-ta-hō-ga-ii-desu**
Section 2 **V_2'-ta-koto-ga-ari-masu**

CHAPTER 9 SECTION 1
V_2'-ta-hō-ga-ii-desu

V_2'-ta is the past tense of a verb, **hō** means "direction" or "way," and **ii-desu** means "good." So **V_2'-ta-hō-ga-ii-desu** literally means "if you did V_2, the way is good." This expression is similar to "you had better do something" in English. It is interesting to note that the past tense is used both in English and in Japanese.

Examples

You had better go at once.	あなたは いますぐ 行ったほう がいいです。 aNAta-wa Ima-SUgu iT-TA-<u>HOo</u>-ga-Ii-desu.
It would be better if you go to bed.	寝 た ほう が いいです。 ne-TA-<u>HOo</u>-ga-Ii-desu.
You'd better go to a doctor.	医者 に 診 て もらっ た ほう がいいです。 iSHA-NI MI-te-moRAT-TA-<u>HOo</u>-ga-Ii-desu.

It would be good if you take some medicine.

薬を飲んだほうがいいです。
kuSURI-O NOn-da-HOo-ga-Ii-desu.

Forget about her, and you are on the right track.

彼女のことは忘れたほうがいいです。
KAnojo-no-koTO-wa waSURE-TA-HOo-ga-Ii-desu.

You'd better think it over.

よく考えたほうがいいです。
YOku kaNGAe-ta-HOo-ga-Ii-desu.

CHAPTER 9 SECTION 2

V_2'-ta-koto-ga-ari-masu

V_2'-ta is the past tense of a verb, **koto** means "fact," and **ari-masu** means "there is." So **V_2'-ta-koto-ga-ari-masu** literally means "there is a fact that I did **V_2**." This useful expression is used when a person is relating his or her experience.

Examples

I have seen the movie before.

その映画は前に見たことがあります。
soNO-Eiga-wa MAe-ni MI-ta-koTO-ga-aRI-MAsu.

I have been to **Kyōto**.

京都に行ったことがあります。
KYOoto-ni iT-TA-koTO-ga-aRI-MAsu.

I have never been to **Nikkō**.

日光に行ったことがありません。
NIkkoo-ni iT-TA-koTO-ga-aRI-MASEn.

I have met Mr. **Tanaka** once before.

田中さんには前に一度お会いした
taNAKA-SAN-NI-wa MAe-ni-iCHIDO o-AI-shi-TA-
ことがあります。
koTO-ga-aRI-MAsu.

Have you ever read "Snow Country" by **Yasunari Kawabata**?

川端康成の「雪国」を読ん
kaWABATA yaSUnari-no "yuKI-guni"-o YOn-
だことがありますか。
da-koTO-ga-aRI-MAsu-KA?

I have eaten **sukiyaki** many times.

すきやきは何回も食べたことが
suKIYAKI-WA NAn-kai-mo TAbe-ta-koTO-ga-
あります。
aRI-MAsu.

I have never forgotten your kindness to me.

あなたのご恩は一度も忘れた
anata-no go-On-wa iCHIDOMO waSURETA-
ことがありません。
KOTO-ga aRI-MASEn.

Chapter 10

The Uses of V_1-nai

V_1-nai is the plain-negative style of a verb, in contrast to **V_2-masen**, which is the polite-negative style. (Refer to CHAPTER 13 Section 1 for a detailed discussion of plain styles.)

	Affirmative	Negative
Plain	V_3 (Root Form)	V_1-nai
Polite	V_2-masu	V_2-masen

Conversion Flow Chart

The flow chart for converting the V_3 form to **V_1-nai** form is shown on the next page. Examples are shown for the representative verbs and the two special verbs, "to do" and "to come."

The reason for the "1" of V_1 is based on the same principle as the V_2 and V_3 naming method. As you see in the flow chart, the non **-iru/-eru** ending groups take the **a**-row of the syllabary chart, and the **a**-row is the first row of the chart.

Note that the **V_1-nai** form for the verb **aru** (to exist) is simply **nai**.

Conversion Chart: V_3 to V_1-nai

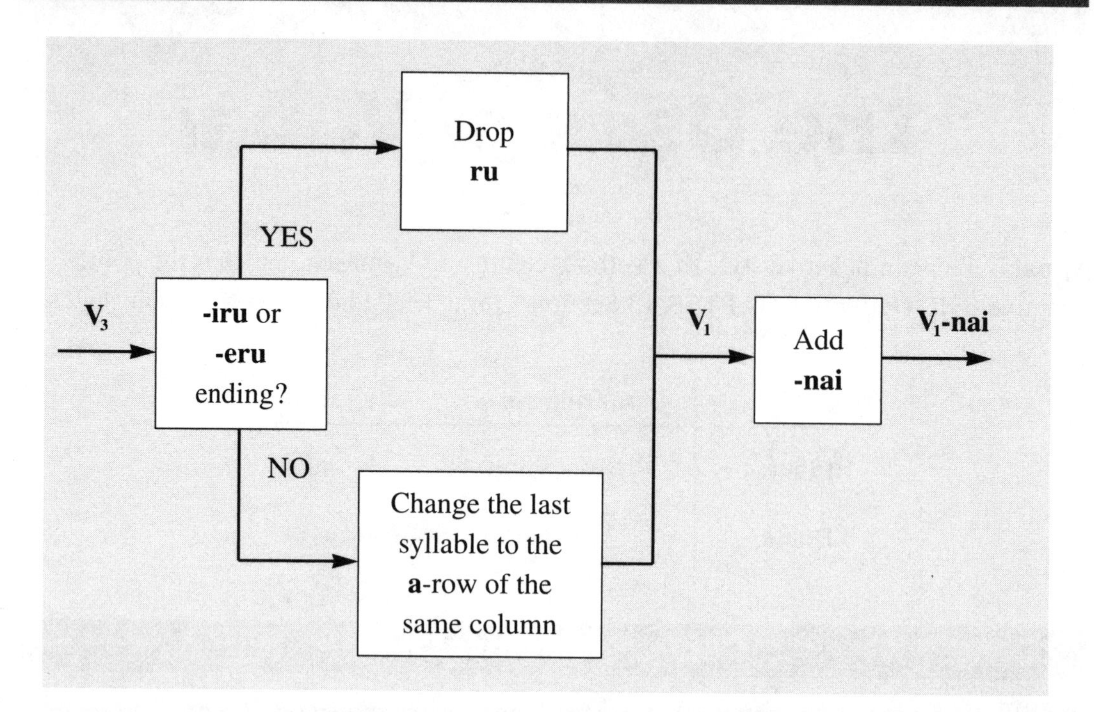

Examples (Representative and Special Verbs)

miru	to see	**mi-nai**
neru	to sleep	**ne-nai**
kasu	to lend	**kasa-nai**
haku	to put on	**haka-nai**
nugu	to take off	**nuga-nai**
matsu	to wait	**mata-nai**
toru	to take	**tora-nai**
kau	to buy	**kawa-nai**
shinu	to die	**shina-nai**
yomu	to read	**yoma-nai**
tobu	to fly	**toba-nai**
suru	to do	**shi-nai**
kuru	to come	**ko-nai**

The Uses of V_1-nai

The suffixes **-tsumori-desu**, **-hazu-desu**, **-sō-desu**, **-de-ii-desu**, **-hō-ga-ii-desu**, **-n-desu**, **-deshō**, **-kamo-shire-masen**, **-koto-ni-shi-mashita**, **-koto-ni-nari-mashita** which are attached to V_3, V_2**'-te**, and V_2**'-ta** forms can also be attached to V_1**-nai** and add the same meanings as these suffixes represent. In CHAPTER 10, we will discuss the following uses which are specific to V_1**-nai.**

Section 1	V_1**-nai-de-kudasai**
Section 2	V_1**-nai-dewa-irare-masen**
Section 3	V_1**-nakereba-nari-masen**

CHAPTER 10 SECTION 1

V_1-nai-de-kudasai

We discussed the **V_2'-te-kudasai** (please do) form in CHAPTER 8 Section 10. **V_1-nai-de-kudasai** is a negative request meaning "please do not."

Examples

Please do not go.	行かないで ください。 iKA-NAi-de-kudasai.
Please do not enter the room.	部屋に入ら ないでください。 heYA-ni haIRA-nai-de-kudasai.
Do not cry any more.	もう 泣か ないで ください。 MOo naKA-NAi-de-kudasai.
Please do not get angry.	怒 らないでください。 oKORA-nai-de-kudasai.
Please do not be surprised.	驚 かないでください。 oDOROKA-nai-de-kudasai.
Please do not run in the house.	うちの中 で走 らないでください。 uCHI-NO-NAka-de haSHIRA-nai-de-kudasai.
Please do not look at me like that.	そんな ふうに私 を見ないで ください。 soNNA-FUu-ni waTASHI-O MI-nai-de-kudasai.
Please do not forget me.	私 を忘 れ ないでください。 waTASHI-O waSURE-NAi-de-kudasai.
Please do not worry.	心配しない でください。 shiNPAI-shi-NAi-de-kudasai.

CHAPTER 10 SECTION 2
V_1-nai-dewa-irare-masen

V_1-nai is a negative form, and means "not doing" or "without doing," and **irare-masen** means "cannot exist." Therefore **V_1-nai-dewa-irare-masen** literally means "cannot exist without doing" or "cannot help doing."

Dewa is necessary because this is a negative sentence, just like the negative version of **watashi-wa isha-desu** is **watashi-wa isha-dewa-ari-masen**. (Refer to CHAPTER 3, Section 8 and CHAPTER 5 Section 1 [5].)

Examples

I cannot help laughing.	笑わないではいられません。 waRAWA-NAi-dewa-iRARE-MASEn.
I could not help crying.	泣かないではいられませんでした。 naKA-NAi-dewa-iRARE-MASEn-deshita.
I could not help getting angry.	怒らないではいられませんでした。 oKORA-nai-dewa-iRARE-MASEn-deshita.
I cannot help meeting her.	彼女に会わないではいられません。 KAnojo-ni aWA-nai-dewa-iRARE-MASEn.
I could not help drinking **sake**.	酒を飲まないではいられませんでした。 saKE-O noMA-nai-dewa-iRARE-MASEn-deshita.

CHAPTER 10 SECTION 3
V_1-nakereba-nari-masen

V_1-nakereba means "if one does not do" and **nari-masen** means "it will not be done." This mouthful expression is, as a whole, equivalent to "must" or "have to" in English.

Examples

I must go.	行かなければなりません。 iKA-NAkereba-naRI-MASEn.
You must hurry.	あなたは急がなければなりません。 aNAta-wa iSOGA-nakereba-naRI-MASEn.

Children must go to bed early.	子供達は早く寝なければなり koDOMO-tachi-wa HAyaku ne-NAkereba-naRI- ません。 MASEn.
I must write a report by tomorrow.	あすまでに報告書を書かなければ aSU-made-ni hoOKOKUSHO-o kaKA-nakereba- なりません。 naRI-MASEn.
You have to study hard.	あなたは一生懸命勉強し aNAta-wa iSSHOOKEnmei beNKYOO-shi- なければなりません。 NAkereba-naRI-MASEn.
I must return the book to the library.	図書館に本を返さなければなり toSHOkan-ni HOn-o kaESA-nakereba- naRI- ません。 MASEn.
You have to take care of your health.	あなたは健康に注意しなければ aNAta-wa keNKOO-NI CHUui-shi-NAkereba- なりません。 naRI-MASEn.

Chapter 11

Derivative Verbs

English verbs have two voices, namely the active voice and the passive voice. For example:

The hammer strikes the bell. — *active voice* (the subject does the action)

The bell is struck by the hammer. — *passive voice* (the subject is the recipient of the action)

In English when one describes an action in the active and the passive voices, one uses the same verb but in a different form ("strike" and "is struck").

By contrast, Japanese verbs have three modes, among which (1) is comparable to the passive voice in English.

(1) the passive mode
(2) the potential mode
(3) the causative mode

The three Japanese modes are all derived from the same original verb. Hence these derived verbs are called "derivative verbs." All the verbs which we have been using so far are considered to be original verbs. For example:

Kare-wa hon-o yomi-masu. — He reads a book.

Yomu (to read) is the original verb from which we can derive three different modes of the verb. Let us examine these derivative verb forms.

Derivative Verbs: Passive Mode

Hon-wa kare-ni yomare-masu. — A book is read by him.

Yomareru (to be read) is the passive mode derivative verb. This form has the same sense as the English passive voice.

Derivative Verbs: Potential Mode

Kare-wa hon-ga yome-masu. He can read a book.

Yomeru (to be able to read) is the potential mode derivative verb. The *potential mode* implies that it is possible to do something.

Derivative Verbs: Causative Mode

Kare-wa kanojo-ni hon-o yomase-masu. He lets her read a book.

Yomaseru (to let someone read) is the causative mode derivative verb. The *causative mode* implies that a person lets or makes somebody do something.

Derivation flow charts for each mode are given in the following sections.

Conjugations

Note that all these derivative verbs are $\mathbf{V_3}$ root forms. Therefore they also conjugate (conversion to $\mathbf{V_1}$, $\mathbf{V_2}$, $\mathbf{V_2}$', etc.) by using the flow charts we have seen already in Chapters 4, 8, 9, and 10.

Examples:

	V_3 (Root)		V_2-masu	V_1-nai
Original Verb	**miru** **yomu**	to see to read	**mi-masu** **yomi-masu**	**mi-nai** **yoma-nai**
Derivative Passive Mode	**mirareru** **yomareru**	to be seen to be read	**mirare-masu** **yomare-masu**	**mirare-nai** **yomare-nai**
Derivative Potential Mode	**mirareru** **yomeru**	to be able to see to be able to read	**mirare-masu** **yome-masu**	**mirare-nai** **yome-nai**
Derivative Causative Mode	**misaseru** **yomaseru**	to let someone see to let someone read	**misase-masu** **yomase-masu**	**misase-nai** **yomase-nai**

CHAPTER 11 SECTION 1
Passive Mode

Let's compare a sentence containing an original verb with a sentence that contains a verb in the passive mode. Pay attention not only to verb forms but also to changes in the postpositions and word order.

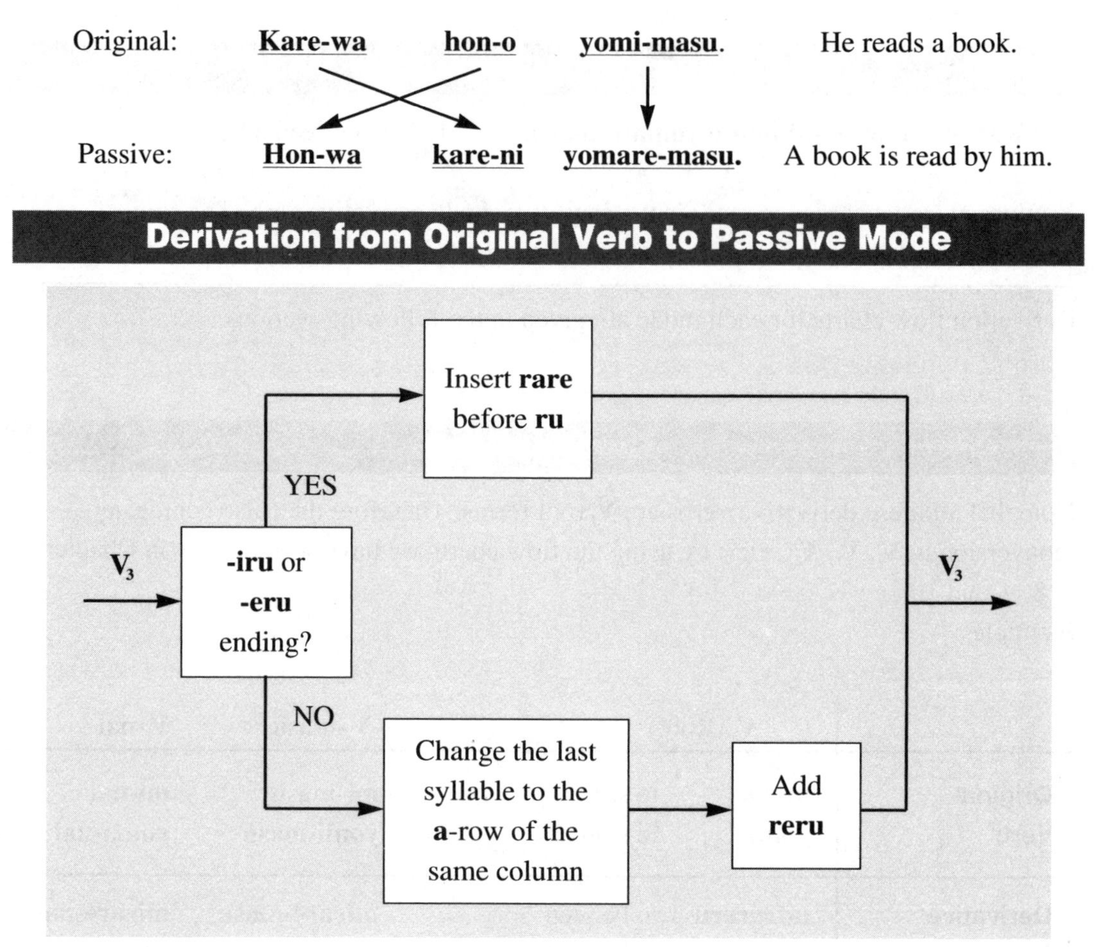

Examples (Representative and Special Verbs)

miru	to see	**mirareru**
neru	to sleep	**nerareru**
kasu	to lend	**kasareru**
haku	to put on	**hakareru**
nugu	to take off	**nugareru**
matsu	to wait	**matareru**
toru	to take	**torareru**
kau	to buy	**kawareru**
shinu	to die	**shinareru**
yomu	to read	**yomareru**
tobu	to fly	**tobareru**
suru	to do	**sareru**
kuru	to come	**korareru**

Translation of "by"

The English preposition "by" in a passive mode sentence can be translated into Japanese in three ways.

(1) **Acting on**

If the nature of the original verb is one in which the subject is acting upon the object, "by" is translated as **-ni**.

For example:

A book is read by him.	**Hon-wa kare-ni yomare-masu.**
Worms are eaten by a bird.	**Mushi-wa tori-ni taberare-masu.**

(2) **Creating**

If the nature of the original verb is one in which the subject is creating the object, "by" is translated as **-ni-yot-te**.

For example:

The novel was written by **Mishima**.	**Sono-shōsetsu-wa Mishima-ni-yot-te kakare-mashita.**
The symphony was composed by Beethoven.	**Sono-kōkyōkyoku-wa Bētōben-ni-yot-te sakkyoku-sare-mashita.**

(3) **Physical or Emotional Transfer**

If the nature of the verb is one in which either a physical or an emotional transfer takes place, "by" is translated as **-kara.**

For example:

The gift was presented by him.	**Sono-purezento-wa kare-kara okurare-mashita.**
She is loved by everybody.	**Kanojo-wa minna-kara ai-sare-te-imasu.**

More Examples

The thief was caught by a policeman.	泥棒は警官につかまえられました。 doROBOO-WA keIKAN-NI tsuKAMAERARE-MAshita.
The song was sung in English.	その歌は英語で歌われました。 soNO-UTA-wa eIGO-DE uTAWARE-MAshita.
My son was scolded by his teacher yesterday.	息子はきのう先生に叱られました。 muSUKO-WA kiNOO seNSEi-ni shiKARARE-MAshita.
She was killed by a young man.	彼女は若い男に殺されました。 KAnojo-wa waKAi-oTOKO-ni koROSARE-MAshita.
He was brought up by his grandmother.	彼はおばあさんに育てられました。 KAre-wa oBAa-san-ni soDATERARE-MAshita.
I was asked the way by a tourist.	旅行者に道を聞かれました。 ryoKOosha-ni miCHI-O kiKARE-MAshita.
The "Mona Lisa" was painted by Leonardo da Vinci.	モナリザはレオナルドダビンチによってかかれました。 moNARIZA-WA reONARUDO-da-BInchi-ni-yoTTE kaKARE-MAshita.
His name will never be forgotten.	彼の名前は決して忘れられないでしょう。 KAre-no-naMAE-WA keSSHITE waSURE-RARE-NAI-DESHOo.
His painting is well known in Japan.	彼の絵は日本でよく知られています。 KAre-no-E-wa niHOn-de YOku shiRARE-TE-i-MAsu.
Nattō is disliked by most non-Japanese.	納豆はほとんどの外国人に嫌われています。 naTTOo-wa hoTOndo-no gaIKOKUjin-ni kiRAWARE-TE-i-MAsu.

CHAPTER 11 SECTION 2
Honorifics (6): Passive Mode

Verbs in the passive mode can be used to indicate respect, although the degree of respectfulness is lower than that of **o-V_2** or **V_2'-te** forms. When used to show respect, the verbs no longer function as "passive" verbs.

In English, intransitive verbs are never used in the passive voice because they do not take objects. This is also generally true in Japanese. However, it is interesting to note that when they are used as respectful words, Japanese intransitive verbs take passive mode form. For example:

Tanaka-san-ga korare-mashita.	Mr. Tanaka came.
Nan-ji-ni okirare-mashita-ka?	What time did you get up?

More Examples

Have you read the book already?	その本はもう読まれましたか。 soNO-HOn-wa MOo yoMARE-MAshita-KA?
Where did you learn Japanese?	どこで日本語を習われましたか。 DOko-de niHON-GO-O naRAWARE-MAshita-KA?
When did you buy this picture?	いつこの絵を買われましたか。 Itsu koNO-E-o kaWARE-MAshita-KA?
Mr. Smith left New York this morning.	スミスさんはけさニューヨークを発たれ SUmisu-san-wa KEsa nyuUYOoku-o taTARE- ました。 MAshita
Have you ever been to **Nara**?	奈良に行かれたことがありますか。 NAra-ni iKARETA-koTO-ga aRI-MAsu-KA?

CHAPTER 11 SECTION 3
Potential Mode

There are two styles to express "to be able to do" in Japanese. For example, let's say "I can speak Japanese" in two styles:

Watashi-wa Nihon-go-o hanasu-koto-ga deki-masu.

Watashi-wa Nihon-go-ga hanase-masu.

We discussed the first style **V_3-koto-ga deki-masu** in CHAPTER 6 Section 9. In this section, we will discuss the second style, which is the potential mode.

Note that both **Nihon-go-o hanasu-koto** of the first sentence and **Nihon-go** of the second sentence take the postposition **-ga**, because these sentences are based on our Sentence Pattern (5).

Derivation from Original Verb to Potential Mode

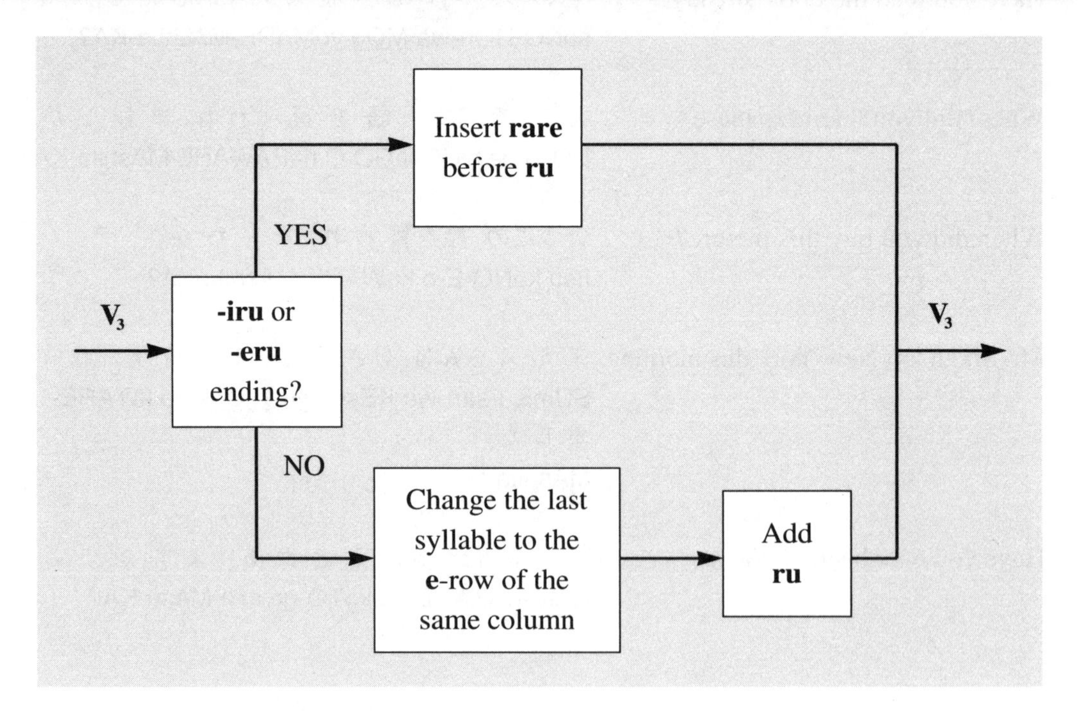

Examples (Representative and Special Verbs)

miru	to see	**mirareru**
neru	to sleep	**nerareru**
kasu	to lend	**kaseru**
haku	to put on	**hakeru**
nugu	to take off	**nugeru**
matsu	to wait	**materu**
toru	to take	**toreru**

kau	to buy	**kaeru**
shinu	to die	**shineru**
yomu	to read	**yomeru**
tobu	to fly	**toberu**
suru	to do	**dekiru**
kuru	to come	**korareru**

Examples

I can write **kanji**.	私は漢字が書けます。 waTASHI-WA kaNJI-GA kaKE-MAsu.
Can you ride a bicycle?	あなたは自転車に乗れますか。 aNAta-wa jiTENSHA-NI noRE-MAsu-KA?
He can swim like a fish.	彼は魚のように泳げます。 KAre-WA saKANA-NO-YOo-ni oYOGE-MAsu.
She can play the piano.	彼女はピアノが弾けます。 KAnojo-wa piANO-GA hiKE-MAsu.
Our baby can toddle along already.	うちの赤ん坊はもうよちよち uCHI-NO aKANBOO-WA MOo YOchi-yochi 歩けます。 aRUKE-MAsu.
She cannot come to the party this evening.	彼女は今夜パーティーに来られません。 KAnojo-wa KOnya PAatii-ni koRARE-MASEn.
This mushroom is edible.	このきのこは食べられます。 koNO-KInoko-wa taBERARE-MAsu.
This water is not safe to drink.	この水は飲めません。 koNO-MIZU-WA noME-MASEn.
We can buy electric products at a low price in **Akihabara**.	秋葉原では電気製品が安く aKIHAbara-dewa deNKI-SEihin-ga YAsuku 買えます。 kaE-MAsu.

CHAPTER 11 SECTION 4
Causative Mode

A verb used in the causative mode expresses the meaning "to let or to make somebody do something." For example:

Watashi-wa kare-o ikase-masu. I will let (make) him go.

Derivation from Original Verb to Causative Mode

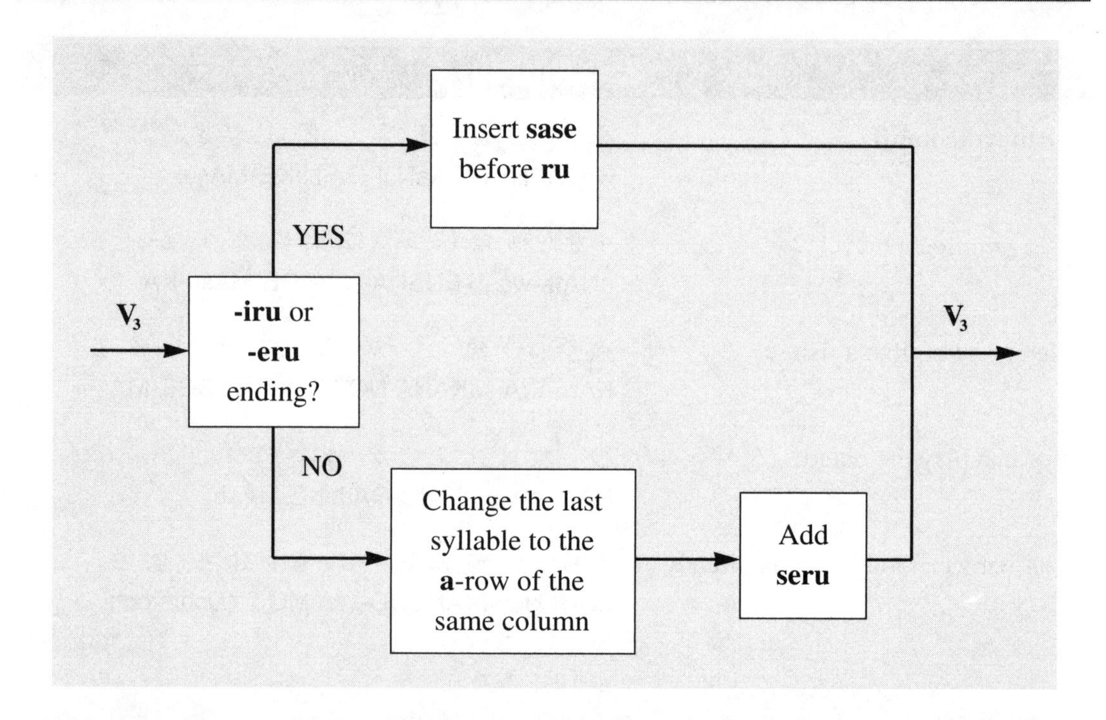

Examples (Representative and Special Verbs)

miru	to see	**misaseru**
neru	to sleep	**nesaseru**
kasu	to lend	**kasaseru**
haku	to put on	**hakaseru**
nugu	to take off	**nugaseru**
matsu	to wait	**mataseru**
toru	to take	**toraseru**

kau	to buy	**kawaseru**
shinu	to die	**shinaseru**
yomu	to read	**yomaseru**
tobu	to fly	**tobaseru**
suru	to do	**saseru**
kuru	to come	**kosaseru**

Examples

Sorry I made you wait.	お待たせしました。 o-MATASE-shi-MAshita.
I made her cry.	私は彼女を泣かせました。 waTASHI-WA KAnojo-o naKASE-MAshita.
She let her dog eat the dog food.	彼女は犬にドッグフードを食べさせました。 KAnojo-wa iNU-ni doGGU-FUudo-o taBESASE-MAshita.
He made her drink whisky.	彼は彼女にウイスキーを飲ませました。 KAre-wa KAnojo-ni uISUkii-o noMASE-MAshita.
I let all my students go home at noon.	昼に全生徒を帰らせました。 hiRU-ni zeN-SEito-o kaERASE-MAshita.
I will have my secretary contact you later.	あとで秘書に連絡させます。 Ato-de HIsho-ni reNRAKU-saSE-MAsu.
I will have my lawyer investigate the issue.	弁護士に問題点を調査させます。 beNGOshi-ni moNDAiten-o CHOosa-saSE-MAsu.
Please let me use your car.	あなたの車を使わせてください。 aNAta-no kuRUMA-O tsuKAWASE-TE-KUDASAi.
Don't make me laugh.	笑わせないでください。 waRAWASE-NAi-de kudasai.
I was forced to write my name and address.	名前と住所を書かせられました。 naMAE-TO JUusho-o kaKASERARE-MAshita.

Chapter 12

Compound Sentences

Simple, Compound and Complex Sentences

Let us look at an example:

simple sentence	Mr. Smith is a lawyer.
simple sentence	Mr. Smith practices in **Tōkyō**.
compound sentence	Mr. Smith is a lawyer and he practices in **Tōkyō**.
complex sentence	Mr. Smith is a lawyer who practices in **Tōkyō**.

Up to this point, we have been dealing with a single independent sentence, which is called a *simple sentence.*

When two simple sentences are combined on an equal footing, the result is called a *compound sentence.*

When two simple sentences are combined in such a fashion that one sentence functions as a principal clause and the other sentence functions as a subordinate clause, the result is called a *complex sentence.* A *subordinate clause* performs a certain role for the *principal clause.* In the above example, the subordinate clause "who practices in **Tōkyō**" performs the role of *modifier* (like an adjective) for the word "lawyer" in the principal clause "Mr. Smith is a lawyer."

Compound sentences are discussed in this chapter, and complex sentences are discussed in CHAPTER 13.

CHAPTER 12 SECTION 1
Alternate Actions

Normally one simple sentence can have only one verb. Therefore, two sentences are normally needed to describe two different actions. However, to express two actions that occur or are done alternately and repeatedly, we can squeeze two verbs into one sentence by using the expression **V_2'-tari V_2'-tari shi-masu**.

For example, if I watch (**miru**) and I listen (**kiku**) and then I watch and I listen again, I can express this in one sentence by saying **mi-tari kii-tari shi-masu**.

More Examples

He stands up and sits down anxiously.	彼は不安そうに立ったり座ったりしています。 KAre-wa fuANSOoni TAt-tari-suWAT-TAri-shiTE-I-MAsu.
The bird goes in and out of the nest.	鳥が巣から出たり入ったりしています。 toRI-GA SU-kara DE-tari-HAit-tari-shiTE-I-MAsu.
The stock price is fluctuating.	株が上がったり下がったりしています。 kaBU-GA aGAT-TAri-saGAt-tari-shi-TE-I-MAsu.
He is in and out of bed. [due to varying condition of illness]	彼は寝たり起きたりしています。 KAre-wa ne-TAri-Oki-tari-shi-TE-I-MAsu.
They ate and drank all night.	彼らは一晩中飲んだり食べたりしました。 KArera-wa hiTOBAN-JUU NOn-dari TAbe-tari-shi-MAshita.

CHAPTER 12 SECTION 2
Ending Modifications

We can combine two simple sentences by modifying the ending of the first sentence. For example:

Kare-wa Tomu-desu.	He is Tom.
Kanojo-wa Keito-desu.	She is Kate.

Now we modify the ending of the first sentence and combine the two sentences like this:

Kare-wa Tomu-de, kanojo-wa Keito-desu.

This, in effect, means "He is Tom, and she is Kate."

Modification

Modification is done in the following manner:

	Ending	→ Modification
(1)	(1st Sentence)	(1st Sentence)-**ga**,
(2)	**N-desu.** **N-deshita.**	**N-de,**
(3)	**A-i-desu.**	**A-ku-te,**
(4)	**A-(na)-desu.**	**A-(na)-de,**
(5)	**V_2-masu.** **V_2-mashita.**	**V_2**, or **V_2'-te,**
(6)	**V_2-masen.** **V_2-masen-deshita.**	**V_1-nai-de,**

Examples

Examples are grouped by the numbers shown in the chart on the previous page.

---

(1) (1st sentence.) ⟶ (1st sentence)-ga,

I saw the movie, and it was very interesting.

その 映画を見 ました が、たいへんおもしろ
soNO-Eiga-o mi-MAshita ga, taIHEN oMOSHIRO-
かったです。
katta-desu.

I want to buy a car, but I haven't got enough money.

車 を買いたいんですが、お金 が 足り
kuRUMA-O kaI-TAi-n-desu ga, o-KANE-GA taRI-
ません。
MASEn.

---

(2) N-desu/N-deshita. ⟶ N-de,

Tom is a doctor, and Bill is a novelist.

トム は 医者 で、ビル は 小 説 家 です。
TOmu-wa iSHA-DE, BIru-wa shoOSETSU-KA-desu.

It was rainy the day before yesterday, and it was cloudy yesterday.

おとといは 雨 で、きのうは 曇 りでした。
oTOTOi-wa Ame-de, kiNOo-wa kuMORI-deshita.

---

(3) A-i-desu. ⟶ A-ku-te,

The summer in **Tōkyō** is hot, and the winter in New York is cold.

東 京 の 夏 は 暑 くて、
toOKYOO-NO-naTSU-wa aTSU-ku-te,
ニューヨークの 冬 は 寒 いです。
nyuUYOoku-no-fuYU-wa saMUi-desu.

The food in this restaurant is delicious, and inexpensive.

この レストランの 食 事は おいしくて
koNO-REsutoran-no-shoKUJI-WA oISHIku-te
安 いです。
yaSUi-desu.

---

(4) A-(na)-desu. ⟶ A-(na)-de,

Tom is ill, and he will be absent from school tomorrow.

トム は 病 気で、あす学 校 を休 み
TOmu-wa byoOKI-DE, aSU gaKKOO-O yaSUMI-
ます。
MAsu.

I was worried about you, and I could not sleep last night.

あなたのことが心配で、ゆうべは寝られませんでした。
aNAta-no-koTO-ga shiNPAI-DE, yuUBE-wa neRARE-MASEn-deshita.

(5) V_2-masu/V_2-mashita. → V_2 or V_2'-te,

Mr. **Itō** plays the violin, and Mrs. **Itō** plays the piano.

伊藤さんのご主人はバイオリンを弾き、奥さんはピアノを弾きます。
iTOO-SAN-NO go-SHUjin-wa baIORIN-O hiKI, Oku-san-wa piANO-O hiKI-MAsu.

We traveled in Japan last year, and enjoyed beautiful scenery and delicious Japanese food.

私達は昨年日本を旅行して、美しい景色とおいしい日本料理を楽しみました。
waTASHI-tachi-wa saKUNEN niHOn-o ryoKOO-SHI-TE, uTSUKUSHIi-KEshiki-to oISHII-niHON-RYOori-o taNOSHIMI-MAshita.

(6) V_2-masen/V_2-masen-deshita. → V_1-nai-de,

Please hold the line, and wait a few more minutes.

電話を切らないで、もうしばらくお待ちください。
deNWA-O kiRA-nai-de, moO shiBAraku o-MACHI-KUDASAi.

Last night, we went to the restaurant without making a reservation.

ゆうべは予約しないで、レストランに行きました。
yuUBE-wa yoYAKU-shi-NAi-de, REsutoran-ni iKI-MAshita.

CHAPTER 12 SECTION 3
Conjunctions

We can interrelate two simple sentences by placing a *conjunction* at the beginning of the second sentence while the first sentence remains unchanged.
For example:

Kare-wa Tomu-desu.	He is Tom.
Kanojo-wa Keito-desu.	She is Kate.

If we place the conjunction **soshite**, which literally means "and," at the beginning of the second sentence, the result is a continuity of flow between the two independent sentences.

Kare-wa Tomu-desu. Soshite kanojo-wa Keito-desu.

Some Conjunctions

and	soSHITE	otherwise	SAmonaito
and also	maTA	in other words	iIKAereba
and then	soREKARA	anyway	TOnikaku
therefore	DAkara, DEsukara	in short	TSUmari, yoOSUruni
accordingly	shiTAGAtte	after all	keKKYOKU
in that case	soRENAra	well	SAte
moreover	SHIkamo, soNOUE	by the way	toKOROde
on the other hand	iPPOo	namely	SUnawachi
but	shiKAshi	for example	taTOeba
however	KEredomo	because	NAzenara
on the contrary	soREDOkoroka	to tell the truth	jiTSUwa
or	aRUiwa, soRETOmo		

Examples

Would you like coffee? Or would you rather have tea?	コーヒーをお飲みになりますか。 koOHIi-o o-NOMI-NI-naRI-MAsu-KA? それとも紅茶になさいますか。 soRETOmo koOCHA-NI naSAI-MAsu-KA?
It's nice weather, isn't it? Well, where shall we go today?	いいお天気ですね。さて、きょうはどこへ行き Ii-oTEnki-desu-NE. SAte, KYOo-wa DOko-e iKI- ましょうか。 MASHOo-ka?

I can eat almost all Japanese foods. For example, I like **sushi** very much. But octopus is my only problem.

日本料理はほとんどなんでも
niHON-RYOori-wa hoTOndo NAn-demo
食べられます。たとえばおすしは
taBERARE-MAsu. taTOeba o-SUshi-wa
大好きです。しかし、タコだけは
DAi-suki-desu. shiKAshi TAko-daKE-wa
どうも苦手です。
DOomo niGATE-desu.

Don't you know him? To tell you the truth, I don't either.

あの人を知らないんですか。
aNO-hito-o shiRA-NAi-n-desu-KA?
実は私もです。
jiTSUwa waTASHI-MO-desu.

She is very beautiful and charming. Moreover her father is a millionaire.

彼女は美人で魅力的です。
KAnojo-wa biJIN-DE miRYOKU-TEKI-DEsu.
しかも彼女のお父さんは
SHIkamo KAnojo-no o-TOo-san-wa
億万長者です。
oKU-MAN-CHOoja-desu.

He tediously gives all kinds of poor excuses. In short, he does not want to go.

彼はくどくどとへたな言いわけを
KAre-wa KUdokudo-to heTA-na iIWAKE-O
言っています。要するに行きたく
iT-TE I-masu. yoOSUruni iKI-TAKU-
ないんです。
NAi-n-desu.

Chapter 13

Complex Sentences

As described in the introduction to CHAPTER 12, two simple sentences can be combined in a single sentence so that one functions as a principal clause and the other functions as a subordinate clause. The result is called a complex sentence. In complex sentences, the subordinate clause performs a certain role for the principal clause, such as a noun, adjective, adverb, or predicate. Subordinate clauses fall into the following groups:

noun clause
adjectival clause
adverbial clause
predicate clause

Important

Politeness can be maintained in complex sentences by using **-desu** and **-masu** endings in the principal clause only. In other words, the plain ("not polite") style of predicates is used in the subordinate clause. (The plain style will be discussed in Section 1.)

The subject in the subordinate clause normally takes either the postposition **-ga** or **-no**.

CHAPTER 13 SECTION 1

Plain Style of the Predicate

Polite Style

The polite-to-the-listener style of the predicate (using **-desu** and **-masu** endings) is commonly used in the business environment, in the public address, and in daily conversation among adults who are not close friends. If you use the plain style in these environments, people may think that you are overfamiliar, rude, or even ill-bred.

Plain Style

On the other hand, the plain style of the predicate is used:

(1) in daily conversation among children, family members, close friends, classmates, and colleagues.
(2) in written works such as books, newspapers, and diaries.
(3) in the subordinate sentence of a complex sentence.

Polite-Plain Comparison Chart

Carefully study the chart on the next page which compares polite and plain styles. Each position of the negative-past triangles on the left side of the page corresponds to the same position of the triangles on the right side. (Refer to CHAPTER 3 Chapter Section 8 for details of the [N]-[P] Triangle.)

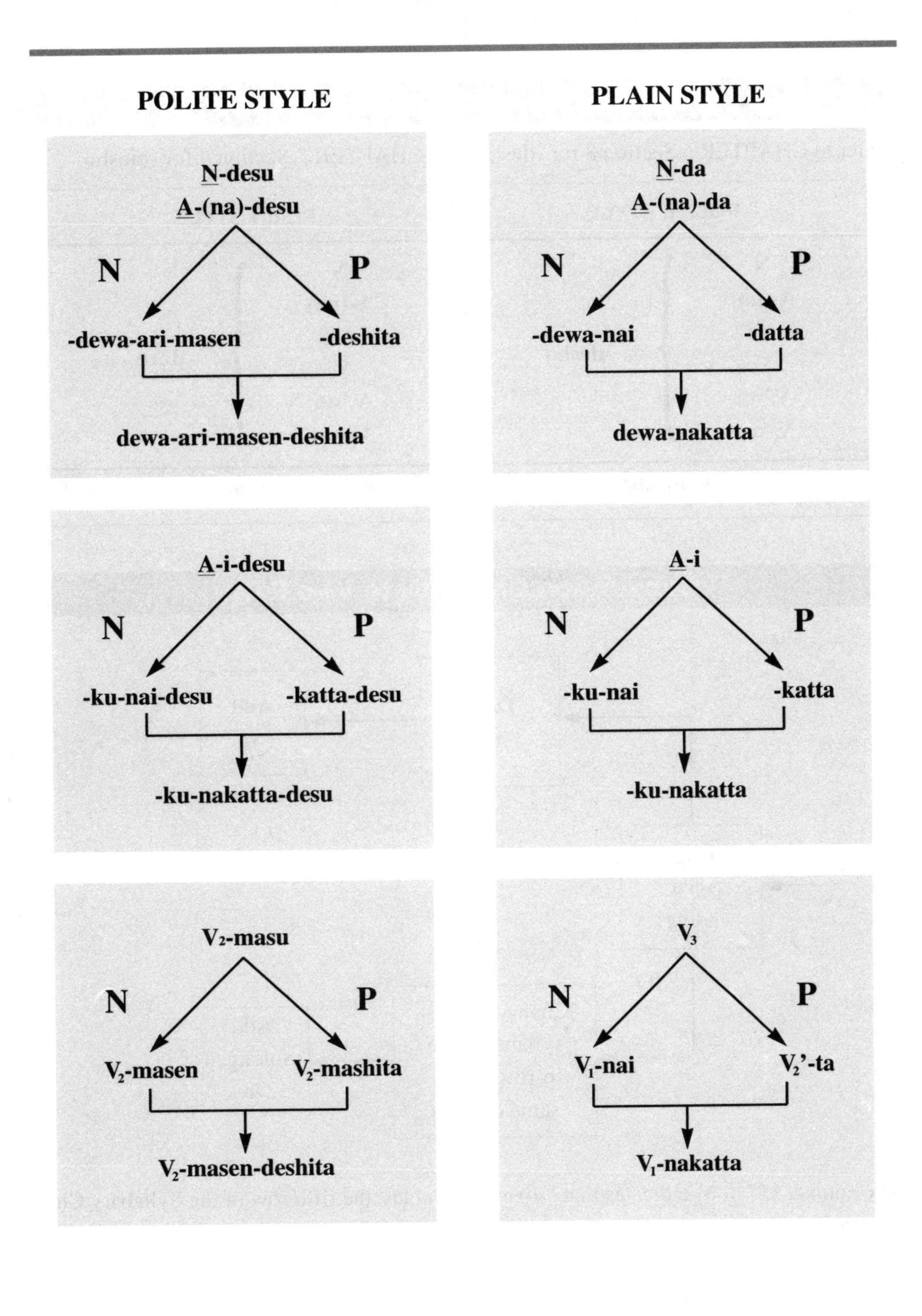
POLITE STYLE
PLAIN STYLE
N-desu
A-(na)-desu
N
P
-dewa-ari-masen
-deshita
dewa-ari-masen-deshita
N-da
A-(na)-da
N
P
-dewa-nai
-datta
dewa-nakatta
A-i-desu
N
P
-ku-nai-desu
-katta-desu
-ku-nakatta-desu
A-i
N
P
-ku-nai
-katta
-ku-nakatta
V2-masu
N
P
V2-masen
V2-mashita
V2-masen-deshita
V3
N
P
V1-nai
V2'-ta
V1-nakatta

Plain Style of -deshō and -mashō

Refer to CHAPTER 6 Section 8 for **-deshō**, and CHAPTER 7 Section 4 for **-mashō**.

POLITE STYLE		PLAIN STYLE	
N **A-(na)** **A-i** **V_3** **V_2'-ta** **V_1-nai**	**-deshō**	**N** **A-(na)** **A-i** **V_3** **V_2'-ta** **V_1-nai**	**-darō**
V_2-mashō		**V_5-o**	

Conversion Chart: V_3 to V_5-o Form

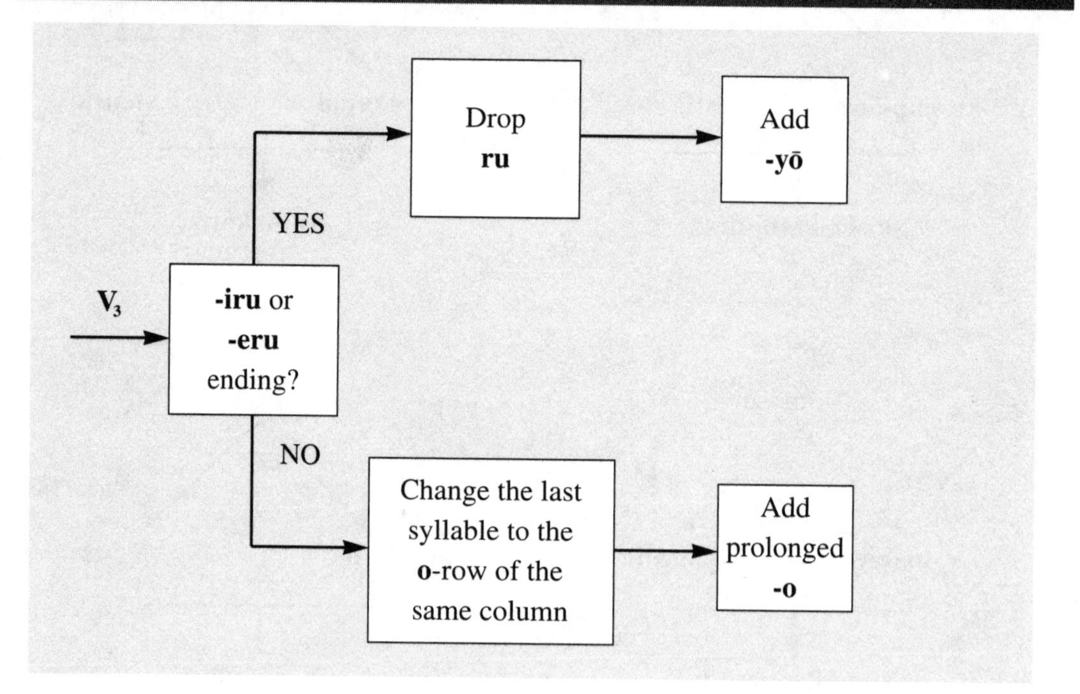

The number "5" of V_5 indicates that "**o-row**" syllables, the fifth row of the Syllabary Chart, are used.

Examples (Representative and Special Verbs)

miru	to see	**mi-yō**
neru	to sleep	**ne-yō**
kasu	to lend	**kasō**
haku	to put on	**hakō**
nugu	to take off	**nugō**
matsu	to wait	**matō**
toru	to take	**torō**

kau	to buy	**kaō**
shinu	to die	**shinō**
yomu	to read	**yomō**
tobu	to fly	**tobō**
suru	to do	**shi-yō**
kuru	to come	**ko-yō**

Examples

Following are some examples of the plain style.

Mr. **Tanaka** is a teacher.	田中さんは先生だ。 taNAKA-SAN-WA seNSEi-da.
This is not my umbrella.	これは私の傘ではない。 koRE-WA waTASHI-NO-KAsa-dewa-NAi.
I was so ashamed.	私はとても恥ずかしかった。 waTASHI-WA toTEMO haZUKASHI-katta.
This neighborhood is very quiet.	このあたりはたいへん静かだ。 koNO-Atari-wa taIHEN SHIzuka-da.
He did not remember me.	彼は私を覚えていなかった。 KAre-wa waTASHI-O oBOe-te-i-NAkatta.
I think it will be cold tomorrow.	あすは寒いだろう。 aSU-wa saMUi-daroo.
I don't think she is coming.	彼女は来ないだろう。 KAnojo-wa KO-nai-daroo.
Let's get off at the next station.	次の駅でおりよう。 tsuGI-no-Eki-de oRI-YOo.
Let's walk for a while.	少し歩こう。 suKOshi aRU-KOo.
Shall I open the window?	窓を開けようか。 MAdo-o aKE-YOo-KA?

CHAPTER 13 SECTION 2
Noun Clauses

When the subordinate clause functions as a noun in a complex sentence, it is called a *noun clause*. For example:

Kisha-ga kuru-no-o mi-mashita. I saw the train was coming.

When **-no** is attached to the subordinate clause, **kisha-ga kuru** (train is coming), it functions as a noun and is the object of the verb **miru** (to see), and therefore takes the suffix **-o.**

Two ending styles of Japanese noun clauses will be discussed:

(1) **-to**

(2) **-koto** or **-no**

(1) -to Ending

Subordinate clauses that function as the object for "I think" or "he says" (a quoted sentence), which have the various ending forms shown below, can be used as noun clauses when the suffix **-to** is attached. In this usage, the subject of the subordinate clause or a quoted sentence may take (theme)-**wa** form.

N-da

A-(na)-da } -to

A-i } -to

V_3 } -to

V_2'-te-iru } -to

V_2'-ta } -to

V_1-nai } -to

V_5-o

Examples

He says, "I will stand by you as your friend."	「僕は君の味方だ」と彼は言います。 "BOku-wa kiMI-NO miKATA-DA"-TO KAre-wa iI-MAsu.
They say that prices of commodities are high in **Tōkyō**.	東京は物価が高いと言います。 toOKYOO-WA buKKA-GA taKAI-to iI-MAsu.

He says, "I am not the culprit."	「私は犯人ではない」と彼は "waTASHI-WA HAnnin-DEwa-NAi"-to KAre-wa 言っています。 iT-TE-i-MAsu.
He says that he is going to leave the company.	彼は会社を辞めると言っています。 KAre-wa kaISHA-O yaMERU-TO iT-TE-i-MAsu.
I don't think she knows the truth.	彼女は真実を知らないと思い KAnojo-wa SHInjitsu-o shiRA-NAI-TO oMOI- ます。 MAsu. (I think she doesn't know the truth.)
I think I will sleep on it.	あす考えようと思います。 aSU kaNGAE-YOo-to oMOI-MAsu.

(2) -koto or -no Ending

Subordinate clauses with various ending forms, as shown below, can be used as noun clauses when the suffix **-koto** or **-no** (meaning "a thing" or "a fact") is attached. (Only **-no** is used with the objects of sensory verbs [see, hear, etc.].)

N-da-to-iu	
A-na	**-koto**
A-i	
V_3	
V_2'-te-iru	
V_2'-ta	**-no**
V_1-nai	

Examples

I didn't know that he was a famous musician.	彼が有名な音楽家だという KAre-ga yuUMEI-NA oNGAKU-KA-DA-to- iU- ことを知りませんでした。 KOTO-o shiRI-MASEn-deshita.
Please tell me what you saw.	あなたが見たことを話してください。 aNAta-ga MI-ta-koTO-o haNAshi-te-kuDASAi.

Taking a walk every day seems to be very good for the health.	毎日 散歩すること は 健康 にとても いいようです。 MAinichi saNPO-SURU-KOTO-wa keNKOO-NI toTEMO li-yoo-desu.
I know that she came home very late last night.	彼女が ゆうべ 遅く 帰ってきた のを知っています。 KAnojo-ga yuUBE-oSOKU KAet-te-KI-ta-no-o shiT-TE-I-MAsu.
I saw the suspect coming out of the room hastily.	容疑者 が その 部屋 から あわてて 出て くるのを見ました。 yoOGIsha-ga soNO-HEYA-kara aWATETE DE-te-kuru-no-o mi-MAshita.

CHAPTER 13 SECTION 3

Noun Modifiers (3) Adjectival Clauses

A subordinate clause that modifies a noun in a complex sentence is called an *adjectival clause*. For example:

Kore-wa kare-ga kure-ta pen-desu. This is the pen that he gave me.

Kare-ga kure-ta (that he gave me) acts as an adjective to describe the pen and is therefore called an adjectival clause in the complex sentence.

Three ending styles of adjectival clauses will be discussed:

(1) No additional suffix
(2) **-to-iu**
(3) **-yō-na**

(1) No Additional Suffix

Subordinate clauses with the various ending forms shown below can be used as adjectival clauses without the addition of a suffix.

This usage is comparable to the English use of a subordinate clause lead by a relative pronoun or a relative adverb modifying the antecedent noun. In the example "This is the pen that he gave me," "that" is the *relative pronoun*. The subordinate clause, "that he gave me," modifies the *antecedent noun*, "the pen."

<u>A</u>-na
<u>A</u>-i
V_3
V_2'-te-iru
V_2'-ta
V_1-nai

Examples

The National Museum is in **Ueno** park, which is famous for its zoo and cherry blossoms.	国立博物館は、動物 koKURITSU-haKUBUTSU-kan-wa, <u>doO</u>BUTSU- 園と桜で有名な上野公園 en-to saKURA-DE <u>yuU</u>MEI-NA uENO-<u>KOo</u>en- の中にあります。 no-NAka-ni aRI-MAsu.
I was born in **Sendai** where the forests are so beautiful.	私は、森のたいへん美しい waTASHI-WA, moRI-NO taIHEN uTSUKUSHIi 仙台で生まれました。 SEndai-de uMARE-MAshita.
Yamato, the restaurant we often go to, is near the airport.	私達がよく行くレストランの waTASHI-tachi-ga YOku iKU REsutoran-no 「やまと」は空港の近くに "YAmato"-wa <u>kuUKOO</u>-NO-chiKAku-ni あります。 aRI-MAsu.
The house I now live in is in the center of **Tōkyō**.	私がいま住んでいる家は都心に waTASHI-GA Ima SUn-de-iru-iE-wa toSHIN-NI あります。 aRI-MAsu.
There was a fire this morning in the hotel where I am staying.	私の泊まっているホテルでけさ waTASHI-NO toMAT-TE-IRU-HOteru-de KEsa 火事がありました。 KAji-ga aRI-MAshita.

The photograph I took in Europe was admitted to the exhibition.	ヨーロッパで撮った写真が入選 yoOROppa-de TOt-ta shaSHIN-GA nyuUSEN- しました。 shi-MAshita.
He only writes novels that never sell.	彼は売れない小説ばかり書いて KAre-wa uRE-NAI shoOSETSU-BAkari KAi-te います。 i-MAsu.

(2) -to-iu Ending

Subordinate clauses that have the ending forms shown below can be used as adjectival clauses by attaching the suffix **-to-iu** (meaning "they say").

N-da
A-(na)-da
A-i
V_3
V_2'-te-iru
V_2'-ta
V_1-nai
V_5-o

} **-to-iu**

Examples

There is a rumor saying that Mr. **Tanaka** will be the next mayor.	田中さんが次の市長だ taNAKA-SAN-GA tsuGI-no SHIchoo-da- といううわさがあります。 to-iu uWASA-GA aRI-MAsu.
There is nobody who says that this movie is interesting.	この映画がおもしろいという人は koNO-Eiga-ga oMOSHIROi-to-iU-hiTO-wa 一人もいません。 hiTORI-MO i-MASEn.
There was a telephone call saying that she would arrive in Japan today.	彼女からきょう日本に着くと KAnojo-kara KYOo niHOn-ni TSUku-to- いう電話がありました。 iu deNWA-GA aRI-MAshita.

I received a memo saying that he would be waiting in the bar.

バーで待っているという彼のメモを受け取りました。
BAa-de MAt-te-iru-to-iu KAre-no-MEmo-o uKETORI-MAshita.

I visited a house, where they say Beethoven used to live.

ベートーベンが住んでいたという家を訪ねました。
beETOoben-ga SUn-de-iTA-to-iu-iE-o taZUNE-MAshita.

The resolution that we would hold the next meeting in **Kyōto** was adopted.

次回の会議を京都で開催しようという決議が採択されました。
jiKAi-no-kaIGI-o KYOoto-de kaISAI-shi-YOo-to-iu-KEtsugi-ga saITAKU-saRE-MAshita.

(3) -yō-na Ending

Subordinate clauses that have the endings shown below can be used as adjectival clauses by attaching the suffix **-yō-na** (meaning "seem like," "as if," or "such as").

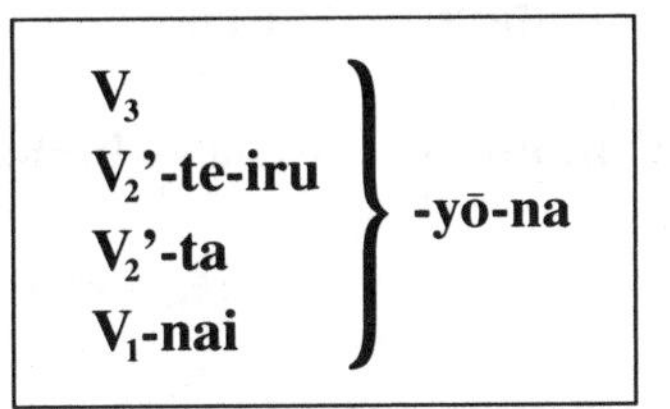

Examples

I don't like people who tell lies.

うそをつくような人は嫌いです。
Uso-o-tsuKU-YOo-na hiTO-wa kiRAI-DEsu.

I feel as if I am dreaming.

夢を見ているような気がします。
yuME-o MI-te-iRU-YOo-na ki-GA SHI-MAsu.

There was a sound as if the lightning had struck.

雷が落ちたような音がしました。
kaMINARI-ga Ochita-yoo-na oTO-ga shi-MAshita.

She confided a secret to me, which I could hardly believe.

彼女は私に信じられないような秘密を打ちあけました。
KAnojo-wa waTASHI-NI shiNJI-raRE-nai-yoo-na hiMITSU-O uCHI-AKE-MAshita.

CHAPTER 13 SECTION 4
Adverbial Clauses

A subordinate clause that functions as an adverb in a complex sentence (that is, it modifies the verb in the principal clause) is called an *adverbial clause.*

The following ending styles of adverbial clauses will be discussed:

(1) Time:	
(a) when:	**-toki(-ni)**
(b) before:	**-mae-ni**
(c) after:	**-ato-de, -kara**
(d) during:	**-aida**
(e) while:	**-nagara**
(f) until:	**-made**
(g) by:	**-made-ni**
(2) Condition:	
(a) General condition:	**-ba, -nara(ba)**
(b) Realistic condition:	**-to**
(c) Unrealistic condition:	**-ta-ra**
(3) Comparative Condition:	**---ba ---hodo**
(4) Reason:	**-node, -kara**
(5) Purpose:	**-tame-ni**
(6) Cause:	**-tame**
(7) Concession:	**-keredo(mo)**
(8) Manner:	**-yō-ni, -tōri-ni**

(1) Time

(1-a) When: **-toki(ni)**

Subordinate clauses with the ending forms shown below can be used as adverbial clauses by adding the suffix **-toki** or **-toki-ni** (meaning "when").

N-no
A-na
A-i
V_3
V_2'-te-iru
V_2'-ta
V_1-nai

} **-toki (ni)**

Examples:

I came to Japan when I was twenty years old.	20歳のとき日本に来ました。 HAtachi-no-TOki niHOn-ni ki-MAshita.
I study when it is quiet.	静かなときに勉強します。 SHIzuka-na-TOki-ni beNKYOO-SHI-MAsu.
Do you use chopsticks when you eat **o-sushi**?	あなたはおすしを食べるときに aNAta-wa o-SUshi-o taBEru-toki-ni 箸を使いますか。 HAshi-o tsuKAi-MAsu-KA?
I was reading a book when he came.	彼が来たとき私は本を KAre-ga KI-ta-toki waTASHI-WA HOn-o 読んでいました。 YOn-de-i-MAshita.
Mr. **Tanaka** came when you were not here.	あなたがいないときに田中さんがみえ aNAta-ga i-NAI-TOki-ni taNAKA-SAN-GA miE- ました。 MAshita.

(1-b) Before: **-mae-ni**

V_3-mae-ni

Examples:

I brush my teeth before I go to bed.	私は寝る前に歯を磨きます。 waTASHI-WA neRU-MAe-ni HA-o miGAKI-MAsu.

The police nabbed the thief before he ran away.	泥棒が逃げる前に警察が doROBOO-GA niGEru-MAe-ni keISATSU-GA 取り押さえました。 toRI-OSAE-MAshita.

(1-c) After: **-ato-de, -kara**

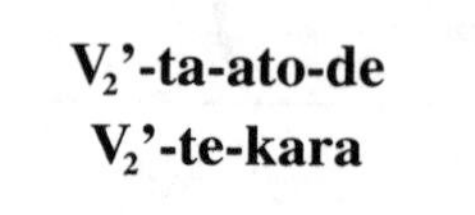

Examples:

I changed my mind after I placed an order.	注文したあとで気が変わり chuUMON-shi-TA-Ato-de ki-GA KAWARI- ました。 MAshita.
I will answer after I have given it some thought.	よく考えてからお答えします。 YOku kaNGAe-te-kara o-KOTAE-shi-MAsu.

(1-d) During: **-aida**

V_2'-te-iru-aida

Example:

My mother attended on me during my stay in the hospital.	私が入院している間 waTASHI-GA nyuUIN-shi-TE-IRU-AIDA 母が付き添ってくれました。 HAha-ga tsuKISOt-te-kuRE-MAshita.

(1-e) While: **-nagara**

V_2-nagara

Example:

My father eats breakfast while he reads the paper.	父は新聞を読みながら朝 CHIchi-wa shiNBUN-O yoMI-NAgara aSA- ご飯を食べます。 GOhan-o taBE-MAsu.

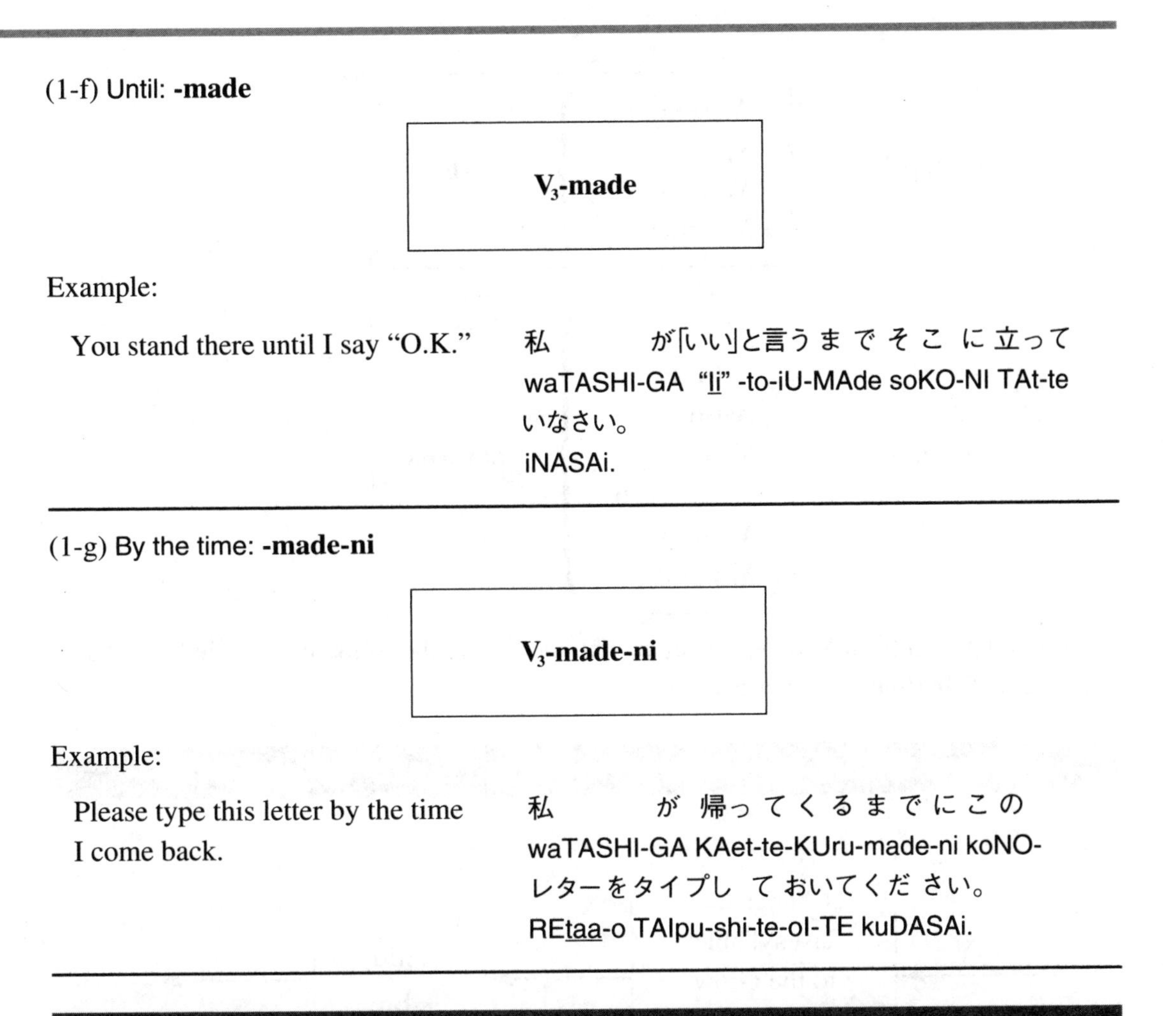

(1-f) Until: **-made**

V_3-made

Example:

You stand there until I say "O.K."

私が「いい」と言うまでそこに立って
waTASHI-GA "Ii" -to-iU-MAde soKO-NI TAt-te
いなさい。
iNASAi.

(1-g) By the time: **-made-ni**

V_3-made-ni

Example:

Please type this letter by the time I come back.

私が帰ってくるまでにこの
waTASHI-GA KAet-te-KUru-made-ni koNO-
レターをタイプしておいてください。
REtaa-o TAIpu-shi-te-oI-TE kuDASAi.

---

(2) Condition

Adverbial clauses of condition are formed in such a way that the condition described in the subordinate clause is necessary in order to bring about the situation described in the principal clause. For example in the sentence, "If you don't put the kettle on to boil, we can't have tea," the action of having tea, described in the principal clause, depends on the condition of the kettle being put on to boil.

(2-a) General condition: **-ba, -nara(ba)**

Subordinate clauses with the various ending forms shown below can be used as adverbial clauses to convey the general condition by attaching the suffixes **-ba**, **-nara**, or **-naraba**.

The first group states a simple "if" condition (basically, if this happens, then that will or will not happen) while the second group gives the condition based on the present situation or the observation of circumstances (if this, as I see, is the case, then...).

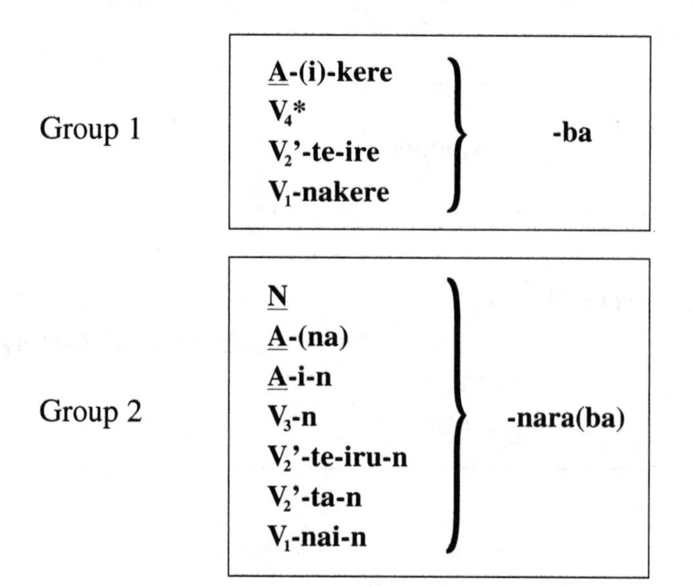

* The conjugation from $\mathbf{V_3}$ to $\mathbf{V_4}$**-ba** can be obtained using the following simple flow chart, regardless of **-iru/-eru** or other endings.

Flow Chart for Converting from V_3 to V_4-ba Form

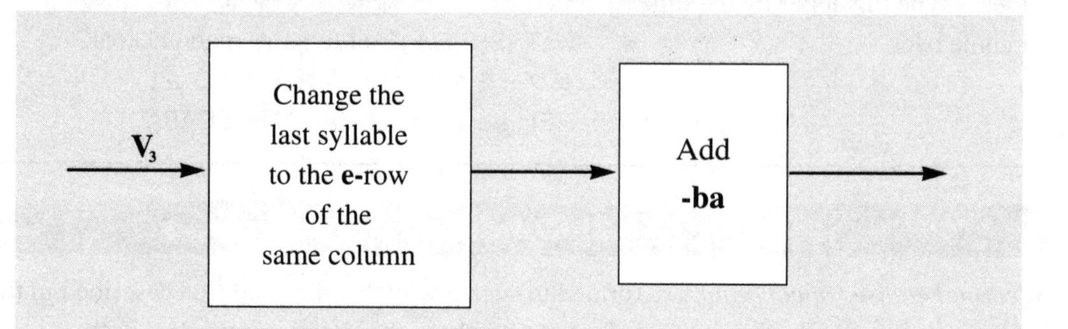

V_3 to V_4-ba (Representative and Special Verbs)

miru	to see	**mire-ba**
neru	to sleep	**nere-ba**
kasu	to lend	**kase-ba**
haku	to put on	**hake-ba**
nugu	to take off	**nuge-ba**
matsu	to wait	**mate-ba**
toru	to take	**tore-ba**
kau	to buy	**kae-ba**
shinu	to die	**shine-ba**
yomu	to read	**yome-ba**
tobu	to fly	**tobe-ba**
suru	to do	**sure-ba**
kuru	to come	**kure-ba**

Examples (Group 1):

If it is cheap I will buy it.

安ければ買います。
yaSU-kere-ba kaI-MAsu.

I will forgive him if he apologizes.

もし彼が謝れば許してやりましょう。
MOshi KAre-ga aYAMAre-ba yuRUshi-te yaRi-MASHOo.

They say, "Every dog has his day."

「犬も歩けば棒にあたる」*といいます。
"iNU-mo aRUke-ba boO-NI aTARU" TO iI-MAsu.
(*The literal translation of this is "Even a dog will hit a pole if he walks"!)

If the light is off, he is not back yet.

もし電気が消えていれば彼はまだ帰っていないんです。
MOshi DEnki-ga kiE-TE-iRE-ba KAre-wa MAda KAet-te i-NAi-n-desu.

If he is not there, I will leave a message.

もし彼がいなければメッセージをおいてきます。
MOshi KAre-ga i-NAkere-ba MEsseeji-o oI-TE-ki-MAsu.

Examples (Group 2):

If that person over there is Mr. **Tanaka**, I must say hello to him.

あそこにいる人が田中さんならあいさつしなければなりません。
aSOKO-NI-iRU-HITO-ga taNAKA-SAN-NAra Aisatsu-shi-NAkereba-naRI-MASEn.

If you feel so anxious, you'd better call him up.

そんなに心配なら電話してみたほうがいいです。
soNNA-NI shiNPAI-NAra deNWA-SHI-TE-MI-ta-hoo-ga Ii-desu.

If you are hot, take off your coat.

暑いんなら上着を脱ぎなさい。
aTSUi-n-nara uWAGI-O nuGI-NASAi.

If you are going, I am going too.

君が行くんなら僕も行きます。
kiMI-GA iKU-n-nara BOku-mo-iKI-MAsu.

If you know, please tell me.	知っているんなら教えてください。 shiT-TE-iRU-n-nara oSHIE-TE-kuDASAi.
If you lost it, look for it yourself.	なくしたんなら自分で探しなさい。 naKUSHI-TA-n-nara jiBUN-DE saGASHI-NASAi.
If you do not understand, please do not hesitate to ask questions.	わからないんなら遠慮なく waKARA-nai-n-nara eNRYO-NAku 質問してください。 shiTSUMON-shi-TE-kuDASAi.

(2-b) Realistic condition: **-to**

This again describes a relationship of dependence between the principal and subordinate clauses, but in this case the subject matter is strictly factual.

Subordinate clauses with the ending forms shown below can be used as adverbial clauses of realistic condition when the suffix **-to** (implying "always true") is attached.

Ending form	Suffix
N-da	**-to**
A-(na)-da	
A-i	
V_3	
V_2'-te-iru	
V_1-nai	

Examples:

If you take an airplane, you will get there earlier	飛行機だと早く着きます。 hiKOoki-da-to HAyaku tsuKI-MAsu.
If you open the window, you will see the harbor.	窓を開けると港が見えます。 MAdo-o aKERU-TO miNATO-GA miE-MAsu.
If you add 2 to 3, you will get 5.	3に2を足すと5になります。 saN-ni NI-o taSU-TO GO-ni naRI-MAsu.
If I listen to Mozart, I feel calm.	モーツアルトを聞いていると気持ちが MOotsuaruto-o kiI-TE-IRU-TO kiMOCHI-GA 落ち着きます。 oCHITSUKI-MAsu.

If you do not show them your ID card, you cannot enter.	身分証明書を見せないと入れ miBUN-shoOMEI-SHO-o miSE-nai-to haIRE- ません。 MASEn.

(2-c) Unrealistic condition: **-ta-ra**

In this form, the condition stated in the subordinate clause, and upon which the action depends, is either contrary to the facts or the probability of the condition is zero or nearly zero.

Subordinate clauses which have any of the various ending forms of the past tense (**-ta** ending) shown below can be used as adverbial clauses of unrealistic condition by attaching the suffix **-ra**.

N-datta
A-(na)-datta
A-(i)-katta
V_2'-te-ita
V_2'-ta
V_1-nakatta
} **-ra**

Examples:

If I were a bird, I would fly to you.	私がもし鳥だったら waTASHI-GA MOshi toRI-DAtta-ra あなたの所へ飛んで行くでしょう。 aNAta-no-toKORO-e toN-DE-iKU-DESHOo.
If I were healthy, I would travel around the world.	もし健康だったら、世界中を MOshi keNKOO-DAtta-ra, seKAI-JUU-O 旅行するんですが。 ryoKOO-suRU-n-desu-ga.
If I were a little younger, I would study abroad.	もう少し若かったら海外に moO suKOshi waKA-katta-ra KAigai-ni 留学するんですが。 ryuUGAKU-suRU-n-desu-ga.
If I win the first prize in the lottery, I will buy you a diamond ring.	宝くじで一等に当たったら、 taKARA-kuji-de iTTOO-NI aTAT-TA-ra, ダイヤモンドの指輪を買ってあげよう。 daIYAMOndo-no yuBIWA-O kaT-TE-aGE-YOo.

If I had studied Japanese earlier, I would have been a fluent speaker by now.	もっと早く日本語を習っていたら いまごろは ペラペラでしょう。 MOtto HAyaku niHON-GO-O naRAt-te-i-TA-ra, iMA-GORO-WA peRA-PERA DESHOo.
If she does not say "yes," what will I do?	もし彼女が「イエス」と言わなかったら どうしよう。 MOshi KAnojo-ga "iEsu" to iWA-NAkat-ta-ra, DOo-shi-yoo.

(3) Comparative Condition ---ba ---hodo

In this construction, the increase or decrease in the condition described in one half of the sentence affects the increase or decrease in that described in the other half. Let's look at an example:

The sooner, the better.

The part "the sooner" is an *adverbial clause of comparable condition*. In Japanese, it is expressed in the following forms.

A-na-ra-ba A-na-hodo
A-(i)-kere-ba A-i-hodo
V_4-ba V_3-hodo

Examples:

The sooner, the better.	早ければ早いほどいいです。 HAya-kere-ba haYA-i-hodo Ii-desu.
The more intricate it is, the more likely it will be to break down.	複雑なら複雑なほど 壊れやすいです。 fuKUZATSU-NAra fuKUZATSU-NA-hoDO koWARE-YASUi-desu.
The higher we climbed, the colder it became.	高く登れば登るほど寒く なってきました。 TAkaku noBORE-ba noBORU-HODO SAmu-ku nat-te-ki-MAshita.
The more I study Japanese, the more interesting I find it.	日本語を勉強すればするほど おもしろくなってきました。 niHON-GO-O beNKYOO-suRE-ba suRU-HODO oMOSHIROku nat-te ki-MAshita.

(4) Reason

Adverbial clauses of reason tell why something happened or will happen.

Subordinate clauses with the ending forms shown below can be used as adverbial clauses of reason by attaching the suffix **-node** or **-kara**.

Ending form	Suffix
N-na	**-node**
A-na	
A-i	
V_3	
V_2'-te-iru	
V_2'-ta	
V_1-nai	

Ending form	Suffix
N-da	**-kara**
A-(na)-da	
A-i	
V_3	
V_2'-te-iru	
V_2'-ta	
V_1-nai	

Examples:

The department store will be closed tomorrow because it is Monday.	あすは月曜なのでそのデパートは閉まっています。 aSU-wa geTSU-YOo-na-node soNO-dePAato-wa shi-MAt-te-i-MAsu.
Because Mr. **Tanaka** speaks English well, you don't need an interpreter.	田中さんは英語がじょうずだから通訳は必要ないでしょう。 taNAKA-SAN-WA eIGO-GA joOZU-dakara TSUuyaku-wa hiTSUYOO-NAi-deshoo.
Please sit down over there, as I want to take your photograph.	写真を撮るからそこに座ってください。 shaSHIN-O TOru-kara soKO-NI suWAT-TE-KUDASAi.
Since I know Mr. **Tanaka** very well, I will write a letter of introduction for you.	田中さんをよく知っているので、紹介状を書いてあげましょう。 taNAKA-SAN-O YOku shiT-TE-iRU-node, shoOKAI-JOO-O KAi-te-aGE-MASHOo.

You'd better take the next train because this one doesn't stop at **Odawara** station.

この 電 車 は 小田原に 止まら ない
koNO-DEnsha-wa oDAWARA-ni toMARA-NAI
から、次 のに 乗った ほう がいいでしょう。
kara, tsuGI-no-ni noTTA-HOo-ga Ii- deshoo.

(5) Purpose -tame-ni

V_3-tame-ni

Examples:

I am going to the airport this afternoon to meet a customer.

お客 様 を 出迎 える ために、
o-KYAKU-SAMA-o deMUKAERU-taME-ni,
午後 空 港 に 行きます。
goGO kuUKOO-NI iKI-MAsu.

Do you live to eat, or do you eat to live?

あなた は 食べ るため に生きています か、
aNAta-wa taBEru-taME-ni Iki-te-i-MAsu-KA,
それ とも 生きるため に 食べ ています か。
soRETOmo iKIru-taME-ni TAbe-te-i-MAsu-KA?

(6) Cause -ta-tame

In this instance, the adverbial clause describes the cause, and the principal clause describes the resulting condition.

Subordinate clauses with various ending forms in the past tense ("**-ta**" ending), as shown below, can be used as *adverbial clauses of cause* by attaching the suffix **-tame**.

A-(na)-datta
A-(i)-katta
V_2'-te-ita
V_1-ta
V_1-nakatta
} **-tame**

Examples:

Because there was a scanty rice harvest, we had to depend on imported rice.

米が不作だったため、輸入米
koME-ga fuSAKU-DAt-ta-tame, yuNYUU-MAI-
に頼らなければなりませんでした。
NI taYORA-nakereba-naRI-MASEn-deshita.

Because I was fast asleep last night, I did not feel the earthquake.

ゆうべはぐっすり寝ていたため、
yuUBE-wa guSSUri ne-TE-I-TA-TAME,
地震に気がつきませんでした。
jiSHIN-NI ki-GA-TSUKI-MASEn-deshita.

Because there was a traffic accident, I was late for school.

交通事故があったため、学校に
koOTSUU-JIko-ga At-ta-tame, gaKKOO-NI
遅刻しました。
chiKOKU-SHI-MAshita

(7) Concession -keredo(mo)

In this form, the matter stated in the principal clause is true despite the perhaps contradictory information described in the subordinate clause.

Subordinate clauses with the endings shown below can be used as *adverbial clauses of concession* when either the suffix **-keredo** or **-keredomo** (meaning "although") is attached.

N-da **A-(na)-da** **A-i** **V_3** **V_2'-te-iru** **V_2'-ta** **V_1-nai**	**-keredo(mo)**

Examples:

Although he is a doctor, he can live on his earnings as a writer.

彼は医者だけれども、作家と
KAre-wa iSHA-DA-keredomo, saKKA-TO-
しても食べていけます。
shi-TE-mo TAbe-te iKE-MAsu.

Although he is young, he is a sound-thinking person.

彼は若いけれど、考えのしっかり
KAre-wa waKAi-keredo, kaNGAe-no shiKKAri-
した人です。
shi-ta-hiTO-desu.

Although I have been studying Japanese for almost two years, I still can't read **kanji**.

もう２年も日本語を勉強し
MOo NI-nen-mo niHON-GO-O beNKYOO-SHI-
ているけれど まだ漢字が読めません。
TE-iRU-keredo, MAda kaNJI-GA yoME-MASEn.

Although I can't write **kanji**, I can read them.

漢字は書けないけれど、読むことは
KAnji-wa kaKE-nai-keredo, YOmu-koTO-wa
できます。
deKI-MAsu.

(8) Manner -yō-ni, -tōri-ni

Adverbial clauses of manner describe the way in which something is done.

Subordinate clauses with the ending forms shown below can be used as adverbial clauses of manner by adding either the suffix **-yō-ni** or **-tōri-ni** (meaning "as" or "like").

V_3 **V_2'-te-iru** **V_2'-ta**	} **-yō-ni** } **-tōri-ni**

Examples:

Try to do just as I do.

私がするようにやってみて
waTASHI-GA suRU-YOo-ni yaT-TE-MI-te-
ください。
kudasai.

She was entranced, as if in a dream.

彼女は夢でも見ているように
KAnojo-wa yuME-demo MI-te-iru-YOo-ni
うっとりとしていました。
uTTOri-to shi-te-i-MAshita.

She arranged the flowers like her teacher did.

彼女は先生が生けたとおりに花を
KAnojo-wa seNSEI-ga Ike-ta-TOori-ni haNA-o
生けました。
iKE-MAshita.

CHAPTER 13 SECTION 5

Predicate Clauses

Let us compare the following two sentences:

(1) **Zō-wa ōkii-desu.**	An elephant is big.
(2) **Zō-wa hana-ga nagai-desu.**	An elephant has a long trunk.

Note that **hana-ga nagai-desu** in (2) (literally meaning "the trunk is long") is a subordinate clause, and it performs the same function as **ōkii-desu** (predicate) in (1).

This grammatical form, in which the subordinate clause functions as a predicate, is unique to the Japanese language. I refer to this usage of a clause as the *predicate clause*.

Theme-wa (predicate clause).

More Examples

The literal English translation of the Japanese is provided in parentheses.

This doll has blue eyes.	この人形は目が青いです。 koNO-niNGYOO-WA ME-ga aOi-desu. (As for this doll, its eyes are blue)
This robot's mouth moves.	このロボットは口が動きます。 koNO-roBOtto-wa kuCHI-GA uGOKI-MAsu. (As for this robot, its mouth moves)
He is tall.	彼は背が高いです。 KAre-wa SE-ga taKAi-desu. (As for him, he is tall)
Tōkyō has a large population.	東京は人口が多いです。 toOKYOO-WA jiNKOO-GA Ooi-desu. (As for **Tōkyō**, its population is large)

This TV's picture is distorted.

このテレビは画像がゆがんでいます。
koNO-TErebi-wa gaZOO-GA yuGAN-DE-I-MAsu.
(As for this TV, its picture is distorted)

His heart beat fast.

彼は胸が高鳴りました。
KAre-wa muNE-ga taKA-NARI-MAshita.
(As for him, his heart beat fast)

This kettle is leaking.

このやかんは水がもれます。
koNO-yaKAN-WA miZU-GA moRE-MAsu.
(As for this kettle, it is leaking)

He has much nerve.

彼は心臓が強いです。
KAre-wa shiNZOO-GA tsuYOi-desu.
(As for him, his heart is strong)

The parents are proud (of their child).

親は鼻が高いです。
oYA-wa haNA-GA taKAi-desu.
(As for his parents, their noses are high)

He is condescending.

彼は腰が低いです。
KAre-wa koSHI-GA hiKUi-desu.
(As for him, his waist is low)

I was offended.

私は腹が立ちました。
waTASHI-WA haRA-ga taCHI-MAshita.
(As for me, my belly stood up)

Appendix 1. Greetings and Simple Expressions

(Refer to CHAPTER 1 Section 2 for accent symbols used here.)

Good morning.	o-HAYOO goZAI-MAsu.
Good day.	koNNICHI-WA.
Good afternoon.	koNNICHI-WA.
Good evening.	koNBAN-WA.
Good night.	o-YASUMI-NASAi.
Good-bye.	saYOO-NARA.
Hi! (men only)	YAa!
Let me introduce Mr. Smith.	SUmisu-san-o go-SHOOKAI-shi-MAsu.
Let me introduce myself.	jiKO-SHOokai-shi-masu.
This is Mr./Mrs./Miss Smith	koCHIRA-WA SUmisu-san-desu.
I am Mr./Mrs./Miss Smith.	(waTASHI-WA) SUmisu-desu.
How do you do?	haJIME-MAshite.
Nice to meet you.	DOozo yoROSHIKU.
I am glad that you have come.	YOku iRASSHAI-MAshita.
See you later.	maTA Ato-de.
See you again.	maTA aI-MASHOo.
Please come again.	maTA DOozo.
Take good care of yourself.	oDAIJI-NI.
Be careful/Look out.	ki-O TSUKE-te.
Do your best!	gaNBAt-te!
Bon voyage.	taNOSHIi go-RYOKOO-O.
Say hello to George.	JOoji-san-ni yoROSHIKU.
How are you?	o-GEnki-desu-KA?
How is Kate?	KEito-san-wa o-GEnki-desu-KA?
How is everybody?	MInasan o-GEnki-desu-KA?
How do you feel?	KIbun-wa iKAga-desu-KA?
How are you doing?	go-KIGEN iKAga-desu-KA?
I am fine.	GEnki-desu.
I am sick.	byoOKI-DEsu.
I am not feeling well.	KIbun-ga waRUi-desu.
Thanks.	aRIgatoo.
Thank you very much.	DOomo aRIgatoo-goZAI-MAsu.

Thanks for asking.	o-KAGE-SAMA-DE.
And you?	aNAta-WA?
You are welcome.	DOo iTASHI-MAshite.
Don't mention it.	iIE, Iin-desu.
Nice day, isn't it?	Ii oTEnki-desu-NE.
Nasty weather, isn't it?	iYAna-oTEnki-desu-NE.
It is hot today, isn't it?	KYOo-wa aTSUi-desu-NE.
It is cold today, isn't it?	KYOo-wa saMUi-desu-NE.
It rains a lot, doesn't it?	YOku fuRI-MAsu-NE.
Who?	DAre? (DOnata?)
What?	NAni?
Which? (of two)	DOtchi? (DOchira?)
Which? (of three or more)	DOre?
When?	Itsu?
What time?	NAn-ji?
Where?	DOko?
Why?	NAze?
How come?	DOo shi-te?
How many?	Ikutsu?
How much?	Ikura?
A few / A little	suKOshi
Many / Much	taKUSAN
More	MOtto
A few more / A little more	moO SUKOshi
Welcome! (to a visitor)	iRASSHAi! (iRASSHAI-MAse!)
It has been a long time since	shiBAraku-desu-NE
May I come in?	HAit-te Ii-desu-KA?
Please come in.	DOozo o-HAIRI-KUDASAi.
Please come in. (taking shoes off).	DOozo o-AGARI-KUDASAi.
Please come this way.	DOozo koCHIRA-E.
After you.	DOozo o-SAKI-NI.
Have a nice weekend.	taNOSHIi shuUMATSU-O.
How was your weekend?	shuUMATSU-WA DOo-deshita-KA?
How was your flight?	hiKOoki-wa DOo-deshita-KA?

It was wonderful.	suBARASHI-katta-desu.
It wasn't bad / It was so so.	MAa-MAa deshita.

Please.	DOozo.
Excuse me.	shiTSUrei-shi-masu.
Excuse me, but ---	shiTSUrei-desu-ga, ---
I say! (getting the attention of a stranger on the street)	MOshi-moshi!
I beg a favor of you.	o-NEGAI-SHI-MAsu.

I am sorry.	suMI-MASEn.
I beg your pardon.	go-MEN-NASAi.
I made a mistake.	maCHIGAE-MAshita.
Sorry to disturb you.	o-JAMA-SHI-MAsu.
Sorry to have disturbed you.	o-JAMA-SHI-MAshita.

O.K.	OOkei.
I see.	waKARI-MAshita.
Is that so?	SOo-desu-ka?
Indeed!	naRUHODO!
Maybe.	TAbun.
Of course.	moCHIROn.
With pleasure.	yoROKOnde.
No problem.	moNDAI-NAi-desu.

That is fine.	KEkkoo-desu.
Really?	hoNTOO-DEsu-KA?
Be sure (to do something).	kiTTO.
No kidding.	MAsaka.
No way!	daME-desu!

That is right.	SOo-desu.
That is wrong.	chiGAI-MAsu.
I think so.	soO OMOI-MAsu.
I don't think so.	SOo-wa oMOI-MASEn.
Probably so.	TAbun SOo-deshoo.
I agree.	saNSEI-DEsu.
I disagree.	haNTAI-DEsu.

I understand.	waKARI-MAsu.
Do you understand?	waKARI-MAsu-KA?
I don't understand.	waKARI-MASEn.

I don’t understand Japanese.	niHONGO-WA waKARI-MASEn.
I don’t know.	shiRI-MASEn.
I don’t mind.	kaMAI-MASEn.
It cannot be helped.	shiKATA-GA aRI-MASEn.
I am in trouble.	koMARI-MAshita.
Congratulations!	oMEDETOO-goZAI-MAsu.
Happy birthday.	taNJOo-bi oMEDETOO.
Happy New Year.	SHInnen oMEDETOO-goZAI-MAsu.
What is the matter with you?	DOo shi-MAshita-KA?
Are you all right?	daIJOobu-desu-KA?
I am all right.	daIJOobu-desu.
Just a moment.	CHOtto MAtte-kudasai.
Will you please wait a while.	shiBAraku o-MACHI-KUDASAi.
Sorry to have kept you waiting.	o-MATASE-shi-MAshita.
I am leaving! (to school, etc.)	iTTE-MAIRI-MAsu!
Take care! (seeing a person off)	iTTE-IRASSHAi!
I am home!	taDAIMA!
Welcome home!	o-KAERI-NASAi!
Thanks for the meal. (when you begin eating)	iTADAKI-MAsu.
Thanks for the meal. (when you finish eating)	goCHISOO-SAMA.
Hello! (on the telephone)	MOshi-moshi.
Is Mr. **Tanaka** in?	taNAKA-SAN-WA i-MAsu-KA?
Who is this please?	DOnata-desu-KA?
This is Mr. Smith (speaking).	SUmisu-desu.
He is not home.	RUsu-desu.
He is in a meeting.	kaIGI-CHUU-DEsu.
He is on another line.	deNWA-CHUU-DEsu.
He has just stepped out.	SEki-o haZUSHITE-I-MAsu.
He is out of the office.	gaISHUTSU-SHITE-I-MAsu.
He is out of town.	shuTCHOO-SHITE-I-MAsu.
Is there anybody who can speak English?	eIGO-NO deKIru-hito i-MAsu-KA?
Is there any message?	deNGON-WA aRI-MAsu-KA?

I will call back.	maTA deNWA-SHI-MAsu.
You have a wrong number.	baNGOO-CHIgai-desu.

I am lost.	miCHI-NI maYOI-MAshita.
Where am I?	koKO-WA DOko-desu-KA?
Where is the station?	Eki-wa DOko-desu-KA?
Where is the bus-stop?	baSU-TEI-WA DOko-desu-KA?
Which way is **Ginza**?	giNZA-WA DOtchi-desu-KA?

Taxi!	TAkushii!
Take me to **Ginza**.	giNZA-MAde.
Take me to TCAT.	haKOzaki-made.
(TCAT: Tokyo City Air Terminal in **Hakozaki**)	
Take me to the Airport.	kuUkOO-MAde.

Turn to the left.	hiDARI.
Turn to the left there.	soKO-O hiDARI.
Turn to the left at the signal.	shiNGOO-O hiDARI.
Turn to the right	miGI.
Go straight.	maSSUgu.
Go slowly.	yuKKUri.
Stop.	suTOppu., toMETE.

Please give me a cup of coffee.	koOHIi-o kuDASAi.
Please tell me.	oSHIETE-KUDASAi.
Please say it again.	moO-ICHIDO iTTE-KUDASAi.
Please speak slowly.	yuKKUri iTTE-KUDASAi.
Please speak in English.	eIGO-DE iTTE-KUDASAi.

Appendix 2. Kanji Radicals

A *radical* is the key part of a **Kanji** which is used when you want to look up a character in a **Kanji** dictionary.

Radical	Meaning	Examples		
入	entrance	入 HAiru (enter)	込 KOmu (to be crowded)	
夕	half moon	夕 yuUBE (evening)	夜 YOru (night)	夢 yuME (dream)
大	person's arms, legs stretched	大 oOKIi (big)	太 fuTOi (thick)	天 TEn (heaven)
子	child	子 ko (child)	学 maNAbu (study)	乳 chiCHI (milk)
川	river	川 kaWA (river)	州 su (sandbank)	
田	rice paddy	田 TA (rice paddy)	男 oTOKO (man)	町 maCHI (town)
目	eye	目 ME (eye)	見 MIru (see)	看 MIru (watch)
亻	person	人 hiTO (person)	住 SUmu (live)	位 kuRAI (rank)
冫	cold, or to put side by side	冷 tsuMETAI (cold)	冬 fuYU (winter)	次 tsuGI (next)
忄	to put together	十 JUu (ten)	協 KYOo (cooperate)	博 hiROi (extensive)

Radical	Meaning	Examples		
口	mouth	口 kuCHI (mouth)	呼 yoBU (call)	味 aJI (taste)
土	soil on the ground	土 tsuCHI (soil)	地 CHI (land)	場 ba (place)
女	woman with her arms crossed	女 oNNA (woman)	婦 oNNA (lady)	妻 TSUma (wife)
弓	bow	弓 yuMI (bow)	引 hiKU (pull)	強 tsuYOi (strong)
彳	go	行 iKU (go forward)	復 maTA (again)	徒 to (on foot)
阝	heaped soil	陸 riKU (land)	降 oRIru (step down)	険 keWASHIi (steep)
忄	heart	性 SEi (character)	情 naSAKE (mercy)	快 koKOROYOi (agreeable)
戸	door	戸 to (door)	所 toKORO (place)	
扌	hand	手 TE (hand)	打 Utsu (beat)	持 MOtsu (grab)
方	plow or flag	方 HOo (direction)	旗 haTA (flag)	族 ZOku (family)

Radical	Meaning	Examples		
日	the sun	日 hi (day)	晴 haRE (sunny)	明 aKARUI (bright)
月	body	腹 haRA (belly)	胸 muNE (breast)	脳 NOo (brain)
木	tree	木 KI (tree)	根 NE (root)	植 uERU (plant)
歹	backbone	列 REtsu (column)	残 noKOru (remain)	死 shiNU (die)
氵	water	海 Umi (sea)	酒 saKE (rice wine)	泣 naKU (cry)
火	fire	火 HI (fire)	灯 aKARI (lamp)	灰 haI (ash)
片	the right half of a tree	片 kaTA (the other half)	版 HAn (printing block)	
牛	cow's head	牛 uSHI (cow)	物 moNO (thing)	牧 maKI (pasture)
犭	dog, animal	犬 iNU (dog)	猿 SAru (monkey)	犯 oKASU (commit crime)
王	three strung balls	玉 taMA (ball)	王 Oo (king)	球 taMA (globe)

Radical	Meaning	Examples		
矢	arrow	矢 YA (arrow)	知 shiRU (know)	短 miJIKAi (short)
石	stone by a cliff	石 iSHI (stone)	砂 suNA (sand)	破 yaBUru (break)
礻	altar	示 shiMESU (indicate)	神 KAmi (god)	社 yaSHIRO (shrine)
禾	crops	秋 Aki (autumn)	種 TAne (seed)	税 ZEi (tax)
米	four rice grains	米 koME (rice)	粉 koNA (flour)	糖 TOo (sugar)
糸	cocoon	糸 Ito (thread)	細 hoSOi (thin)	絹 KInu (silk)
耳	ear	耳 miMI (ear)	取 TOru (take)	聞 kiKU (hear)
舟	ship	船 FUne (ship)	航 KOo (voyage)	
衤	neck band of **kimono**	衣 koROMO (clothes)	複 fuKU (layers)	製 SEi (make)
角	horn of an animal	角 tsuNO (horn)	解 TOku (solve)	

Radical	Meaning	Examples		
言	sharp knife and mouth	言 iU (say)	話 haNAsu (speak)	語 kaTAru (talk)
豆	high-legged dish	豆 maME (bean)	頭 aTAMA (head)	豊 YUtaka (abundant)
貝	shellfish	貝 KAi (shell)	財 ZAi (assets)	買 kaU (buy)
足	leg	足 aSHI (leg)	路 miCHI (street)	
車	cart	車 kuRUMA (car)	転 koROGARU (roll)	輪 WA (wheel)
酉	pot	配 kuBAru (distribute)	酸 SAn (acid)	酒 saKE (wine)
里	rice paddy and soil	里 saTO (hamlet)	野 NO (field)	
金	grains contained in soil	金 KIn (gold)	銀 GIn (silver)	鉄 teTSU (iron)
青	grass and spring water	青 aOi (blue)	静 SHIzuka (quiet)	
食	cereals on a plate	食 taBEru (eat)	飲 NOmu (drink)	飯 HAn (meal)

Radical	Meaning	Examples		
馬	horse	馬 uMA (horse)	駅 Eki (station)	験 KEn (examine)
刀	sword	刀 kaTANA (sword)	切 KIru (cut)	分 waKEru (separate)
刂	sword	別 waKAREru (part)	刻 kiZAMU (carve)	割 waRU (break)
力	flexed arm muscles	力 chiKARA (power)	動 uGOku (move)	助 taSUKEru (help)
匕	sitting person	化 baKEru (disguise)	比 kuRABERU (compare)	死 shiNU (die)
又	hand	取 TOru (take)	収 oSAMEru (obtain)	受 uKEru (receive)
夂	two legs	夏 naTSU (summer)	各 Onoono (each)	処 toKORO (place)
阝	heaped soil	都 miYAKO (capital)	部 BU (part)	郵 YUu (post)
戈	halberd (a type of spear)	戦 taTAKAI (war)	成 NAru (complete)	我 WAre (I)
攵	do	教 oSHIERU (teach)	数 kaZOEru (count)	改 aRATAMEru (revise)

Radical	Meaning	Examples		
斗	measure	科 KA (distinguish)	料 haKAru (measure)	
斤	ax	新 aTARASHIi (new)	所 toKORO (place)	断 TAtsu (disconnect)
月	new moon	月 tsuKI (moon)	明 aKARUI (bright)	青 aOi (blue)
欠	bent body	欠 kaKERU (lack)	歌 uTAU (sing)	欲 hoSSURU (desire)
殳	do	殺 koROSU (kill)	段 DAn (step)	穀 koKU (grain)
見	eyes and person	見 MIru (see)	視 MIru (stare)	観 KAn (observe)
長	long hair streaming in wind	長 naGAi (long)	帳 CHOo (curtain)	張 haRU (spread)
鳥	bird	鳥 toRI (bird)	鳴 naKU (chirp)	
隹	bird	雑 ZAtsu (mixed)	難 NAn (mishap)	集 aTSUMAru (gather)
頁	head	頭 aTAMA (head)	顔 kaO (face)	頂 iTADAKI (summit)

Radical	Meaning	Examples		
𠆢	roof	会 Au (meet)	食 taBEru (eat)	金 kaNE (money)
冖	cover	写 uTSUsu (copy)	軍 GUn (military)	
宀	roof	家 iE (house)	室 shiTSU (room)	宿 yaDO (inn)
山	mountain	山 yaMA (mountain)	岩 iWA (rock)	炭 suMI (charcoal)
艹	grass	草 kuSA (grass)	花 haNA (flower)	茶 cha (tea)
耂	old person leaning on a cane	老 ROo (old)	考 kaNGAEru (think)	者 moNO (person)
癶	pair of legs	発 HAtsu (depart)	登 noBORU (climb)	
穴	hole	穴 aNA (hole)	空 kaRA (empty)	窓 MAdo (window)
罒	net	買 kaU (buy)	置 oKU (put)	罪 TSUmi (crime)
⺮	two bamboo canes	竹 taKE (bamboo)	笛 fuE (flute)	管 KUda (pipe)

Radical	Meaning	Examples		
羊	sheep	羊 hiTSUJI (sheep)	美 uTSUKUSHIi (beautiful)	群 muRE (group)
羽	two feathers	羽 haNE (feather)	習 naRAu (learn)	翌 yoKU (next)
自	nose of a person	自 MIzukara (myself)	息 Iki (breath)	鼻 haNA (nose)
⻗	rain drops from sky	雨 Ame (rain)	雲 KUmo (cloud)	雪 yuKI (snow)
儿	person's body	兄 Ani (brother)	児 ko (child)	元 MOto (origin)
八	holding with both hands	共 TOmo (together)	具 soNAWAru (possess)	典 noRI (rule book)
寸	hand	寸 SUn (little)	射 Iru (shoot)	導 miCHIBIku (guide)
巾	cloth	布 nuNO (cloth)	帯 Obi (belt)	幕 maKU (drapery)
心	heart	心 koKORO (heart)	思 oMOu (think)	愛 Ai (love)
毋	woman's breasts	母 HAha (mother)	毎 MAi (every)	毒 doKU (poison)

Radical	Meaning	Examples		
灬	fire	熱 neTSU (heat)	燃 moERU (burn)	赤 aKAI (red)
皿	plate	皿 saRA (plate)	益 maSU (increase)	盛 MOru (fill)
厂	cliff	原 HAra (field)	厚 aTSUI (thick)	
尸	sitting person, or roof	居 iRU (exist)	屋 YA (house)	層 SOo (layer)
广	house	店 miSE (store)	庫 kuRA (ware house)	庭 niWA (garden)
疒	sick person in bed	病 YAmai (sickness)	痛 iTAMI (pain)	
廴	advance	建 taTEru (build)	延 noBAsu (lengthen)	
辶	walk forward	進 suSUMU (advance)	道 miCHI (road)	速 haYAi (quick)
走	person's legs stretched	走 haSHIru (run)	起 oKIru (get up)	
冂	cover	内 uCHI (inside)	円 En (circle)	周 SHUu (around)

Radical	Meaning	Examples		
匚	storage place	区 KU (mark off)	医 i (cure)	
囗	enclose	囲 kaKOMU (surround)	国 kuNI (country)	園 soNO (garden)
弋	stick	代 kaWARU (replace)	式 SHIki (method)	
彳亍	crossroad	行 iKU (go)	街 maCHI (downtown)	衛 maMOru (guard)
門	gate	門 MOn (gate)	開 aKERU (open)	閉 shiMEru (close)

Appendix 3. Numbers

Cardinal Numbers

(a) 0 through 9,999

0	**rei, zero**	零
1	**ichi**	一
2	**ni**	二
3	**san**	三
4	**yon, shi**	四
5	**go**	五
6	**roku**	六
7	**nana, shichi**	七
8	**hachi**	八
9	**kyū, ku**	九

10	**jū**	十
11	**jū-ichi**	十一
12	**jū-ni**	十二
13	**jū-san**	十三
14	**jū-shi, yon**	十四
15	**jū-go**	十五
16	**jū-roku**	十六
17	**jū-shichi, nana**	十七
18	**jū-hachi**	十八
19	**jū-ku, kyū**	十九

20	**ni-jū**	二十
21	**ni-jū-ichi**	二十一
22	**ni-jū-ni**	二十二
23	**ni-jū-san**	二十三
24	**ni-jū-shi, yon**	二十四
25	**ni-jū-go**	二十五

30	**san-jū**	三十
40	**yon-jū**	四十
50	**go-jū**	五十
60	**roku-jū**	六十
70	**nana-jū**	七十
80	**hachi-jū**	八十
90	**kyū-jū**	九十

100	**hyaku**	百
200	**ni-hyaku**	二百
300	**san-byaku**	三百
400	**yon-hyaku**	四百
500	**go-hyaku**	五百
600	**rop-pyaku**	六百
700	**nana-hyaku**	七百
800	**hap-pyaku**	八百
900	**kyū-hyaku**	九百

1000	**sen**	千
2000	**ni-sen**	二千
3000	**san-zen**	三千
4000	**yon-sen**	四千
5000	**go-sen**	五千
6000	**roku-sen**	六千
7000	**nana-sen**	七千
8000	**has-sen**	八千
9000	**kyū-sen**	九千

Examples:

365	**san-byaku roku-jū go**
1,481	**sen yon-hyaku hachi-jū ichi**
3,672	**san-zen rop-pyaku nana-jū ni**
9,848	**kyū-sen hap-pyaku yon-jū hachi**

(b) Numbers above 10,000

Observe carefully the difference between English and Japanese counting methods.

In English, a large number is divided into three-digit groups (base group and subsequent groups of thousand, million, billion, trillion, and so on) as shown above. The counting method from 1 to 999 is repeatedly used for each group.

So the number above reads:

one hundred (and) twenty-three trillion,
four hundred (and) fifty-six billion,
seven hundred (and) eighty-nine million,
eight hundred (and) seventy-six thousand,
five hundred (and) forty-three

The Japanese counting method is like this.

兆 **chō**	億 **oku**	万 **man**	
123	4567	8987	6543
hyaku jū	sen hyaku jū	sen hyaku jū	sen hyaku jū
百 十	千 百 十	千 百 十	千 百 十

In Japanese, a large number is divided into four-digit groups (base group and subsequent groups of **man**, **oku**, **chō** and so on) as shown above. The counting method from 1 to 9,999, which has been discussed on the previous page, is repeatedly used for each group.

So the number above reads:

hyakuni-jū san chō
yon-sen go-hyaku roku-jū nana oku
has-sen kyū-hyaku hachi-jū nana man
roku-sen go-hyaku yon-jū san

(c) Note the following special cases:

I. Years
1998: **sen kyū-hyaku kyū-jū hachi nen** (**nen** = year) (Do not read as "nineteen ninety-eight.")

II. Telephone Numbers
3275-6904: **san-ni-nana-go-no roku-kyū-zero-yon** (**-no** is attached to the exchange number.)

III. In reading postal codes, room numbers, road numbers, machine type numbers, etc., **maru** (which means "circle") is often used instead of **zero**. (just like "oh" in English). So "106" reads **ichi-maru-roku**.

Traditional Yamato-Kotoba counting

A traditional **Yamato-kotoba** counting method (1 through 10 only) is also used in the casual language. (**Yon** and **nana** in normal counting [p.245] are derived from the traditional counting.)

1	**hitotsu**	6	**muttsu**
2	**futatsu**	7	**nanatsu**
3	**mittsu**	8	**yattsu**
4	**yottsu**	9	**kokonotsu**
5	**itsutsu**	10	**too**

Ordinal numbers

Ordinal numbers are expressed by inserting a cardinal number in place of X in the following formula:

dai-(X)-ban-me (**dai, me** or **ban-me** can be left out)

Examples:

the 1st **dai-ichi-ban-me, ichi-ban-me, ichi-ban, dai-ichi**
the 2nd **dai-ni-ban-me, ni-ban-me, ni-ban, dai-ni**
the 3rd **dai-san-ban-me, san-ban-me, san-ban, dai-san**

Also used are:
saisho (the first)
saigo (the last)

Months of the year

January	**ichi-gatsu**	一月
February	**ni-gatsu**	二月
March	**san-gatsu**	三月
April	**shi-gatsu** (not **yon-gatsu**)	四月
May	**go-gatsu**	五月
June	**roku-gatsu**	六月
July	**shichi-gatsu** (not **nana-gatsu**)	七月
August	**hachi-gatsu**	八月
September	**ku-gatsu** (not **kyū-gatsu**)	九月
October	**jū-gatsu**	十月
November	**jū-ichi-gatsu**	十一月
December	**jū-ni-gatsu**	十二月

Days of the month

1	**tsui-tachi**	一日	17	**jū-shichi-nichi**	十七日
2	**futsu-ka**	二日	18	**jū-hachi-nichi**	十八日
3	**mik-ka**	三日	19	**jū-ku-nichi**	十九日
4	**yok-ka**	四日	20	**hatsu-ka**	二十日
5	**itsu-ka**	五日	21	**ni-jū-ichi-nichi**	二十一日
6	**mui-ka**	六日	22	**ni-jū-ni-nichi**	二十二日
7	**nano-ka**	七日	23	**ni-jū-san-nichi**	二十三日
8	**yō-ka**	八日	24	**ni-jū-yok-ka**	二十四日
9	**kokono-ka**	九日	25	**ni-jū-go-nichi**	二十五日
10	**too-ka**	十日	26	**ni-jū-roku-nichi**	二十六日
11	**jū-ichi-nichi**	十一日	27	**ni-jū-shichi-nichi**	二十七日
12	**jū-ni-nichi**	十二日	28	**ni-jū-hachi-nichi**	二十八日
13	**jū-san-nichi**	十三日	29	**ni-jū-ku-nichi**	二十九日
14	**jū-yok-ka**	十四日	30	**san-jū-nichi**	三十日
15	**jū-go-nichi**	十五日	31	**san-jū-ichi-nichi**	三十一日
16	**jū-roku-nichi**	十六日			

Special names:

January 1	**gan-jitsu**	元日
the last day of each month	**miso-ka**	みそか
December 31	**oo-miso-ka**	おおみそか

Counting units

Compared with the counting units used in English (mile, yard, metre, feet, gallon, litre, dollar, cent, etc.), Japanese counting units are much more extensive and complex, many having no English equivalent. I did my best in trying to group them, as shown below.

Group 1: Plain counting units
(a) Plain units with no exceptions
(b) Plain but exceptional "4" (**yo** instead of **yon**)

Group 2: Double consonants
(a) Double consonants "k" for 1, 6, and 10.
(b) Double consonants "s" or "t" for 1, 8, and 10.
(c) Double consonants "k" or "s" and voiced 3
(d) Double consonant "pp" to replace consonant "h" or "f" for 1, 6, 10, and voiced 3

Group 3: Traditional counting

Examples:

Group 1 (a): Plain counting units with no exceptions
Examples: **ichi-mai, ni-mai, san-mai, yon-mai, go-mai, roku-mai, nana-mai... jū-yon-mai... ni-jū-yon-mai...**

mai	枚	used to count flat objects like paper, bank notes, stamps, disks, shirts, etc.
dai	台	machines like cars, bicycles, cameras, telephones, computers, etc.
wa	羽	birds, rabbits

Group 1 (b): Plain but exceptional "4" (**yo** instead of **yon**)
Examples: **yo-en, jū-yo-en, ni-jū-yo-en, yo-ji, yo-nin**

en	円	¥, Japanese currency
ji	時	o'clock
jikan	時間	period of time in hours
nin	人	persons (exceptions: 1 person=**hitori**, 2 people=**futari**)
nen	年	years
nen-kan	年間	period of time in years

Group 2 (a): Double consonants "k" for 1, 6, and 10
Examples: **ik-ko, ni-ko, san-ko, yon-ko, go-ko, rok-ko, nana-ko, hachi-ko, kyū-ko, jik-ko, jū-ik-ko**, and so on

ko	個	used to count something small and round, like balls, apples, eggs, stones, etc.
kai	回	number of times like "once," "twice,"
ka-getsu	か月	Period of time in months

Group 2 (b): Double consonants "s" or "t" for 1, 8, and 10
Examples: **is-sai, ni-sai, san-sai, yon-sai, go-sai, roku-sai, nana-sai, has-sai, kyū-sai, jis-sai, jū-is-sai... it-ten, hat-ten, jit-ten...**

sai	才	age (exception: **hatachi** for 20 years old)
satsu	冊	books, notebooks, dictionaries, etc.
shūkan	週間	period of time in weeks
shō	勝	number of wins in games, sports, etc.
ten	点	number of points in a test, game, etc.
tsū	通	letters
tō	頭	big animals like horses, cows, lions, elephants

Group 2 (c): Double consonants "k" (1, 6, 10) or "s" (1, 8, 10) and voiced 3
Examples: **ik-kai, ni-kai, san-gai, yon-kai, go-kai, rok-kai, nana-kai, hachi-kai, kyū-kai, jik-kai... is-soku, ni-soku, san-zoku, yon-soku, go-soku, roku-soku, nana-soku, has-soku, kyū-soku, jis-soku...**

kai	階	floor of a building
ken	軒	houses
soku	足	shoes, socks, stockings

Group 2 (d): Double consonant "pp" to replace consonant "h" or "f" for 1, 6, 10, and voiced 3
Examples: **ip-pon, ni-hon, san-bon, yon-hon, go-hon, rop-pon, nana-hon, hachi-hon, kyū-hon, jip-pon**

hon	本	something slender like pencils, trees, bottles
hiki	匹	small animals like dogs, cats, fishes
hai	杯	number of glasses of a drink
fun	分	minutes
hai	敗	number of losses in games, sports, etc.
haku	泊	overnight stays in a hotel, etc.

Group 3: Traditional counting

Small parts (one up to about four) of the traditional counting method are used to form prefixes with certain units. For example: **hito-hako, futa-hako, mi-hako, yo-hako, go-hako, rop-pako, nana-hako, hachi-hako, kyū-hako, jip-pako, jū-ichi-hako...**

ri	人	person (1: **hito-ri**, 2: **futa-ri** only)
hako	箱	boxes, packs of cigarettes
kire	切れ	slices of fish, bread, etc.
kumi	組	sets, pairs
toori	通り	ways of doing something
tsuki	月	months
ban	晩	nights

Appendix 4. Verb Conjugation Chart

This chart shows **V_3** (root), **V_2-masu** (polite), **V_2'-te** (present participle), **V_1-nai** (plain-negative), **V_4-ba** (conditional), and **V_5-o** (volitional) forms for the eleven representative verbs and two special verbs.

V_3		V_2-masu	V_2'-te	V_1-nai	V_4-ba	V_5-o
MIru	to see	mi-MAsu	MI-te	MI-nai	MIre-ba	mi-YOo
neRU	to sleep	ne-MAsu	ne-TE	ne-NAI	neRE-ba	ne-YOo
kaSU	to lend	kaSHI-MAsu	kaSHI-TE	kaSA-NAI	kaSE-ba	kaSO-o
haKU	to put on	haKI-MAsu	haI-TE	haKA-NAI	haKE-ba	haKO-o
NUgu	to take off	nuGI-MAsu	NUi-de	nuGA-nai	NUge-ba	nuGO-o
MAtsu	to wait	maCHI-MAsu	MAt-te	maTA-nai	MAte-ba	maTO-o
TOru	to take	toRI-MAsu	TOt-te	toRA-nai	TOre-ba	toRO-o
kaU	to buy	kaI-MAsu	kaT-TE	kaWA-NAI	kaE-ba	kaO-o
shiNU	to die	shiNI-MAsu	shiN-DE	shiNA-NAI	shiNE-ba	shiNO-o
YOmu	to read	yoMI-MAsu	YOn-de	yoMA-nai	YOme-ba	yoMO-o
toBU	to fly	toBI-MAsu	toN-DE	toBA-NAI	toBE-ba	toBO-o
suRU	to do	shi-MAsu	shi-TE	shi-NAI	suRE-ba	shi-YOo
KUru	to come	ki-MAsu	KI-te	KO-nai	KUre-ba	ko-YOo

Note

(1) **V_2'-te** form of iKU (to go) is iT-TE.

(2) **V_1-nai** form of Aru (to exist) is simply NAi.

V_2-masen (polite-negative), **V_2-mashita** (polite-past), **V_2-masen-deshita** (polite-negative-past), **V_2'-ta** (plain-past), and **V_1-nakatta** (plain-negative-past) forms, which can easily be derived from the chart, are not shown.

Index

T

U

V

W

Y

Hiragana Syllabary

あ a	か ka	さ sa	た ta	な na	は ha	ま ma	や ya	ら ra	わ wa
い i	き ki	し *shi*	ち *chi*	に ni	ひ hi	み mi	い *i*	り ri	い *i*
う u	く ku	す su	つ *tsu*	ぬ nu	ふ *fu*	む mu	ゆ yu	る ru	う *u*
え e	け ke	せ se	て te	ね ne	へ he	め me	え *e*	れ re	え *e*
お o	こ ko	そ so	と to	の no	ほ ho	も mo	よ yo	ろ ro	を *o*

が ga	ざ za	だ da	ば ba	ぱ pa
ぎ gi	じ *ji*	ぢ *ji*	び bi	ぴ pi
ぐ gu	ず zu	づ *zu*	ぶ bu	ぷ pu
げ ge	ぜ ze	で de	べ be	ぺ pe
ご go	ぞ zo	ど do	ぼ bo	ぽ po

ん n

きゃ kya	しゃ sha	ちゃ cha	にゃ nya	ひゃ hya	みゃ mya	りゃ rya
きゅ kyu	しゅ shu	ちゅ chu	にゅ nyu	ひゅ hyu	みゅ myu	りゅ ryu
きょ kyo	しょ sho	ちょ cho	にょ nyo	ひょ hyo	みょ myo	りょ ryo

ぎゃ gya	じゃ ja	ぢゃ ja	びゃ bya	ぴゃ pya
ぎゅ gyu	じゅ ju	ぢゅ ju	びゅ byu	ぴゅ pyu
ぎょ gyo	じょ jo	ぢょ jo	びょ byo	ぴょ pyo

•Exceptions in **rōmaji** spelling are marked in italics.